Globalisation and Finance at the Crossroads

Adrian Blundell-Wignall · Paul Atkinson
Caroline Roulet

Globalisation and Finance at the Crossroads

The Financial Crisis, Regulatory Reform and the Future of Banking

palgrave
macmillan

Adrian Blundell-Wignall
University of Sydney and OECD
(consultant advisor to the Secretary General, and former Director of the Financial and Enterprise Affairs Directorate)
Paris, France

Caroline Roulet
Organisation for Economic Co-operation and Development
Paris, France

Paul Atkinson
NHA Economics, Ltd.
Paris, France

ISBN 978-3-030-10249-4 ISBN 978-3-319-72676-2 (eBook)
https://doi.org/10.1007/978-3-319-72676-2

Softcover re-print of the Hardcover 1st edition 2018

Cover illustration: DKart, iStock/Getty Images Plus

Printed on acid-free paper

This Palgrave Macmillan imprint is published by the registered company Springer Nature Switzerland AG
The registered company address is: Gewerbestrasse 11, 6330 Cham, Switzerland

For Lucy Mushita, Mubeccel Gevher, Iftekhar Hasan and those few key people who supported us by letting the evidence be heard in the face of all that regulatory capture working against it.

The views in this book and any errors herein are those of the authors alone. The opinions expressed and the arguments employed do not purport to reflect those of the OECD, the OECD Secretary General, or any members countries

Foreword

Policy makers, international organisations, central banks and Treasury departments were caught off guard during the financial crisis of 2007–2008. This was mainly due to a poor understanding of the connectivity between major trends in the global economy, such as deregulation, leverage, financial innovation and the rise of savings outside of OECD countries. The crisis was a manifestation of the inconsistency between these global trends. And this journey is not over.

This book *Globalisation and Finance at the Crossroads*—by former and current OECD officials—aims to provide the reader a with good understanding of what happened during the crisis, what is currently happening, as well as some of the tools that current and future practitioners will need to analyse and understand financial risk going forward.

Groupthink amongst policy makers and regulatory pushback from banks are blocking sensible financial regulation. In some jurisdictions, banks are still dealing with the aftermath of the crisis, while in others banks' profits are back to pre-crisis levels even as they continue pushing back on regulations. While the Basel Committee has done good work on capital and leverage reforms, not so much has been done to change the business models of large systemic banks, which the authors have shown in research spanning a decade to be much more important. It is hard to judge when the right balance will be achieved, but it is safe to say we are not there yet and more work needs to be done.

In this respect, the regulatory landscape best suited to the global collective interest in the future is a central concern for the OECD. In general, progress towards a world that operates on a level playing field and based on a set of common principles has been very slow. One has to agree with the authors that without consistency, new forms of risks will always emerge; worryingly, today we see plenty of inconsistencies between financial jurisdictions in OECD countries and between different policy approaches in advanced and in emerging countries. In addition, in certain developing countries debt is building up quickly, including that associated with infrastructure investment in Belt-and-Road-related countries; and there are also echoes of the 2008 financial crisis in some emerging countries in the extent to which large off-balance sheet exposures of banks have been building up. The authors argue that the connections between globalisation and finance have reached a crossroads where the pressures for policy changes are building up anew.

But how do we know which issues matter most and what policies are best suited to deal with them? The world is not in any state to withstand another crisis, given the extremes to which monetary and fiscal support were pushed in major economies since 2008. This book aims to provide students, historians, researchers and policy makers with some necessary tools and a way of thinking about problems in globalisation and finance based on real-world experience, in both the policy world and private sector finance. One of the main strengths of this book is that the proposals being put forward are based on empirical support.

The knowledge being shared within these pages is invaluable. I am happy to say this based on my own experience with some of the authors at the OECD, where the case for an imminent crisis was presented internally and in published forms in the two years prior to the 'Lehman moment' in late 2008. This view was based both on knowledge of, and bottom-up research on, banks' activities. Since 2012, the

OECD has incorporated some of this thinking into its overall work on New Approaches to Economic Challenges (NAEC). I would encourage others interested in reform to benefit from the breadth of the insights in this book.

Paris, France
April 2018

Angel Gurría
OECD Secretary General

Contents

List of Figures

List of Tables

Glossary of Acronyms and Concepts

Alt-A Alternative A-paper, a mortgage security riskier than prime, but better than subprime.

AMLF Asset-backed Commercial Paper Money Market Mutual Fund Liquidity Facility.

Amortised Cost Accounting a method of valuing a portfolio of assets (e.g. loans) based on historic cost, less repayments, adjusting for write-offs (including intangibles) like goodwill or accretions. It is used for instruments whose main purpose is to collect contractual cash flows (payments of principal and interest), to be distinguished from Fair Value through Profit or Loss accounts.

Bank acceptances bills issued by companies that instruct the bank to pay a specified sum to a third party at a specified date. The bank acts as a guarantor, but unless the bill is discounted it doesn't appear on the bank balance sheet. If it is discounted before the due date—cashed in at a discount—it will appear on the bank balance sheet.

Basel Rules housed within the BIS, located in Basel, Switzerland, a banking committee meets to set minimum rules that banks in member jurisdictions should meet with respect to capital and liquidity. 'These include **Basel I, Basel II, and Basel III**.

Belt and Road Initiative (BRI) a project by China, covering 72 countries (and rising), which involves an extensive infrastructure investment programme funded mainly by Chinese Communist Party development and commercial banks. It is aimed at securing resources, shifting excess capacity and creating a cooperation and trade platform with (a high value added) China at its centre.

BIS Bank for International Settlements.

Broker-Dealer an intermediary, often owned by a bank. Acting as a broker is executing trades on behalf of a client as their agent; as a dealer executing trades on the firm's own account.

Capital Asset Pricing Model (CAPM) an equilibrium relationship whereby the expected return on a stock requires a linear combination of a risk premium and the risk-free rate (normally the government bond yield). Investors are able to invest without risk in the bond and require a premium to invest in the riskier asset.

CBOE Chicago Board of Options Exchange.

CBOT Chicago Board of Trade.

CDO Collateralised Debt Obligation. These take debt such as loans and mortgages that generate cash flows which are then used to create securities within a special purpose entity. The securities are promises to pay in a sequence based on seniority (from AAA to junk bonds and equity). Returns are higher for the risky tranches which, in case of default in the underlying debt, incur the first losses, thereby protecting more senior tranches. Synthetic CDOs are constructed with derivatives.

CEA Commodities Exchange Act, 1936.

CFIUS Committee on Foreign Investment in the United States.

CFMA Commodity Futures Modernisation Act, 2000.

CFTC Commodity Future Trading Commission.

CMO Collateralised Mortgage Obligation.

CoCos contingent convertible bonds. These can be converted to common equity in a crisis.

Collateral high-quality assets like cash or government debt that are held by a lending counterparty as a buffer against default. Rules apply to collateral (e.g. under Basel III) in the form of 'haircuts' (e.g. $100 of securities that collateralises a loan of $90 has a 10% haircut).

Collateralised Synthetic Obligations (CSO) These are essentially like CDOs, but instead of holding physical loans and bonds, it invests in derivatives (swaps, CDS, etc.) to gain exposure to fixed income assets.

Common Equity Tier 1 (CET-1) a 'going concern' loss absorber for banks made up of issued common stock, retained earnings and only some qualifying minority interests.

Covered Bonds is where a bank issues bonds linked to a cover pool of assets; most often this is dynamic cover, whereby the bank updates for the best assets to back the bonds.

Credit Default Swap (CDS) The buyer pays a premium and the seller insures the security against default according to contractual terms for an agreed notional amount net of the recovery value of assets following a default. The securities can be traded, depending mainly on the probability of default, a discount rate and the period of time.

CSE Consolidated Supervised Entities; a regulatory programme for acceptance of regulation in EU jurisdictions.

Curvature Risk in Basel when calculating market risk including options, it captures the nonlinear risk not captured by 'delta' when a portfolio is subject to a spot price stress scenario (second derivative effect).

CVA Credit Valuation Adjustment, a Basel concept related to counterparty valuation shifts.

Delta-adjusted in options the delta refers to the sensitivity of the derivative value to the underlying price of the security. If the portfolio is based on derivatives, its value is sensitive to and adjusted for price changes of the underlying names.

Derivatives These are contracts to buy and sell underlying assets, indexes, interest rates and currencies according to specific conditions: notably notional amounts, definitions, maturity dates and margin requirements. They are mainly over the counter (OTC) due to their specificity, but there is a regulatory push towards more uniform contracts that are traded on exchanges. The price of the derivative is linked to the price movements of the underlying security. Typical derivatives are swaps, options, futures and forwards.

DFAST Dodd-Frank Act Stress Test.

Distance-to-Default (DTD) for a bank, this is a statistical measure of the gap between the market value of the bank's assets (calculated as that implied by market data) and the book value of its liabilities. The default point is zero, and higher values indicate a safer bank.

Dodd-Frank Act authored by Senator Chris Dodd and Rep. Barney Frank is the 'Wall Street Reform and Consumer Protection Act'. It deals with all aspects of the US financial system needing reform following the 2008 crisis.

EBITDA Earnings before Interest, Taxes, Depreciation and Amortisation.

EMIR European markets infrastructure regulation.

Entrusted Loans Common in China. Companies with idle funds provide finance to each other with a return above the deposit rate at a bank. The bank in principle is an intermediary only and regulations in China require it not to offer guarantees.

Exchange Rate the bilateral price between 2 currencies. A trade-weighted exchange rate index (TWI) weights together various bilateral currencies according to their importance in a specific country's trade with the other countries.

Fair Value through Profit or Loss accounting for financial instruments that cannot be classified for amortised cost accounting methods. Assets values are based on fair value (current market value). They are assets held for trading purposes or designated as such by the nature of the asset (such as equities and derivatives). Gains and losses are recognised in the income statement.

FASB Financial Standards Accounting Board, which issues the Generally Accepted Accounting Standards (GAAP) mainly referring to US company accounts.

FDI Foreign Direct Investment.

FHFA Federal Housing Finance Agency.

FOMC Federal Open Market Committee.

Forward (derivative) is an OTC derivative contract between 2 parties to buy or sell an asset/currency at a specified future date at a price set today. The contract may be traded before expiry and may or may not include margin requirements.

FSB Financial Stability Board. The FSB is the successor of the Financial Stability Forum, suggested by Hans Tietmeyer as a means for the official family to discuss financial issues.

Future (derivative) is like a forward, but is standardised, usually liquid and traded on an exchange with frequent margin requirement top-ups.

GATT General Agreement on Tariffs and Trade.

GICS Global Industrial Classification Standard.

Gross Market Value (GMV) of derivatives, as opposed to the notional value, this the dollar value of the cost of replacing the derivatives at current prices.

GSEs Government Sponsored Enterprises, United States context, See Fannie Mae and Freddie Mac.

GSIB Global Systemically Important Bank, as defined by the FSB.

Hedge Fund lightly regulated managers of private capital that use an active investment approach to play arbitrage opportunities that arise when mispricing of financial instruments emerge. Extensive use of leverage and derivatives is a common feature of hedge funds.

ISDA International Swaps and Derivatives Association.

LCR Liquidity Coverage Ratio, a Basel regulatory rule

Leverage in financial balance sheets is the use of borrowed funds to enhance returns. More highly leveraged banks have higher debt-to-equity ratios (see also the different concept of synthetic leverage).

Liquidity (depth) of a security is the ease with which it can be transacted without affecting its price. Depth requires uniform securities traded on exchanges. Depth is measured by the size of an order need to move the market.

Living will regulatory proposals where a bank must outline detailed plans for how it should be resolved in the event of a default.

IFRS International Accounting Standards Board, used in most countries outside of the USA (which uses FASB standards).

IMF International Monetary Fund.

Intermediate Holding Company (IHC) A 2014 Federal Reserve rule requiring larger foreign banks with subsidiaries in the USA to set up separately capitalised holding companies to be subject to the same capital rules as US bank holding companies.

Intrinsic Value long-term discounted cash flows which may differ from current market value.

IOSCO International Organization of Securities Commissions.

Margin is a form of collateral posted by derivative counterparties to protect against default. The defaulter's collateral is forfeited to offset some part of the loss. They are required for both exchange cleared and OTC derivatives under BCBS and IOSCO rules developed in response to a G20 request after the crisis. Margins help ensure the non-defaulters capital is protected, but also raise the cost of derivative transactions and use up valuable liquidity for the poster of the margin.

Market Making broker-dealers hold inventories of securities on balance sheet the prices of which are displayed for sale to customers as buy and sell quotations.

MBS Mortgage-Backed Securities.

MFN Most Favoured Nation. A status granted to a trade partner which must be equal to the most favoured of its trading partners.

MPA Macro-prudential Assessment Framework, in China.

MR Market risk, a notation used in Basel trading book capital rules.

NAFTA North American Free Trade Agreement.

Non-Operating Holding Company (NOHC) is a legal structure for bank holding companies whereby the parent can raise capital and debt and invest in subsidiaries, but these are firewalled from the parent and each other. The structure is to ensure that the creditors of anyone cannot pursue the capital or assets of any of the others.

Notional Value referring to derivatives is an exposure measure calculated as the number of contracts multiplied by the price of a contract at the start date. Payments related to the contract are based on the notional value.

NSFR Net Stable Funding Ratio, a proposed Basel rule.

OECD Organisation for Economic Cooperation and Development.

OFHEO Office of Federal Housing Enterprise Oversight (now defunct).

Option is a derivative contract between 2 parties whereby the buyer pays a fee or premium to the seller in exchange for keeping an offer to buy or sell a security at a specific price over a specified period of time. Bought **call options** are the right (but not the obligation) to exercise the option before or at expiry. A bought **put option** is the right to sell a security in the same manner.

Originate-to-distribute model banks originate loans, securitise them and distribute them to investors.

OTC over the counter, applying to non-standard derivatives exchanged between two counterparties.

PBOC Peoples Bank of China.

Prime Broking the special services given by bank broker-dealers to prime clients such as hedge funds. This includes rapid allocation of securities to investors usually via inventory and intermediating securities lending.

QSPE Qualified Special Purpose Entity. A US bank SPE with risk fully transferred to a third party. They are passive entities that purchase assets and pass through cash flow to investors and are not consolidated. During the crisis, banks sometimes regarded their reputation as an obligation to lend support to QSPEs even if they were not legally obliged to do so.

Rehypothecation collateral is pledged to an intermediary (i.e. that can be seized in the event of default) is hypothecation. If that collateral is then repledged to a third party, it is rehypothecation (which occurs if a segregated account has not been asked for in the transaction).

REMIC Real Estate Mortgage Investment Conduit.

Repo A repurchase agreement involves an immediate sale of securities and a simultaneous agreement to repurchase them at a pre-specified future price and date. The intent is to borrow cash/liquidity.

Reverse Repo Opposite of a Repo. It is the purchase of securities and a simultaneous agreement to resell them at a specified date and price.

Risk Weighted Assets (RWA) Banks are allowed to weight assets according to their purported riskiness, using either a default set of external weights for smaller less sophisticated banks or weights set by running sophisticated internal models. The Basel capital rules apply to RWA as opposed to the larger total assets.

RMBS Residential Mortgage-Backed Securities.

SEC Securities and Exchange Commission.

Securitisation is the generic term for pooling commercial loans, mortgages, consumer debt, etc., and selling their cash flows as securities such as CDOs.

SFT Securities Financing Transaction (like a repo).

SIV Structured Investment Vehicle.

SOE State-owned Enterprise.

SPV/SPE Special Purpose Vehicle or Special Purpose Entity. These are legal entities like a company with a narrow purpose to isolate the originating company from financial risk—by sitting off the balance sheet. Whether or not the parent has some form of control determines how they should be consolidated for accounting and regulatory purposes.

Structured Product a generic term for the structuring of securities such as equities, bonds and loans to achieve tailored outcomes for clients, such as better yields and directional bets on markets (many offering downside capital protection). Derivatives are commonly used in their construction. A CDO is one of many different types of structured financial products.

Subprime Mortgage Loans to lower-income households with poor credit histories that don't qualify for conventional mortgages and pay higher-than-prime lending rates due to the risk.

Swap, (interest rate) Two parties swap cash flows, in a normal vanilla transaction involving fixed and floating rate legs. A company may want to lock in a fixed rate and receive floating to match its floating rate debt. The other side might be an investor. Notional amounts are constant, and the market risk to counterparties depends on what happens mainly to the fixed rate over the period of the contract. A rise hurts the fixed rate receiver.

Synthetic Leverage using derivatives to gain exposures the size of which depends on the future price movements of underlying assets.

TALF Term Asset-Backed Securities Loan Facility. A US crisis measure.

TARP Troubled Assets Relief Program. A US crisis measure.

'Teaser' Interest Rates and Resets To attract subprime borrowers rates were set below that reflecting the true risk for the first few years, which would then be reset to the higher rate later on.

Tier 1 Capital is made up of CET-1 capital and '*Additional Tier 1 Capital*', where the latter is other perpetual capital instruments not secured or covered by guarantees that enhance its seniority and which are not callable for a minimum time period which must be approved by supervisors. Examples include preferred shares and CoCos.

Tier 2 Capital this is supplementary 'gone concern' issued capital instruments (that can't be included in Tier 1) but usable to settle liabilities in default. It includes: undisclosed reserves, asset valuation reserves, provisions, hybrids (debt/equity) and subordinated debt (NB Tier 3 doesn't exist under Basel III).

TLAC Total Loss Absorbing Capacity. Adds debt to capital for GSIBs to make up a minimum (see text).

Total Return Swap a swap in which one party makes payments based on a fixed or floating rate, while the other's is based on the income and/or capital gains of an underlying assets.

Tri-partite Repo where a third party administers and runs all the services associated with the repo transaction.

Trust Company Loan Trust companies are financial entities that may be owned by a bank, which administer funds (e.g. inheritances, endowments) on behalf of a third party. As such, they are off-balance-sheet transactions for a bank (a China context).

Underwriting investment banks raise capital for companies or governments that are issuing securities (bonds and equity), usually in a syndicate, each taking responsibility for its allotment. This carries capital risk if prices change before finalisation.

Vega whereas delta measures the sensitivity of a derivative value to a change in the underlying price, vega measures its sensitivity to a change in the volatility of the underlying asset price.

VIE Variable Interest Entity. US bank SPE (SPV) with risk not fully transferred to a third party. The company has some form of control (not necessarily voting rights) and is consolidated in the company accounts.

WMP wealth management product—China common usage.

WTO World Trade Organisation.

Introduction

Globalisation and the governance of the international financial system have arrived at the crossroads. Either a coherent global level playing field for the cross-border activities of banks and multinational enterprises must emerge or the likelihood of another crisis will rise over time. This level playing field must extend to both the advanced countries that dominated the world economy during the second half of the twentieth century and the emerging countries that have shifted the world's economic centre of gravity from Europe to Asia, especially China and economies in its immediate sphere of influence.

Sovereign governments acting on what they believe to be in the national interest of their citizens have not served the collective global interest. The result has been a series of financial disturbances or crises, from the Latin American debt problems of the 1980s, the 'peso' crisis of the mid-1990s and the Asia crisis of the late 1990s to the post-millennium subprime debacle and euro crisis. These episodes have been managed in the main with monetary and fiscal policy responses, restrictive where the IMF has been in control and by easing elsewhere, usually accompanied by emergency bailouts and supports. Follow-up regulatory responses to avoid repeating the latest crisis have usually been negotiated with banks at the centre of the crises themselves. This has served only to roll the crisis from one country, region or sector to another without dealing with the underlying structural problems.

The 2007–2008 crisis did not happen in isolation with a few banks behaving badly. It resulted from the collision of a number of inconsistent economic and financial trends. The first of these is globalisation and the rapid development of emerging markets based on high national saving and state-owned enterprise-based investment. Two different economic systems began to butt-up against each other: one based on the principle of markets determining outcomes; the other based on the state playing the key role in the economy. Soon after the millennium, vast financial flows from countries recovering from the Asian crisis and, slightly later, from China to the USA, served to link the US mortgage market to emerging Asia. This intersected with the second major trend: financial innovation and deregulation that allowed leverage to expand in new ways (notably synthetic leverage via derivatives and structured products). Leverage rose—interacting with asset prices while increasing connectivity and counterparty risks within the financial system in Europe and the USA—until the financial pyramid collapsed upon itself. As of today, the response to the crisis has not solved the underlying problems and, looking forward, risks appear to be rolling into new sectors and regions (and possibly into China and its Belt and Road Initiative).

When thinking about policy and future markets outcomes, there are always one or two moving parts that really matter at any point in time. These will change from one phase to the next, with the actions of agents and structural changes conditioning what will happen next. It is important to avoid basing views on long-run average relationships or 'equilibrium' conditions. Even if everything can be confidently assumed to revert to equilibrium eventually in response to disturbances, adjustment processes along the way can be very damaging. Underlying forces, institutions, incentives, interconnections, and dynamics need to be understood.

This book is aimed at young policy makers learning their trade, private sector analysts and students (at the masters or doctorate level) looking to learn where and how to look for the key moving parts. It reviews the historical roots of today's globalised financial world and, based on what has happened, it explores the interconnectedness of the factors involved in the crisis. These include structural change, regulations and what agents did and will continue to do as these interactions change and move forward. The chapters will often refer to the real-time published work of the authors and the processes followed in giving views and advice from the start of 2007. The book blends academic training, experience of private sector money management and policy making in central banks, Treasuries, the Institute of International Finance and the Organisation for Economic Cooperation and Development (OECD).

Policy Makers Blindsided by Inconsistent Global Trends on a Collision Course

By the start of 2007, there was a general view in official circles that hedge funds were highly levered and constituted the main risk to stability—there was a fear that they weren't regulated and supervised by authorities as were the banks.[1] The OECD Financial Directorate disputed this, arguing that hedge fund leverage was only just above 3 times equity, that they played a key role in providing liquidity in the face of volatility, and that investment banks were protected (via collateral/margins) in regard to hedge fund risk. The argument was that the latter are managed actively and can close down risks while, by way of contrast, structured products originated by banks are 'passive' in nature and are: '*highly exposed to downward price gaps in the risky assets used in their construction*'.[2]

Policy makers had no idea that it was in the banking system where an 'atomic bomb' was primed to explode. The OECD Secretary General was nervous about the financial situation. He called the key staff into his office in March 2007. One view was that US losses related to structured products would be more than $300 billion, and that: '… *write offs*

[1] See Financial Stability Forum (2007).

[2] See Blundell-Wignall (2007).

of these magnitudes… will constrain the ability of prime brokers and banks to expand their balance sheets, … It is the potential instability in the credit supply process that is the key issue'. The other view stated: '*In its 'Economic Outlook' last Autumn, the OECD took the view that the US slowdown was not heralding a period of worldwide economic weakness, unlike, for instance, in 2001. Rather, a "smooth" rebalancing was to be expected, with Europe taking over the baton from the United States in driving OECD growth. Recent developments have broadly confirmed this prognosis. Indeed, the current economic situation is in many ways better than what we have experienced in years*'.[3]

The IMF had published descriptive material about structured products such as collateralised debt obligations (CDOs) in technical boxes and papers, but the systemic risks they posed did not make it through to the 'front office' view. The April 2007 *Financial Stability Report* concluded in its global assessment (p. 7): '*This weakness has been contained to certain portions of the subprime market (and, to a lesser extent, the Alt-A market), and is not likely to pose a serious systemic threat. Stress tests conducted by investment banks show that, even under scenarios of nationwide house price declines that are historically unprecedented, most investors with exposure to subprime mortgages through securitized structures will not face losses*'.[4]

The BIS *Annual Report* of 2007 (pp. 108–110) too was quite sanguine about the economic and financial situation despite more concerned views within its ranks[5]: '*The rally in credit markets was twice interrupted by periods of market turbulence, which turned out to be relatively brief in duration. Sound corporate fundamentals, as well as strong investor demand for structured credit products and greater investor risk appetite, seemed to be important forces behind the rally*'. And later:

[3] OECD (2007), p.7.

[4] See IMF (2007). The irony of this is that the IMF was placing faith in simulations carried out by none other than Lehman Brothers, the investment bank that fifteen months later would become the most famous casualty of the crisis.

[5] See, for example White (2006). White correctly pointed to globalisation connections and the unprepared nature of policies to deal with crises should such defaults require management and resolution in the future.

'*Whether and how the problems in the US subprime mortgage market may spill over into other markets remains unclear. In part, the risks are limited because of the relatively small size of the subprime market*'.[6]

Ben Bernanke, to whom the world owes something of a debt for his courageous responses to the crisis later on, seemed to have little idea of what was happening before the event. In a speech in Chicago in May 2007, he stated: '*Importantly, we see no serious broader spillover to banks or thrift institutions from the problems in the subprime market; the troubled lenders, for the most part, have not been institutions with federally insured deposits*'.[7]

In March 2007, the Financial Stability Forum met for the last time before the real tremors of the crisis started.[8] There had been a strong bout of market volatility in February, and it would be fair to say that the preponderance of opinion was that the markets had worked well, liquidity providers had come in, and it was all reasonably reassuring. It would be unfair to say there was no concern about the extent of subprime defaults, though it was felt this was more a concern for borrowers than for financial markets. Easily the biggest concern was the work being done on highly levered financial institutions which were taken to be the unregulated hedge funds and private equity sectors. Only a few were concerned about the regulated (and vastly more leveraged) banking system.

This snapshot of views at the time is not an unfair cherry-picking. The problems with financial policy making were (and likely remain) quite systematic. Trawling through hundreds of official documents concerning the policy advice of international organisations shows that: '*The general pattern here is that the most pointed questions and useful warnings were largely made relatively early, when risks may have seemed abstract or highly unlikely. Not only were they generally not reflected in the main editorial sections designed to focus high-level attention, but as excesses*

[6] See BIS (2007).

[7] See Bernanke (2007).

[8] Probably in August with BNP Paribas freezing accounts based on subprime structured products. Others argue that the real start was the earlier collapse of the two Bear Stearns hedge funds in July.

accumulated over time concern seems to have diminished rather than increased'.[9] When the risk of crisis is remote, criticisms are more strident but clear and present danger is, for whatever reason, put to one side.

Policy makers did not understand the interconnectedness of financial innovations and structural changes in the world economy. Globalisation (particularly China's role) and financial innovation were, together, interacting to change the normal parameters within which inflation, monetary policy, regulation and supervision operated. These trends were on a collision course.

The Broad Aims of this Book

Few policy makers or bankers accepted responsibility for the crisis. It was as though the crisis was an 'exogenous phenomenon' that came out of nowhere. It did not. When economists talk about 'causality', they usually have some notion of 'exogeneity' in mind; that relatively independent factors changed and caused endogenous things to happen—in this case the biggest financial crisis since the Great Depression. The crisis itself was not independent, but originated from the distortions and incentives created by past policy actions. Poor regulation and supervision in the face of structural change are shown to be the prime causes of the crisis. Evidence-based research about what happened should guide regulatory reform.

However—having been blindsided and authorities finding themselves in uncharted waters—the emergency response was to pump liquidity and capital into banks (with the USA in the lead here), while regulatory reforms then proceeded without the benefit of evidence-based research. Furthermore, the new regulations were developed in full consultation with the banks whose influence (particularly in Europe) was very effective. The letters written by the big players at the centre of the crisis

[9] See Shigehara and Atkinson (2011).

make interesting reading. In broad terms and paraphrasing, they have the following themes in common:

- *'be very careful about the unintended consequences and cumulative effects of regulation in our complex businesses'*;
- *'do not place simple leverage constraints at the centre of regulations'*;
- *'be careful about things you make us deduct from equity'*; *and*
- *'don't unduly constrain us with regulations in our crucial role in supporting the economic recovery'*.[10]

The subtext of all this was that banks, having socialised their losses via the emergency measures in the crisis, needed to restore profits and share prices as quickly as possible for the more narrow benefit of senior staff and major shareholders.

The first broad aim of this book, then, is to examine the reforms put in place and to compare these with what the emerging empirical evidence has to say concerning risks in the financial system.

A second aim of the book is to broaden the perspective of the reader as to the interconnectedness between structural changes in the global economy, monetary policy responses, ongoing innovation, re-regulation and market outcomes. The history of the crisis and its aftermath teaches that there are indeed unintended consequences—there always are. Regulating to control the causes of the previous set of issues leads to innovations and business model changes that roll risks into new sectors and jurisdictions—particularly when a level playing field has not been established. The line between banks and what is often referred to as '*shadow banking*' begins to shift. Jurisdictions with more lenient variants of the Basel rules, and those believing they can operate with impunity behind capital controls and other so-called macro-prudential instruments find leverage and risky products are entering in new ways. The reality has always been that until all financial instruments are taxed and regulated in the same way, and in all locations, financial markets will find a way to arbitrage the differences

[10] See Bank for International Settlements (2009).

in regulatory and tax parameters. This should be seen as '*principle number one*' of any regulatory theory. The world is still very far away from this ideal.

Finally, the book aims to share some of the practical research tools and methods for looking at the emerging issues in globalisation and finance. At any moment in time, there are a few moving parts that matter much more than others in driving markets and risks. The art of both managing money in the private sector and financial policy making is to identify what these are at the present point in time. For this, a strong view throughout the book is that bottom-up empirical analysis of micro company data, specific regulations, security instruments and products is the key to understanding the linkages between finance and the real economy. The ability to recognise inconsistent developments and risks that drive turning points and crises will help the practitioner understand what the next issue will be.

References

Bank for International Settlements. (2007). *Annual Report*. Basel.

Bank for International Settlements. (2009). *Comments Received on the Consultative Documents 'Strengthening the Resilience of the Banking Sector' and 'International Framework for Liquidity Risk Measurement, Standards and Monitoring'*. http://www.bis.org/publ/bcbs165/cacomments.htm.

Bernanke, B. S. (2007, May). The Subprime Mortgage Market. *At the Federal Reserve Bank of Chicago's 43rd Annual Conference on Bank Structure and Competition*. Chicago, IL. https://www.federalreserve.gov/newsevents/speech/bernanke20070517a.htm.

Blundell-Wignall, A. (2007, June). An Overview of Hedge Funds and Structured Products. *OECD Journal Financial Trends, 2007*(1), pp. 37–57.

Financial Stability Forum. (2007). *Update of the FSF Report on Highly Leveraged Institutions*, Basel, May. http://www.fsb.org/wp-content/uploads/r_0705.pdf.

IMF. (2007, April). *Global Financial Stability Report*. Washington, DC.

OECD. (2007, June). *OECD Economic Outlook, Volume 2007*(1), No. 81, June.

Shigehara, K., & Atkinson P. (2011). *Surveillance by International Institutions: Lessons from the Global Financial and Economic Crisis* (Economics Department Working Paper No. 860). Paris: OECD.

White, W. R. (2006). *Opening Address, Financial Globalisation.* 5th Annual BIS Research Conference, Brunnen, June. Available at: http://www.bis.org/speeches/sp060619.htm.

1
Globalisation Sets the Background to the Crisis

Introduction to Globalisation

Globalisation concerns the opening up of trade, cross-border investment and inter-connected production and financing between countries, a process which underpinned much of the success of advanced countries in the post-war period. The world by the 1960s had essentially split into three: the OECD-integrated market (including Japan and West Germany); the centrally planned world led by Russia; and the developing countries that were not centrally planned like Russia, but which were significantly autarchic and did not rely on open market arrangements due to high tariffs, border controls on trade, high levels of state-ownership of industry, and controls on foreign exchange and capital flows. The way that globalisation unfolded in this latter group was to play a key role in the 2007–2008 crisis.[1]

[1] See Blundell-Wignall et al. (2013) for a more detailed study of some of these points.

The original version of this chapter was revised: Misspelt author name has been corrected.
The erratum to this chapter is available at https://doi.org/10.1007/978-3-319-72676-2_10

A. Blundell-Wignall et al., *Globalisation and Finance at the Crossroads*,
https://doi.org/10.1007/978-3-319-72676-2_1

The OECD Countries Open Up

Amongst the OECD countries, post-war reconstruction efforts were designed to encourage trade and greater integration. The Marshall Plan announced in 1947 engaged the USA in the European rebuilding process. It also oversaw the administration of the European Payments Union which facilitated the re-emergence of a multilateral trading system. From 1948, the Global Agreement on Tariffs and Trade (GATT) led to more trade liberalisation, mainly in the OECD area, with four 'rounds' of multilateral negotiations completed by 1956 and a fifth by 1961. With the retreat of European empires, successive GATT rounds became more global, with participation rising from 26 countries in the Dillon Round (1960–1961) to 62 in the Kennedy Round (starting in May 1964) and 123 in the Uruguay round (the last to be completed in 1994). Major expansions of trade followed in each case.

In Europe, the trend towards greater integration was even faster. The Treaty of Rome in 1957–1958 became the basic legal framework ultimately for the establishment of the European Union (EU) single market. European current account convertibility came into effect in 1958 and the process of import licensing ended. By 1968, a full customs union was established, with tariffs and quotas on internal trade being abolished and a common external tariff on third countries coming into effect. Capital account deregulation and the ending of financial repression of domestic financial markets were, on the other hand, notoriously much less rapid.[2]

Propping up fixed or managed exchange rate regimes was one primary reason for not promoting faster financial integration. Persistent dollar weakness from 1958 to 1973 (despite current account balance of payments surpluses) led to US controls such as: the Interest Equalisation Tax (IET) in 1963; the voluntary foreign credit restraint

---

[2]See Bakker (1996) and Wyplosz (2001). McKinnon (1973) amongst other uses the term 'financial repression', for systems, often with interest rate controls, that keep saving yields below inflation enabling governments to incur more debt for development paid for in part by an inflation 'tax'.

(VFCR) in 1965; foreign direct investment (FDI) limitations; and extensive diplomacy to support the dollar. At the same time, surplus countries (such as Germany and Switzerland) imposed capital account restrictions, in order to maintain domestic monetary control and a fixed exchange rate in the face of inflows. Capital flow management was driven by the direction of flows in the early 1970s: the USA, the UK, Denmark, France, Italy and Sweden imposed measures to control outflows, while Germany, Switzerland, Australia, Japan, Austria and Finland focused on measures to prevent inflows.

The fixed exchange rate system was eventually abandoned in 1973, leading to the floating of the major exchange rates. This coincided with a rapid rise in inflation nearly everywhere and the oil price shock in 1973–1974, with OPEC achieving a much greater share of the economic rent from its cheap production costs. Most developed countries found themselves wrestling with inflation, high unemployment, huge budget deficits and large external imbalances. Heavy use of eurocurrency markets to recycle oil surpluses followed, and there was strong official support for this, notably through the IMF.

With the end of the commitment to fixed exchange rates, the trend to financial repression and capital controls began to be reversed in the 1970s, a process which was accelerated in the 1980s by policy and structural changes that made regulations less effective. Central banks were formulating new approaches to monetary control, facilitated by separating their functions from the budget process and relying on market instruments. The extensive use of interest rate swaps, options, forwards and other derivatives separated the notion of exposure and capital flows across exchanges to which many controls applied. Institutional investors and international banks lobbied hard for deregulation to avail themselves of the increased range of products. Germany ended the repression of banks to prevent money from coming in by 1975 (see OECD 2002; Dooley and Isard 1980). The USA removed capital controls in 1974, and the Depository Deregulation Act followed in 1980 (which phased out interest rate ceilings). The UK abolished all capital controls and foreign exchange restrictions in 1979. In 1980, Japan formally ended its exchange controls in one move. By 1981–1982, all of the four major currency countries liberalised exchange controls and domestic financial markets. Other OECD countries soon followed.

From 1981 to 1983, the French under Francois Mitterrand tried independently to stimulate via fiscal and monetary policy during the Volcker squeeze and restrictive German policies. This was followed by capital flight and the imposition of strict controls on outflows to defend the franc. However, recurrent crises in France forced them to change gear after 1983, and France moved to liberalise from 1983–1984, completing the process by 1986.[3] Jacques Delors left the French government around this time and went to the EU Commission to complete the single market project. The Single European Act was signed in 1986, committing countries to remove all controls on goods and capital by 1992. The Second Banking Directive came into effect in 1992—while recognising national regulatory approaches, countries could no longer restrict entry into their domestic market. Australia and New Zealand signed the Closer Economic Relations treaty in 1983, freeing up all trade and capital restrictions between them. The USA signed a free trade agreement with Canada in 1987 and the North American Free Trade Agreement (NAFTA) added Mexico in 1994. Much less progress in formal terms occurred in Asia.

The Case of Japan

Japan deserves some focus for two reasons: first, its spectacular growth prior to 1973 has to a large extent provided something of a model for how to achieve an 'Asian miracle'; and second its cultural values, industrial structures and policies have been very different to those of other OECD countries, so that changing regulations and controls '*on the books*' do not have the same implications for openness. For example, Japan has had the lowest FDI inflow of all OECD countries for many years, most likely due to the lack of a market for corporate control. Boards are reticent to allow hostile foreign takeovers via M&A activity, and legal teams

[3] See OECD (2002), for a full description of measures and dates.

to support such action are hard to find. Accountability in the corporate governance framework is unclear, and inflexible employment and termination rules and restrictions on the entry of foreign workers also serve as a barrier.[4] Thus while foreign ownership was allowed on paper from 1970, and exchange controls and capital account restrictions were eased, in practice the potential benefits of regulatory openness were blunted.

As in China and the Asian Tigers subsequently, the state played the key role in accelerating Japanese growth in the early post-war period. The Ministry of International Trade and Industry (MITI) was perhaps the most important key actor in the planning process.[5] Local industry was protected at the outset, and heavy investment in key industries through the Fiscal Investment and Loan Program (FILP) played a key role. The other parallels are striking too. As growth accelerated, poor social security and financial repression measures encouraged a sharp rise in saving. Relationships between large firms were strong, based on cross-shareholdings and the *Kieretsu* supply chain structure for intermediate inputs. The bulk of finance for new investments was provided by Japan's development banks. As industrial policies succeeded, a bank-oriented financial system emerged in the form of the '*main bank system*'.[6] While Japan made the yen convertible as early as 1960, it did not remove exchange controls and severe capital account restrictions during the 'miracle' growth phase. Indeed capital controls played an important part in the desire to engineer an undervalued exchange rate.[7]

The first oil shock and the breakdown of the fixed exchange rate system ended the very high growth phase of the Japanese miracle. By this time Japan had completed the catch-up phase of capital investment and technology transfer from the West. Japan adapted well as the terms-of-trade shifted against it. While growth slowed substantially it remained above most of the rest of the advanced countries as unemployment remained low and many of its industries emerged as

---

[4]See OECD (2015).

[5]See C. Johnson (1982).

[6]Each major company formed a long-term relationship with a 'main bank'.

[7]See Fukao (1990).

global leaders by successfully adapting advanced technologies in fields such as steel, motor vehicles and electronics. Throughout the 1970s, Japan did not open its capital account as the floating exchange rate era arrived. It experienced some wide swings in the yen as it successfully managed a rapid disinflation while avoiding the recession experienced elsewhere following the second oil price rise and the Volcker squeeze of 1979–1982.

The partial removal of foreign exchange controls in 1980 was a watershed event for Japan. Capital outflows accelerated and as US rates and the dollar rose with the Volcker disinflation the yen was able to weaken, ensuring the competitiveness of the yen. But signing the *Plaza Accord* in September 1985—whereby major central banks were to use coordinated intervention[8] to drive the overvalued US dollar down—proved to be problematic for Japan. The yen appreciated strongly, and in 1987 the *Louvre Accord* was agreed to halt the fall in the dollar. Buying dollars was combined with further deregulation of outflows that permitted pension funds and insurance companies to own more foreign assets. The easing of Japanese monetary policy to support these efforts was to plant the seeds of an asset bubble in both equity and real estate prices which reached a peak at the start of the 1990s. The reversal of this bubble occurred as US monetary policy eased and the dollar weakened, contributing to a further sharp rise in the yen. The collapse in asset prices had serious implications for bank balance sheets which the authorities were reluctant to address, resulting in lost decades of economic performance.

The problems for Japan arose from four important sources: first, failing to deal with bank bad loans while recapitalising them; second, trying to manage the exchange rate through monetary policy and intervention strategies while increasingly liberalising the capital account, which created monetary control problems and asset price inflation;

[8]'Intervention' refers to the practice of choosing a target level for the exchange rate by the central bank which stands read to buy or sell the currency at that price. To hold the exchange rate down in the face of buying pressure usually results in the accumulation of foreign currency reserves at the central banks, and the sale of the local currency, which finds its way into the domestic banking system and expands the money supply.

third, liberalising the capital account while maintaining a set of cultural values that worked against a market for corporate control, and maintained the inflexible relationships between firms that weakened the creative destruction process (whereby stronger innovating companies drive out their weaker competitors); and fourth, excluding immigration in the face of a declining population while maintaining inflexible labour market practices.

Mexico Crises

The collapse in commodity prices during the early 1980s led to the first emerging markets crisis. Following the first oil price rise in 1973–1974, fiscal policies in many developing countries remained expansionary. In particular outside Asia, state-owned enterprises (SOEs) often played a large role in economic strategies focused on import substitution while export bases remained narrow. With IMF encouragement, many countries borrowed on international financial markets to fund their budget deficits and at the same time to avoid adjusting to the terms-of-trade loss experienced by oil importers. This strategy of 'recycling' oil revenues by accumulating generally US dollar-denominated floating rate debt seemed to work well so long as US monetary policy was relaxed.

However, when the second oil price rise triggered by the Iranian revolution was followed by the Volcker monetary policy squeeze in the USA to fight inflation during 1979–1981, the deficiencies of this strategy became transparent. Both the dollar and US interest rates rose sharply, prices of oil and commodities soon fell (eroding export receipts) and the position of most large US dollar-denominated debtors became untenable. In the summer of 1982, Mexico effectively defaulted, triggering a widespread flight of capital from developing countries. Where countries had strengthened their export orientations to adjust to rising oil prices during the 1970s, mainly the Asian Tigers, they coped relatively well with the financial market pressures. But elsewhere, especially in Latin America, debt servicing and capital flight were persistent problems for the rest of the decade. Governments and the IMF dealt with the crisis by trying to ensure debtor countries were able to continue to service their debts to the Western banks rather than forgiving that debt. A severe recession was followed by poor macroeconomic performance throughout what has widely been termed a 'lost decade'.

A second crisis, focused more narrowly on Mexico, occurred in 1994–1995. The huge Mexican current account deficit with a fixed exchange rate was financed by issuing *Tesobonos*, denominated in pesos but indexed to dollars. As borrowing risks rose, securities were sold by international investors, Mexican dollar foreign exchange reserves ran out and the exchange rate in the end collapsed. The USA (with Robert Rubin of Goldman Sachs as Treasury Secretary) and the IMF mobilised enough funds to bail out the US banks and other creditors entirely. Rubin used the Treasury's Exchange Stabilisation Fund, so that President Clinton did not have to obtain Congressional approval. The US Treasury/IMF was becoming a vehicle to bail out Wall Street to an even greater extent than in the 1980s, essentially guaranteeing banks recovery of their capital and not just its servicing. This contributed to reinforcing a too-big-to-fail (TBTF) perception that would come back to haunt policy in 2007–2008, in both the USA and Europe, with even greater needs to support financial institutions.

Washington Consensus

Globalisation began to take hold from the end of the 1980s and, after the collapse of the Soviet Union, the market-integrated model of the OECD and the Washington Consensus had seemingly won the argument about successful global economic governance.[9] These principles were about stabilisation, liberalisation and structural adjustment. They involved some combination of fiscal stabilisation and tax reform; liberalising interest rate and establishing realistic exchange rates; openness in trade and investment; and legal arrangements conducive to property rights.[10] The IMF, the World Bank (WB) and the WTO became the

[9]See Williamson (2004). The emerging economy import substitution model had failed.

[10]Much of the discussion originated with a focus on the experience of the 'Southern Cone' of Latin America and took place in the context of the contrasting success of the Asian Tigers. A synthesis of these ideas gradually came to be known as the 'Washington Consensus'.

institutional side of promoting these principles with WB Structural Adjustment Programs (SAPs) implemented in developing countries, and lending was conditional on adherence.

Centrally planned economies suffering from stagnation in the 1980s also began to break up and move in part towards the OECD model. After the Soviet Union collapsed in 1991, many of the ex-Soviet satellites wanted to detach from Russia and join the European Union.

When Fukuyama (1989) wrote that the world had reached the end of history with respect to Communism versus the West, he did not foresee the arrival of China. How wrong this declaration would prove to be once China gained access to most favoured nation (MFN) status in the USA in 1994 and to the World Trade Organisation (WTO) seven years later. This opening up in the West was in itself a good thing for China's growth and for the countries that trade with China. But the implications for advanced countries are far reaching, and the world is in the process of dividing into two very different systems of global governance.

Emerging Asia

Asia was more export-oriented and had a more diversified industrial base than Latin America, and did somewhat better, particularly in the 1990s. Net private capital portfolio flows to emerging markets soared at this time, and FDI managed to stabilise and then recover. FDI inflows imparted resilience to net capital flowing to emerging economies, despite volatility in portfolio and other 'hot' money flows.

The Asian Tigers (Hong Kong, Taiwan, Korea and Singapore), Thailand, Malaysia, Philippines and Vietnam were at first successful in combining a key role for the state while opening up to foreign investment from advanced countries.[11] These countries had pegged their currencies to the dollar and industrialised rapidly financed by net private foreign borrowing. However, during the first half of the 1990s there

[11]The role of the state varied in intensity across these countries.

was a significant build-up of foreign debt.[12] A lot of the finance went into companies characterised by '*crony capitalism*', where related party transactions and poor corporate governance were a common feature. The policy of fixing against the dollar worked well for many years as the dollar weakened persistently against the yen (i.e. from 1985). This favoured emerging Asian industries increasingly in competition with Japan for third markets while Japanese industries increasingly outsourced cost-sensitive activities to the region. The dollar was especially weak during the second Mexican crisis in 1995. But as Mexico stabilised the dollar recovered and rallied strongly as the tech boom took off in the USA. This created increasing competitiveness problems in the Asia region.

As the yen fell back after 1995, non-Japan Asia experienced increasing trade pressure because their currencies were linked to the rising dollar. Hedge funds and portfolio managers began to withdraw funds as the economic fundamentals deteriorated. Thailand (and others) had let '*hot money*' in, and when these flows reversed, a vicious circle mechanism set in (falling asset prices, reserves loss and economic contraction).[13] The IMF organised a series of bailouts, tying packages to reform and structural adjustment (cuts in fiscal policy; higher interest rates to protect the exchange rate; forcing insolvent financial institutions to fail; pushing for Western-style bank business models; and reducing restrictions on foreign ownership).

The policy of allowing insolvent institutions to fail in Asia was in sharp contrast to the way US and European banks were treated in the peso crisis, and for that matter in the more recent global

[12]Many have used the Asia crisis as an excuse justifying capital controls. See, for example, J. Stiglitz and S. Yusuf (2001), and articles therein. The real problem, however, is managing the exchange rate, and monetary policy accommodating speculation as a result of exchange market intervention. Australia is in Asia and has followed policies of free capital flows and floating exchange rates since 1983. It suffered no financial crisis in 1997 or subsequently. Others have rightly argued for the need to restructure the global financial architecture. See B. Eichengreen (1999). But how to do this remains elusive.

[13]See Corsetti et al. (1998).

turmoil—where the US Treasury and the IMF ensured that such a scenario would not happen to US banks. Similarly, the recession that followed the higher interest rates and fiscal cuts in Asia was in strong contrast to the vigorous easing of monetary policy and relaxation of bank rules that the USA and Europe imposed following the 2001 recession and the recent crisis. Many Asian borrowers couldn't pay their debts as the economy went into recession. This created a very bad image in Asia, causing the region to veer away from the IMF/World Bank approach to governance, and looked to find Asian solutions to deal with Asian problems.

The Chiang Mai Initiative set up regional bilateral swap arrangements between the central banks of ASEAN, China, Japan and South Korea. This has been followed by the Asian Bond Markets Initiative (to set up local currency bond markets to help avoid the build-up of currency mismatch in portfolios). Capital controls have remained a strong feature of policies throughout Asia following the crisis of the late 1990s and FDI flows have been relatively modest as a consequence, in spite of impressive growth.[14] These episodes of the 1990s reinforced the view in China that the OECD/Washington Consensus model was certainly not going to be appropriate for them. China has been able to take advantage of mixed feelings in Asia about the Washington Consensus to launch the ambitious *One Belt One Road* Initiative (discussed in Chapter 9) in 2015.

The China Growth Phase

With some historical merit, China sees itself as a global civilisation—the middle kingdom *Chung Kuo*. While it might have been overshadowed by the past 250 years of industrial revolutions in the West, its own pre-eminence has a much longer history. It was first unified in 221 BC and then always reunified after periodic scissions. Culturally

[14]See S. Radelet and J. Sachs (1998).

(with Confucian values) and militarily, China dominated surrounding countries (in script, language and/or culture, including in Japan, Korea and Vietnam) for 2000 years. The patterns of industrialisation in the West that had contributed to China's previous weakness militarily vis-a-vis Britain, Russia and Japan could be copied—by building infrastructure, obtaining foreign technology and supporting industry with subsidies, tariff and foreign investment protections. This progressed rapidly under the leadership of Deng Xiaoping.

During the late 1970s, the centrally planned (Soviet-style) development approach in China was terminated. Deng had become a paramount leader from 1978 to 1992 and chose a more decentralising approach to planning delegated to the provinces. He dismantled collective farms, established free economic zones and wooed foreign capital into them where technology transfer needs were the greatest. These policies were known as 'hide and bide'. What China needed most abroad was stable access to foreign markets. China would thus '*bide our time and hide our capabilities*'.[15] Access to external markets was a priority that China proved very adept at acquiring (see below).

Unlike the early centralised planning of the Soviet Union, China's reforms under Deng Xiaoping, with self-contained local governments responsible for production targets (akin to the multidivisional form in business), were highly successful: first in agriculture, and then extending to other sectors. China has always had a clear strategy set out in 5-year plans to which new phases are added following the success of the preceding phase. Following China's entry into WTO in 2001, it has moved quickly to become the largest exporter in the world and, for the moment, second only to the USA in terms of GDP.

The common elements of successive Five-Year Plans are that the state plays the most important role in the economy. This includes *inter alia*: financial repression to build a large saving base; investment via SOEs to drive the industrial strategy; subsidies via the tax system and cheap funding from large state banks; and the pricing of exports to gain

[15]See Allison (2015). He points out that China's military leaders interpret this as 'wait before getting even'.

market share (the 'China price'). A major new phase is under way since the crisis in the Belt and Road Initiative that does not go in the direction of multilateral openness—a topic that will be discussed in detail in Chapter 9.

In Summary

The correlation between national savings and investment is a well-known indicator for measuring openness, evidence from which is presented in Chapter 9.[16] Open trade and investment should see no correlation between resident's saving and profitable investment in the country concerned. Savings and investment did become less correlated on average in large countries following the 1980s, led by European integration.[17] The Asian Tigers and China had begun to grow and current account imbalances became larger—and particularly so for that between China and the USA—but the size of this was small compared to the vast size of saving and investment. Emerging economies have never been seduced into opening their trade and investment and, particularly in the BRICS (i.e. Brazil, Russia, India, China and South Africa), into changing cultural values that allow level playing field foreign participation in their economies. In both cases, their national saving and investment have always remained highly correlated (see Chapter 9).

One possible reason for this is the experience of Japan and some of the early attempts amongst developing countries to attract foreign capital often resulted in problems. Sometimes this was because they relied on exports from a narrow commodity base which are very cyclical (oil, copper and coffee). Such countries often attempted to implement an 'import-substitution model' of development to diversify away from commodities and attempted to attract foreign funding while pegging exchange rates and maintaining capital controls. But this mix of policies often led to crises.

[16]See Feldstein and Horioka (1980).

[17]See Chapter 9 for a discussion of these issues.

The China Path to Prosperity and the US Financial Crisis of 2007–2008

The interaction between globalisation trends in Asia and financial system innovation and deregulation in the West combined to be fundamental causes of the crisis. The Asia/China development model set off a global supply shock with a number of elements that would drive towards low interest rates and rising asset prices just as financial deregulation and product innovation were occurring in ways that would allow banks and investors to take maximum advantage. The policies to bring about the Asian miracle had a number of moving parts that link to the events that followed:

- Exchange rate management and export pricing policies which were to drive import penetration by Asian countries and particularly China on an unprecedented scale into Western markets—the needed access to foreign markets—which would affect jobs and living standards in the West.
- A savings glut resulting from the financial repression policies needed to generate funding for investment that did not rely on open capital markets and capital flows from the West—which was to keep downward pressure on global real interest rates.
- Foreign exchange market intervention resulting from the export pricing strategies that would lead to unprecedented buying of US Treasury securities—which was to help drive nominal interest rates down towards the low real rates.
- The competitive response of Western companies to the challenge from Asia, which took the form of accelerating the Schumpeterian process of innovation in strong companies and the exit of weaker firms—this was to add to severe pressure on jobs and living standards when combined with import penetration.

The result of the twin forces of import penetration and advanced country innovation (such as automation through digitalisation) was to squeeze the middle classes through corporate restructuring, kill wage pressures and set in train deflation pressures and an historic monetary response that would drive asset prices upwards and bond yields down (discussed for the post-crisis period in Chapter 9). Low inflation, bond buying and easy monetary policy drove down the entire term structure of interest rates, from the long end of which US mortgages are priced. These preconditions were to combine with financial deregulation and innovation in a disastrous fashion by 2007–2008.

Export Success and Import Penetration Strategies

The development model of the Asian Tigers, like Japan before them, focused on strong saving and trade expansion combined with supportive capital account and exchange rate management. Hong Kong was something of an exception in choosing a currency board and an 'investment openness' approach. India, Pakistan, Indonesia, Turkey, large parts of Latin America and Africa chose more autarkic routes in these earlier years. The 'Tigers' benefited enormously from Asian trade regionalism and the post-1960s success of Japan. Their strategic location allowed them to benefit from investment and trade trends following globalisation events of the early 1980s. These countries expanded their share of world merchandise exports rapidly, achieving an 8% share of global trade at their peak.

Japan had signed the Japan–China Trade Agreement in 1974, which mutually granted MFN status for trade (customs, export and imports), and a bilateral investment treaty in 1988 through which it obtained National Treatment status within China (improving scope for local production abroad as opposed to exports). The US MFN status for China had to be renewed each year by Congress prior to 2001. But China's accession to the WTO in December 2001 enabled an unprecedented acceleration of their exports and freed companies not to have to sell via state intermediaries (except for certain goods like cereals, tobacco, fuels and minerals and some services, such as restrictions on transport and distribution logistics inside the country). It also gave China access to cheaper imports of raw material and capital goods, thereby improving competiveness.

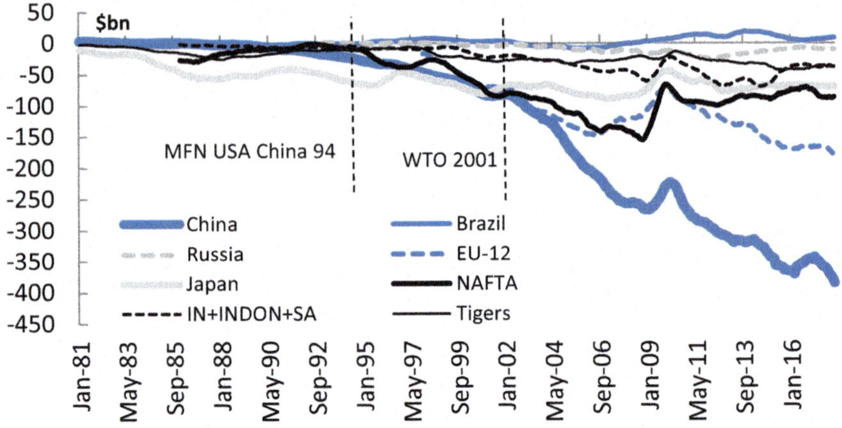

Fig. 1.1 US bilateral trade balances with selected countries (12-month basis) (*Source* Thomson Reuters, authors)

China's total merchandise exports as a share of the world total rose sharply and in recent years, it has become the world's largest exporter and is especially dominant in manufacturing. Figure 1.1 shows the 12-month-ended trade balances of the USA with a selection of countries and groups. The US trade balance has never stopped deteriorating with China, and by the crisis years it reached 90% of all of the other countries shown added together. After China joined the WTO, the US trade balance with it diverged even from the large deficit with European countries.

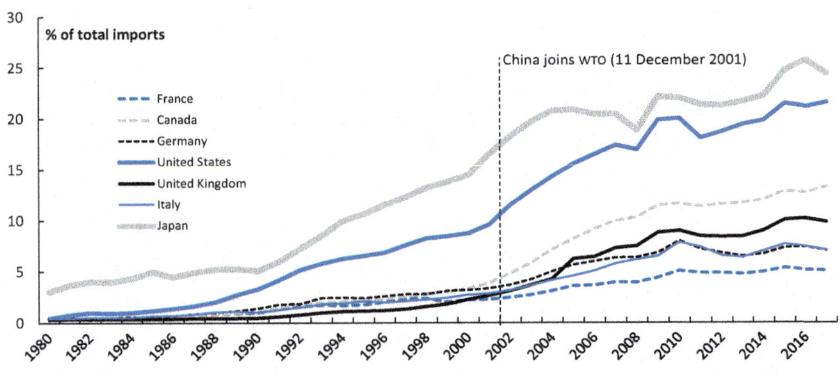

Fig. 1.2 China's shares of selected country imports (*Source* IMF data, authors)

Both the USA and Japan had already seen a rise in import penetration from China prior to 2001, in contrast to Europe where this was delayed until WTO entry (see Fig. 1.2). Import shares from China rose in all regions after 2001 and this, as will be touched on below, has affected labour markets in these countries.

Exchange Rate Management and Pricing for Market Share

Exchange rate management and targeting traded goods prices in these years prior to the crisis played an important role in rapid export expansion. A country may hold its exchange rate at a level that is undervalued compared to fundamentals, which favours exporters unfairly and discriminates against imports. This is usually achieved by the country picking an exchange rate and having its central bank stand ready to buy or sell dollars against its own currency at that price. Because flows can at times be large, possibly destabilising the money supply, this policy is usually accompanied by capital controls and related regulations to reduce the flows and make the task easier.[18] Economists sometimes refer to this as a '*beggar-my-neighbour*' policy, and it is the subject of disputes between countries.[19]

Undervaluation is difficult to define. In principle a purchasing-power-parity (PPP) real exchange rate is compared to some fundamentals-based '*norm*' such as GDP per capita to estimate where it should be.[20] These real econometric measures are subject to great uncertainty however. For the discussion here what matters is the policy countries were pursuing to contain their exchange rates compared to where they might otherwise have moved without capital controls and/or foreign

[18]Capital account management can be by residence—domestic versus foreign. But it can also be by currency, including restrictions on the forward foreign exchange markets, as imposed by Korea in 2010.

[19]For example United States Department of the Treasury (2016).

[20]As in the Harrod-Balassa-Samuelson effect. In a survey of the empirical literature to 2006, Tica et al. (2006) found that 49 out of 58 empirical studies supported the presence of the effect. More recently Berka et al. (2014) found evidence for the effect in the context of European data. Rodrik (2008) uses this approach.

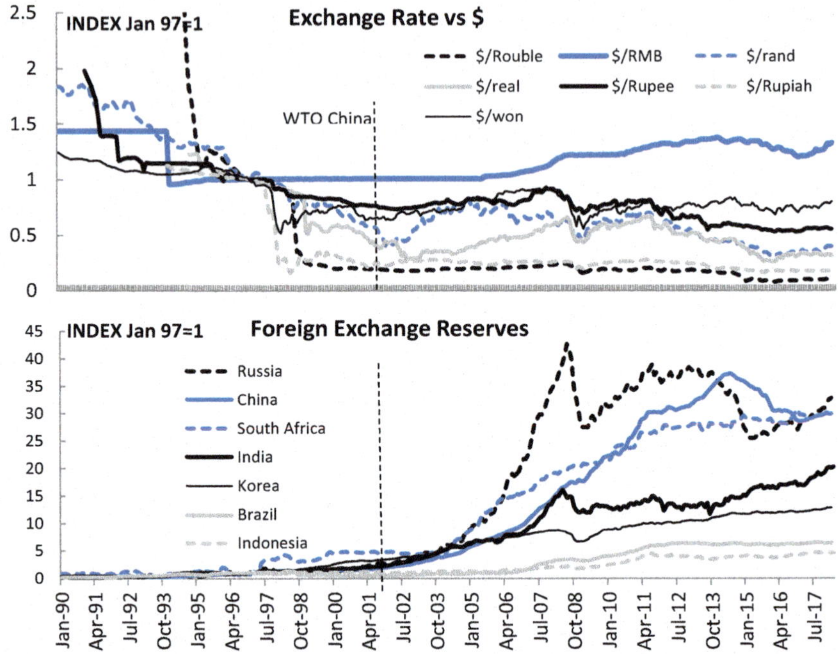

Fig. 1.3 Emerging exchange rates and foreign exchange reserves (*Source* Thomson Reuters, authors)

exchange intervention. In this sense, exchange rates need to be looked at alongside movements in the level of international reserves.

This is done for selected countries in Fig. 1.3. Most of the countries shown managed to keep their currencies down versus the dollar, and heavy accumulation of reserves occurred (though less in the economies with strong capital controls). Russia and Indonesia have been particularly 'successful'. China carried out a large devaluation just prior to the launch of the WTO, but since its own accession it did not devalue any further. However, the net capital flows into China associated with this process would have seen the exchange rate rise sharply, thwarting its push to expand exports. Consequently, it chose to maintain capital controls and to intervene heavily in the foreign exchange market to keep the rate from rising. This policy is closely aligned with other methods for keeping traded goods prices focused on market share.

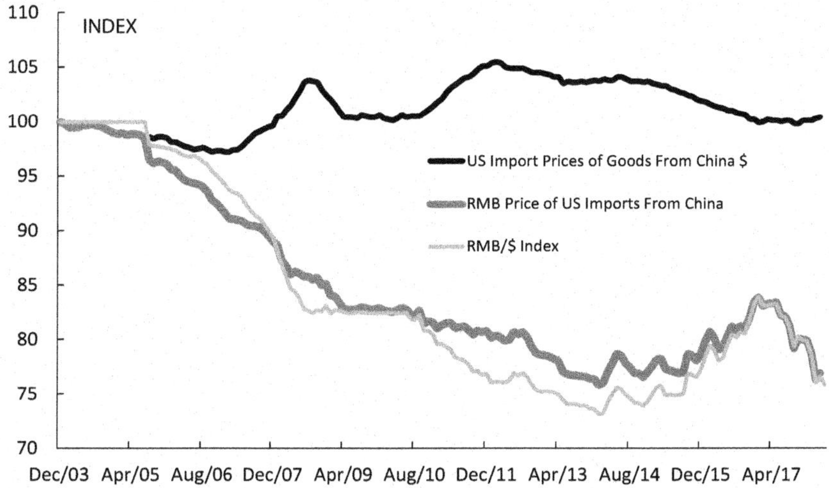

Fig. 1.4 US import prices from China (*Source* Thomson Reuters, authors)

Keeping the exchange rate at a steady level allows policy then to focus on keeping its traded goods prices competitive versus other exporters (the so-called *China Price*). This requires some manipulation of the price of traded goods in foreign currency via China's SOEs. Figure 1.4 shows the US price index for imports from China in dollars, the RMB exchange rate and the implied price received by exporters in RMB, all expressed as deviations from the December 2003 base of 100. From 2003 to the end of 2016, there has been no net increase in prices, despite wage increases at home and an appreciation of the exchange rate. This can be achieved by export companies accepting margin falls at home rather than losing market share. This would place enormous pressure on companies if margins are squeezed too much, including their ability to meet debt liabilities. For this reason, other policy tools are used to support the export sector. Factors cited in addition to the exchange rate that support competitive pricing of exports with variable mark-ups include: export tax rebates; loans from SOE banks and other subsidies; low wages, network clustering (hubs) for efficiency aided by tax concessions for FDI; lower occupational safety and environmental protection costs; and the occasional illegal use of foreign technologies and counterfeit products.

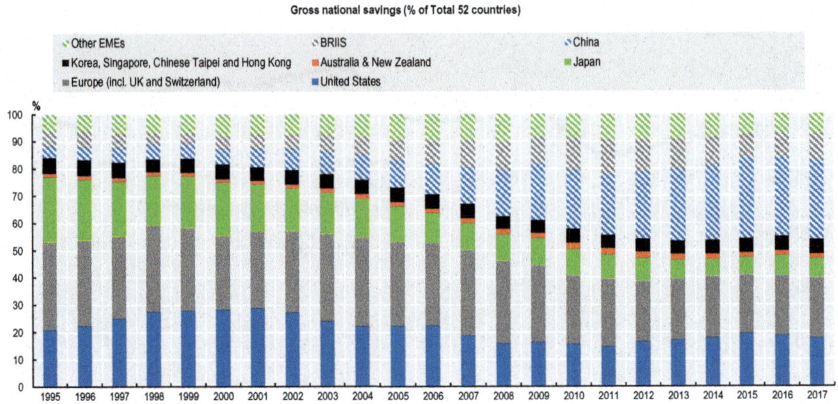

Fig. 1.5 Shares of world national saving (*Source* IMF data. Shares covering 52 countries)

The Saving Glut and Real Interest Rates

China's capacity to produce and export was facilitated by a boost of saving and investment. While ageing and cultural values play a role in saving, these trend factors do not seem to be enough to explain the sudden move up in saving (and investment) from the early 2000s, as shown in Fig. 1.5 (shown as a share of global saving). From 6% of the world total in 2000, just as WTO status was achieved, China's national saving rose to be 31% of the world total by 2015.

This saving change came about from three primary factors. First, state-driven investment under financial repression (selective capital controls, interest rate ceilings and credit rationing) bottles up domestic saving and increases the correlation between national savings and investment. Second, to facilitate investment the state fully or partly privatised around two-thirds of its SOEs and state assets between 1995 and 2005. From 1998 to 2004, six in ten SOE employees, some tens of millions of workers, were laid off.[21] This boosted corporate profits in the state

[21]See Liu (2005) and Cai et al. (2008).

and private sectors and hence company saving. Third, pension reforms at the end of the 1990s were taking effect. This reform reduced benefits, increased contributions and became partially *funded*, requiring increased household saving.[22]

This swing in world saving has led to a current account surplus in China and to a deficit in the USA. Despite the hope that one-day consumption will play a greater role in Chinese policy to remove this source of tension, the likelihood is not very optimistic. First, by embarking on the Belt and Road Initiative (discussed in Chapter 9), the investment needs in China are greater than ever. Second, even if consumption-led growth were possible, the current account surplus will likely not fall. A study based on OECD trade input–output data suggests that this could actually worsen the trade imbalance.[23] This is because investment in China is much more import-intensive than consumption, which the Chinese are well placed to satisfy themselves.

Current account surpluses have to be financed by an equal and opposite capital flow. In financial repression economies, it is most often the government via the central bank (rather than the private sector) that finances the current account surplus with an equal and opposite capital account flow. A savings glut in China, invested in the USA, lowers real interest rates and encourages investment there to exceed US national saving—see Box 1.1.[24] There is nothing wrong with this if the saving funds productive investment to repay the debt down the track. But this didn't happen as the facilitating factor of the savings glut interacted with other policies to fund in large part (unproductive) subprime mortgages in the USA. More will be said about the genesis and evolution of the financial crisis in the USA in subsequent chapters. Suffice it to say here that China was the source of an essential enabling flow of saving that helped to fuel the US subprime crisis.

[22]See Ma and Wang (2010).
[23]See Ma et al. (2016).
[24]See Bernanke (2005).

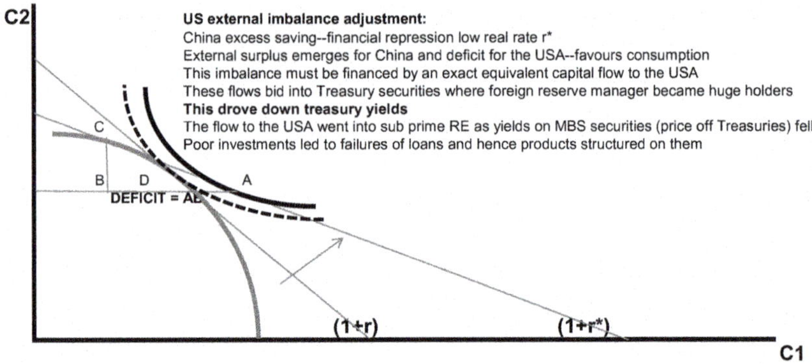

Fig. 1.6 Savings glut and real interest rates (*Source* Author's representation)

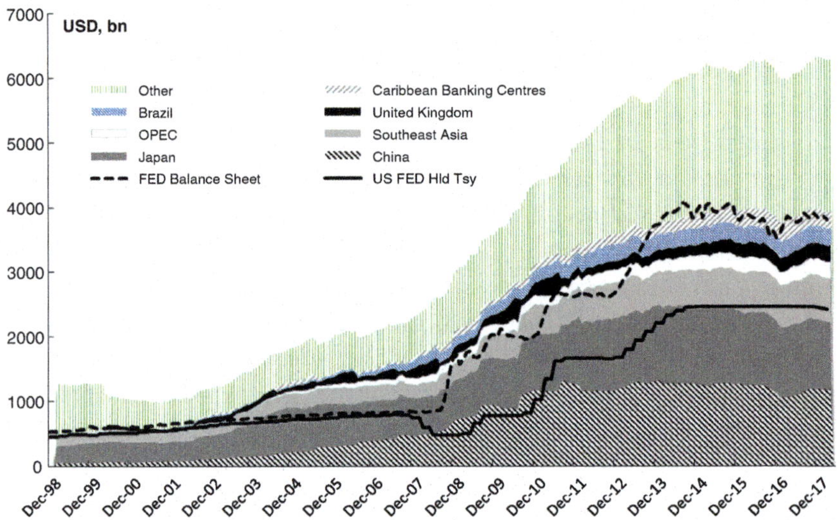

Fig. 1.7 Foreign holdings of US Treasuries compared to the Fed holdings (*Source* Datastream, authors)

Box 1.1: Schematic for China Saving Glut Funding Subprime Housing

The high saving glut financial repression economy has the low real interest rate r*. The figure shows the production possibility curve between consuming today and consuming tomorrow for the closed economy case. In the autarky case, the higher real interest rate r leads to equilibrium at D. But there is a glut of savings available at a much lower real rate r* due to

China, so the USA can improve welfare (move to a higher indifference curve) by investing further and moving production to point to C and consumption to point A. The amount AB is the current account deficit (=China surplus). Welfare is improved if investment is pushed to the point where the return on investment falls from r to r*. The idea fails if the deficit is not associated with productive investment (Fig. 1.6).

Capital Inflows, Foreign Exchange Intervention and Bond Buying

The China policy of allowing FDI inflows to build value chain hubs/agglomerations in free economic zones, while not permitting free outflow of investment (a part of the financial repression policy), puts upward pressure on the exchange rate, and would risk overvaluation without foreign exchange market intervention (see also Box 1.2). The extent of intervention versus the dollar in the lead up to the crisis, simultaneously invested in US Treasuries, is illustrated in Fig. 1.7. This shows the vast holdings of US Treasury securities by non-US countries (mainly governments). Japan was first to accelerate buying in the early 2000s, and this was soon followed by China after 2004. Once the crisis began, official and private scrambling for US Treasuries (the most liquid securities in the world) accelerated across the board, and the Federal Reserve joined into the buying as part of their Quantitative Easing response to the crisis. Foreign holdings are now over $6tn, of which over half sits in the Asian region (much larger than the Fed holdings).

Box 1.2: Exchange Market Intervention and the Trilemma

Financial repression policies include exchange rate and capital account management, non-convertibility of the currency, high bank reserve requirements, interest rate ceilings and strong controls on foreign direct investment (FDI). These financial policies are essentially a tax on the financial economy. This acts to bottle up savings because companies, households and pension funds can't buy or sell foreign assets, and government control of banks leads to directed credits and investments according to government objectives thought to be necessary for economic development. The relatively small size of consumption compared to GDP means that industrial goods must be exported, and this in turn has required pricing for market share (discussed earlier). This process became economically meaningful after China was allowed to join the WTO in late 2001.

In the case of a country wishing to stabilise its exchange rate with export objectives in mind resisting FDI inflow (or outflows) reduces ex ante pressure on the exchange rate, and hence the size of foreign exchange intervention needed to meet the relevant exchange rate peg. Maintaining a stable nominal exchange rate requires the central bank to become 'the market' at the target price: i.e. buying (or selling) US dollars and selling (or buying) domestic currency at the fixed price. The dollars accrued (in the case of inflows) are then lent to the rest of the world by investing them in liquid government securities (usually US dollars).

Foreign reserve accumulation in this way has occurred for a long period with a sequence of Asian countries intervening to manage the exchange rate: first Japan and then Korea and Taiwan, and most recently China from 2004. Russia, Brazil, South Africa and India have also been strong in this activity. Foreign exchange intervention (in the face of inflows) expands credit because buyers invest the local currency acquired in their projects and the money finds its way into the domestic banking system. This is the source of the so-called trilemma: that it is not possible to control the exchange rate, the money supply and avoid capital controls at the same time. Most developing and emerging countries have capital controls to slow down inflows and, in crisis situations, to stop sudden outflows. These crises are often of their own making and are easily solved by floating the exchange rate. For example, Australia is a country in the Asian region which depends on foreign funding of its banks. If commodity prices fall sharply, and investors wish to withdraw funds, Australia lets the exchange rate adjust down until it is sufficiently attractive for new buyers to come into buy $A assets. The problems for Asian countries are caused by the pegging to the US dollar combined with the threat that existing investors would be restricted from withdrawing funds in a crisis—so investors move quickly in such countries.

For the purposes of understanding the 2007–2008 crisis and its aftermath, the massive purchase of US Treasuries drove bond prices up and yields down right across the yield curve (via the usual term-structure arbitrage activity) compared to what they would have been in the absence of such activity—joining forces as it were with monetary policy responses to deflation pressure and the savings glut pressures. US mortgages are priced off US long-term bonds, and the bubble here was to play a key role in the crisis.

The Impact of the Rise of Asia on the West

The Competitive Response of Western Companies to Competition from Asia

Innovation and the adoption of new technology are inextricably linked with trade. Firm-based trade theories link the importance of economies of scale accessed by expanding sales abroad to the adoption of new technology and innovations that jointly drive productivity growth. To understand the pressures on labour markets in the West, it is not sufficient to focus on import penetration alone. The entry of major Asian companies into global trade supported by variable margin pricing, subsidies and cheap funding has posed a serious threat to all companies.[25]

Recent thinking links trade and technology adoption in a dynamic manner at the firm level. Heterogeneous firms within industries have different skills and research capabilities which, sometimes combined with luck, drives innovation and striving for 'leanness'. More productive firms expand and become more intensive in their use of high-skilled labour within industries. Industry productivity rises as less effective firms exit via acquisition (in the main) or failure. There are substantial overheads in establishing export markets (distribution networks) and/or to invest in foreign subsidiaries that (both) allow more productive firms to achieve economies of scale. The successful firms are better able to manage these costs of expanding via exports or its equivalent in setting up to produce abroad.[26]

These economies of scale allow firms better to compete for market share against successful firms from other countries. This process involves corporate restructuring with increases in demand for skilled workers and the reallocation of supply chains within industries and between countries. Production processes are broken up and reallocated in global value chains. Previously separated boundaries are crossed in new ways

[25]Even companies lower down in the value-added chain, such as the Maquiladoras on the Mexican border, are having to restructure due to China/Asia pressure.

[26]See, for example, Helpman et al. (2004) and Melitz and Redding (2012). The underlying idea is that only highly productive firms are able to make sufficient profits to cover the large fixed costs required for export operations.

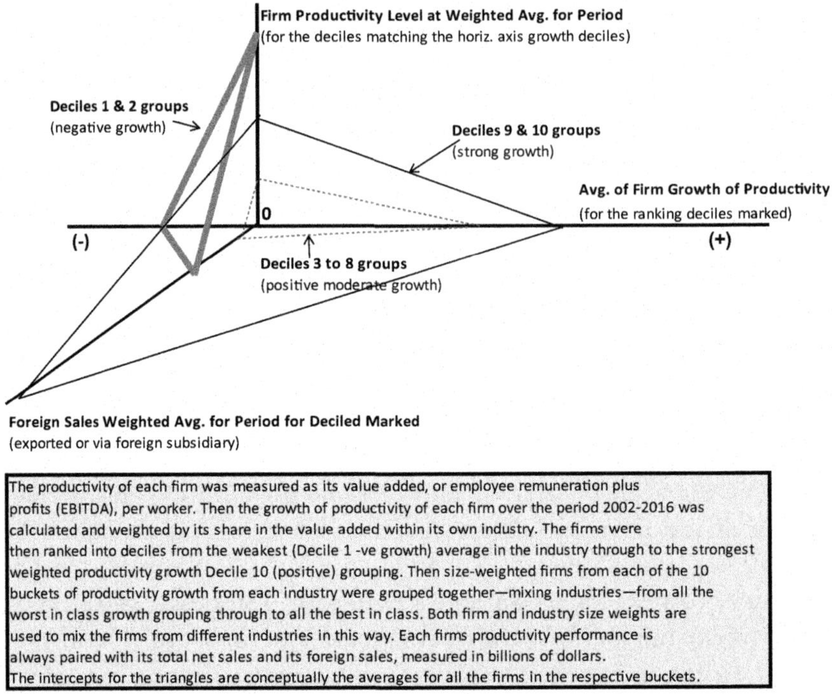

Fig. 1.8 Firm productivity and foreign sales (*Source* Authors, updated and based on their work for the OECD Business and Finance Outlook 2017)

with digitalisation and automation, including via robotics.[27] The non-level playing field competition from Asia has accelerated these natural selection pressures on Western companies.

A recent OECD study has attempted to examine what this process looks like using micro-data for 11,000 of the largest global companies across 21 GICS industrial sectors (excluding Financials and REITs). It

[27]Unmanned factories are already operational in North America. Amazon is about to launch unmanned stores, so that even lower-skilled service sector jobs are at risk. Any activities that can be broken up into calculations and/or repetitive activities can be digitalised and linked up across the internet and applied to everything in the end: production, innovation and design, inventory control and logistics, and driverless road, rail, sea and air transport. Robotics, cloud computing and the internet of things (where objects can communicate information about themselves to feed into the above processes) are platforms for innovation that are unstoppable in businesses that want to survive in the modern competitive world.

examined their weighted productivity growth rates and ranked them into groups of ten (deciles) within their industries. It then collected the matching decile groups for each industry to have companies ranked from worst (decile 1's) to best (decile 10's) in terms of productivity growth. The characteristics of each grouping were looked at (their level of productivity, wage growth, wage levels, R&D spending and so on).[28]

The reader is invited to look at the original study, but at a general level these firm groupings look something like the conceptual picture shown in Fig. 1.8. According to the OECD study, R&D spending is always important for driving productivity growth. But as recent trade theory suggests, the very best-in-class in terms of productivity growth are those companies that develop large foreign markets. The worst group is summarised by the triangle on the left. When the names are examined, these firms tend to be well-known companies that achieved past growth and a high level of productivity in their home market, but they have become stuck. Productivity growth is on average negative for the group—the level is falling. The largest group of companies by numbers is summarised by the smaller triangle in the middle of the diagram. These companies have moderate productivity growth and levels and small international markets—often zero. They tend to depend on supply chain work from larger companies. The most outstanding group is summarised by the large triangle to the right. These companies, often well known, have very fast growth and productivity is rising. Their huge success in penetrating foreign markets is the key driver (along with R&D spending and sometime M&A restructuring).

More and more of these larger global firms are forced to restructure (digitalise, use robotics, use supply chain innovation, etc.) to defend their domestic sales and try to gain better access to world markets in competition with others, via exports or foreign production investment. Sometimes M&A is a mechanism to do this and, in this respect, Chinese firms are spending very large sums in recent years to move up the value-added chain, while Western companies have always been

[28]See OECD (2017).

leaders in this area. These issues are taken up and data provided in Chapter 9, which looks towards the future. The main point of this part of the discussion concerns the way in which emerging market import penetration interacts with technology and innovation to keep companies lean and mean, and that this feeds through into labour markets, wages and prices of consumer goods—inflation and monetary policy.

The Impact of Import Penetration and Firm Innovation on Western Labour Markets

The positive achievements of Asian industrialisation on such a large scale were bound to affect other economies in terms of trade shares and impact on the labour market. A paper about the '*China Shock*', by Autor et al. (2016), provides an empirical *tour de force* on debunking the idea that Chinese import penetration has not cost US jobs. US local labour market geographies most exposed to import penetration from China were found to be affected in the following ways:

- They suffered the largest falls in manufacturing jobs, which resulted in increased unemployment or withdrawal from the labour force (at all education levels) rather than reallocation to other firms and sectors. All up 2.4 million jobs are estimated lost, ignoring aggregate demand and non-local input–output spillover effects (the inclusion of which would make the numbers much larger).
- For below-college-education employees, non-manufacturing jobs were also lost within the labour market commuting zone, likely due to negative demand spillovers.
- Tracing individual workers over time in longitudinal studies, there was very little geographic migration in response to the trade shock.
- Displaced workers move into job churning with fewer years working than non-displaced workers, and they remain in the same trade-exposed industry (since their industry-specific human capital is destroyed leaving them badly placed). After some 16 years, 43% are still 'churning' in the same exposed industry.

- The authors also reference a number of studies for other countries that suggest these effects are not confined to the USA.

This was not supposed to happen. Trade leads to specialisation, for example in capital-intensive production in capital-rich countries and in labour-intensive activity elsewhere.[29] If lower-skilled labour becomes less valued in rich countries, there may be transitional disruption. But this can be helped along by unemployment insurance and trade-exposed adjustment support packages.[30] As developing countries urbanise and generate saving for investment, productivity should rise in their traded goods sectors (e.g. manufacturing), and real wages in that sector will also begin to improve. Rising real wages creates demand for the output of the low-productivity non-traded sectors causing prices there to rise—and hence the real exchange rate will appreciate over time. This, in turn, should encourage a substitution towards demand for foreign goods.[31] Technology transfer between rich and poor countries will see productivity continue to rise, so that all countries gain from open trade. The picture that unfolded over the 2000s was very different from this '*everyone wins*' view of the world.

The loss of jobs in the West—and the fear of job loss—when combined with cheap imports from China and other emerging market economies (EMEs)—meant that global deflation pressure became everywhere more pronounced—other than for resources (such as iron ore, copper, rare metals, oil) needed for the industrialisation process in Asia, whose prices rose during periods of strong demand. This was very good for countries like Australia, Canada, Brazil and South Africa. But a very different picture emerges for countries with significant manufacturing firms competing with China. Rising import penetration together with the technology response of advanced companies to rising global

[29]The Heckscher-Ohlin and Stolper-Samuelson theorems are well known in undergraduate courses.

[30]See, for example, Box 1 of OECD, ILO, World Bank and WTO (2010).

[31]The Harrod-Balassa-Samuelson effect: wages will also tend to rise in the non-traded sector in order to retain workers, and this is passed on in higher non-traded prices. As this occurs over long periods of time, the general price level will rise versus the price of goods overseas.

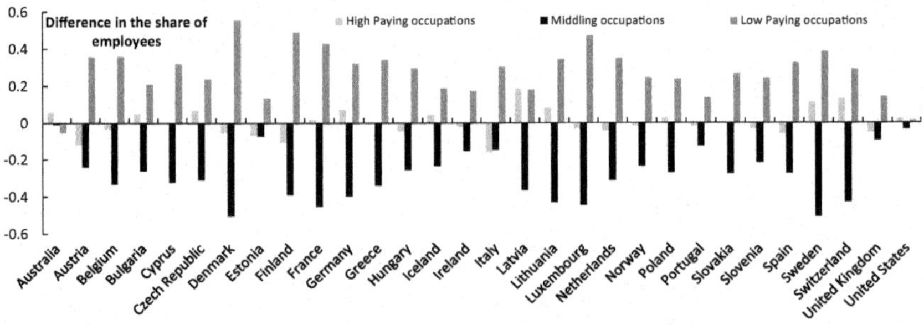

Fig. 1.9 Hollowing out: Changes in shares of employment by pay category, 2000–2015 (percent). The chart shows changes in employment shares over the years 2000–2015. The data include all persons aged 15–65 who reported employment in the sample reference year, excluding those employed by the army. Occupations are first assigned by International Standard Classification of Occupations (ISCO) categories that are consistent over the whole period. These occupations are then grouped into three broad categories by wage levels, as in Goos et al. (2014) (*Source* Data are from the International Labour Organisation and US Bureau of Labor Statistics)

competition began to cost jobs in middle-paying occupations. Squeezed between import penetration from China and induced corporate restructuring in advanced countries, middle-class workers have suffered a loss in living standards.

Figure 1.9 shows the changes in employment shares for high-skilled, middle-skilled and low-skilled workers.[32] In nearly all countries the share of middle-paying jobs has fallen between 2000 and 2015.[33] Relative employment growth has been strongest in the highest paying more technologically demanding jobs. The share of lower-skilled jobs is rising. Other than for highly skilled workers, deflation pressures are present in all countries.

[32]This updates Fig. 11 from Acemoglu and Autor (2011) for the USA, which is also based on the Goos et al. (2009) study for Europe. An additional 10 years of data are included.

[33]While these patterns imply employment income distribution would worsen, it need not worsen after tax and transfer payments. This study is concerned with the pressures from globalisation and not the redistributive policies that they might improve income distribution.

Deflation Pressures in Firms Most Affected by Globalisation

As global competition has increased, in the form of the cross-border activities of (mainly) SOEs from China and the Asian Tigers, firms less able to adjust in the face of the un-level playing field are forced into structural adjustment. Stagnant or falling productivity puts downward pressure on wages per worker. This has put further pressure to drive for better processes and efficiencies.

When wages per employee are matched to the same company groupings as in Fig. 1.8, the picture that emerges goes some way to explain some of the pressures being felt by workers all over the world—which has already had a strong impact on political outcomes.[34] Those companies in the two worst groupings (usually incumbents with high-productivity levels but exhibiting negative productivity growth) have falling average wages per capita.[35] This group is summarised by the triangle of averages (productivity and wage growth per capita and wage levels) in the lower left of Fig. 1.10. The largest numbers of companies are represented by the triangle for the moderate productivity growth groups (deciles 3–8). These tend to exhibit moderate average wage levels and growth. Finally, the companies in the two best productivity growth groups have positive wage increases. However, the level of wages is lower than the first grouping and the wage increases still occur at rates lower than the firm's productivity growth. This of course will see profits rising at the expense of employee wages in these companies. In all cases, the micro-data show that wages do not grow in line with productivity even in the best firms and tend to fall faster in negative productivity growth firms.[36] In short, deflation pressure is evident in the global firm-based data.

[34]Such as: Brexit, the election of the US President, the rise of right wing politics in Europe, and referendum outcomes in Switzerland.

[35]Recall that these companies use employees from countries in multiple national and international locations.

[36]See also *Divided We Stand* (OECD 2011) which shows that the top decile wages grew faster than the bottom decile in all OECD countries from the mid-1980s to the late 2000s.

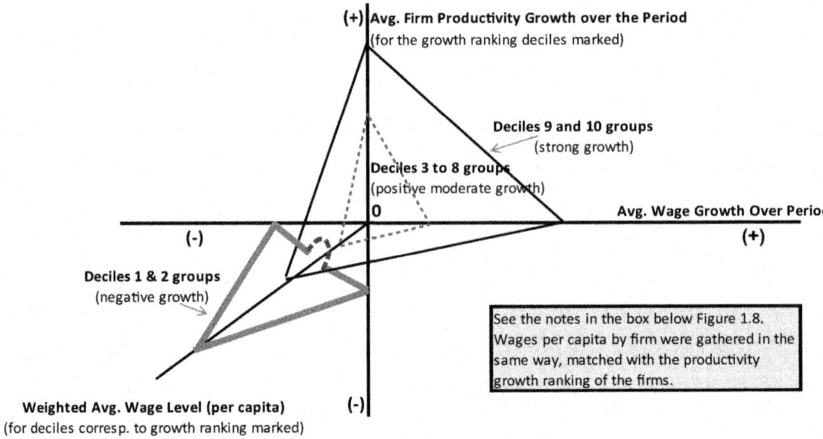

Fig. 1.10 Company productivity and wage trends in advanced countries (*Source* Based on OECD (2017))

The OECD study points out that these divergences are more extreme in some company sectors than others. In particular, there are wider productivity and wage growth differences between firms in:

- *The large 'materials' sector*: this consists of diverse industries such as chemicals, fertilisers, industrial gases, construction materials, metal (steel), glass containers, paper packaging, aluminium, diversified materials, mining, gold, precious metals and minerals, forest products and paper products.
- *The large 'Industrials' sector*: which consists of capital goods, transportation, and commercial and professional services.

These industries contain many of the trade—and technology-exposed workers, i.e. they include large numbers of the lower-skilled jobs where emerging market countries are making progress. They also include industries prone to the digitalisation of routine tasks and the use of robotics.

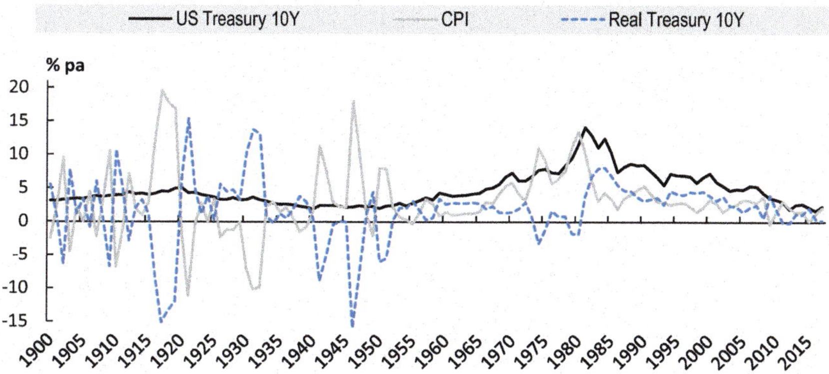

Fig. 1.11 US Treasury bond yields (*Source* Maddison, Thomson Reuters, author calculations)

Summing up the Globalisation Background to the Crisis in the USA

The Great Bond Rally

Figure 1.11 shows 115 years of history of the US 10-year government bond rate in nominal and real terms and CPI inflation. Prior to globalisation in the 2000s, the domestic money supply was thought to be the prime cause of inflation, a domestic central-bank-driven phenomenon, with a natural rate of unemployment and inflation expectations affected by central bank credibility. Globalisation appears to have changed all that, because the supply and demand for labour and goods have become more global: the workforce of Asia became integrated into global value chains. It seems likely that a global Phillips Curve has emerged. The effect of these phenomena was not perceived quickly enough by central banks, which had come to the consensus view that low inflation must be due to their own policy credibility. In some ways, this was a legacy of the past and, because of this, central banks kept interest rates too low.

In terms of the above analysis, real and nominal bond yields fell due to the interaction of a number of factors all working in the same direction: the savings glut in Asia, deflation pressures, monetary policy easing in response to those pressures and unprecedented foreign buying of US Treasury securities.

The debate over this issue can be thought about as an *ex ante* prediction:

- In the face of a global supply shock, a *too easy* monetary policy would see low inflation and increased asset price inflation, with investors taking advantage of low rates to buy assets.
- If monetary policy had been appropriately tight, with low inflation due to central bank credibility, there would also have been low inflation, but asset price inflation should have remained absent.

In the event, the former scenario is the one that unfolded. The yield on the US Treasury 10-year bond fell in both nominal and real terms from about 2001, well after the Volcker disinflation had settled CPI inflation into the 2–5% range. This corresponds with the entry of China into WTO, and the start of the above-combined factors. Once the crisis set in, inflation took another leg down and risk aversion and the demand for safe liquid assets from pension and sovereign wealth funds joined currency managing central banks in buying even more US Treasuries.

Some empirical evidence on the factors that drove US bond rates is presented in the Appendix to this Chapter. The main effect of short rates on bond yields came almost immediately after the crisis began (the drop in short rates from over 5 to 0.3% reduced the 10-year rate by over 1 percentage point immediately). But the effect of foreign buying of Treasuries began much earlier. By January 2007, the effect subtracted around 165 basis points from the 10-year bond rate. Subsequently, this effect nearly doubled after the crisis, when the Federal Reserve joined into the buying, and purchases reached the maximum amounts shown in Fig. 1.7.[37]

[37]This variable is correlated with excess saving reflected in the current account surplus: since current accounts have to be financed, and official lending through reserves accumulation was the principle channel for this.

The Great House Price Rally

US house prices played a critical role in the US subprime crisis. The outcomes for this asset class (due to many of the issues discussed earlier) are shown (by region) in Fig. 1.12. By boosting house prices, very low-interest rates contributed to the leverage and financial fragility problems that followed. From 2000 to the start of 2007, house prices in the Pacific region rose by 128%. From the crisis trough to the early 2018 average prices rose around 46% for the whole of the USA.

It should not be forgotten too that house prices likely contributed to the lack of adjustment in labour markets in the face of import penetration. People like to own their homes, and moving between regions requires workers to sell their homes and buy new ones in the places where the jobs are available. Trade-exposed workers sit in localities often found in: the East-North-Central (Michigan, Ohio, etc.); East-South-Central (e.g. Alabama, Kentucky and Tennessee); and West-North-Central (e.g. Iowa, Kansas, Missouri). Jobs may be available in California, but monetary policy has failed to boost house prices to the same extent as it did for the Pacific region because of the poor underlying supply and demand conditions. Workers wanting to own their own home don't want to move.

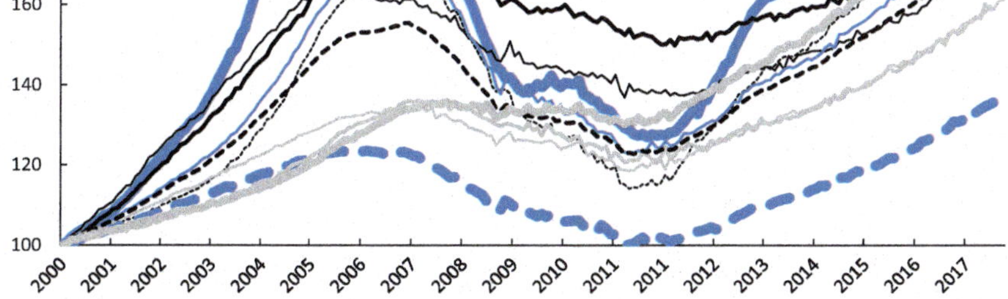

Fig. 1.12 US house prices (*Source* Thomson Reuters, author calculations)

If unemployment fails to adjust to easy policy in the regions where it is most needed, this creates the incentive to keep monetary policy rates lower for longer. Leverage builds up further, and people on low incomes are induced to take on loans that they won't be able to afford at higher rates. These loans are analysed in the next few chapters and tie in with all of the other complex factors that played critical roles in the crisis—financial innovation, securitisation, derivatives, the measures taken for dealing with the crisis and the attempts at negotiating with banks for reform.

Appendix to Chapter 1: Modelling the Effect of Foreign Buying on US Bond Yields

Table 1.1 shows the Engle-Granger co-integration and error-correction model estimates for the 10-year US Treasury bond rate, where CPI is the consumer price index, LIBOR is the US 3-month rate and Treasury securities holdings by foreigners and by the US Federal Reserve are expressed as a per cent of GDP.[38]

According to this model, the contributions to the overall fall in the US bond yield are:

- The move up in foreign and Federal Reserve holdings of US Treasuries as a percentage of GDP. This was 15.4% in January 2002 (worth 125 basis points off the yield) and rose to 21.2% (165 basis points off the 10-year rate), by January 2007. This variable peaked most recently at over 40% (worth a full 3 percentage points off the yield).
- Libor just prior to the crisis was just over 5% and fell to around 0.3%. This would account for a 1.1 percentage point fall in the 10-year bond rate.
- The fall in inflation, from around 4% to just less than 2% over this period, on average, subtracted around 50 basis points from bond yields over the period.

[38]See Blundell-Wignall and Roulet (2014), and references therein.

Table 1.1 US 10-year bond model

Cointegration equation (1)	**Equation (1)** (2000–2016 monthly)	**Equations (2)** (2000–2016 monthly)
CPI Inflation, Monthly % Change	0.230** [-1.98]	–
3-month LIBOR	0.226*** [10.42]	–
Foreign Holdings of US Treasury Securities %GDP	−0.078*** [-16.87]	–
Error correction equation (2)		
Lagged residual	–	-0.107*** [-3.70]
Change in CPI variable	–	0.013 [0.25]
Change in LIBOR from 3 months ago	–	0.136** [2.11]
Change in foreign treasury holdings %GDP	–	−0.003 [-0.08]
Constant	0.049*** [33.12]	-0.001 [−0.72]
Test statistics		
F-Statistic	441.08	3.36
Probability (*F*-Statistic)	0	0.01
Durbin Watson	0.24	1.6
Wald *F*-Statistic	430.59	5.1
Total Observations	214	214

Source Datastream, Authors. Phillips–Perron (PP) unit root test is employed, which corrects, in a nonparametric way, any possible presence of autocorrelation in the standard ADF test. Tests are showing that all variables are non-stationary series at levels but stationary series at first differences. The significant error-correction result establishes the presence of a co-integrating relationship between the bond rate and the explanatory variables, and the lag structure demonstrates causality. It suggests a 7-month lag for the full effects to work through from a change in the co-integrating variables to the observed 10-year bond rate
*** indicate significance at the 1% level
** indicate significance at the 5% level
* indicate significance at the 10% level

References

Acemoglu, D., & Autor, D. H. (2011). "Skills, Tasks and Technologies: Implications for Employment and Earnings", *Handbook of Labor Economics, 4b*, 1043–1171.

Allison, G. (2015, September). The Thucydides Trap. *The Atlantic.*

Autor, D. H., Dorn, D., & Henderson, G. H. (2016). *The China Shock: Learning from Labour Market Adjustment to Large Changes in Trade* (NBER Working Paper No. 21906). National Bureau of Economic Research.

Bakker, A. F. P. (1996). *The Liberalization of Capital Movements in Europe*. Dordrecht and Boston: Kluwer Academic.

Berka, M., Devereux, M. B., & Engel, C. (2014, September). *Real Exchange Rates and Sectoral Productivity in the Eurozone* (NBER Working Paper No. 20510). National Bureau of Economic Research.

Bernanke, B. (2005). The Global Saving Glut and the U.S. Current Account Deficit. Federal Reserve Board. *Homer Jones Lecture*.

Blundell-Wignall, A., & Roulet, C. (2014). Problems in the International Financial System. *OECD Journal, Financial Trends, 2014*(2).

Blundell-Wignall, A., Atkinson, P. E., & Roulet, C. (2013). Integration Versus Interdependence and Complexity in Global Trade and Finance in the Post-war Period. In Morten & Gnan (Eds.), *50 Years of Money and Finance: Lessons and Challenges*. SUERF 50th Anniversary Volume. Larcier.

Cai, F., Park, A., & Yao, Z. (2008). The Chinese Labour Market in the Reform Era. In L. Brandt & T. Rawski (Eds.), *China's Great Economic Transformation*. Cambridge: Cambridge University Press.

Corsetti, G. P., Pesenti, P., & Roubini, N. (1998). *What Caused the Asian Currency and Financial Crisis: The Policy Debate* (NBER Working Paper No. w6834). National Bureau of Economic Research.

Dooley, M., & Isard, P. (1980, April). Capital Controls, Political Risk, and Deviations from Interest-Rate Parity. *Journal of Political Economy, 88*(2), 370–384. University of Chicago Press.

Eichengreen, B. (1999). *Towards a New International Financial Architecture: A Practical Post-Asia Agenda*. Washington: Institute for International Economics.

Feldstein, M., & Horioka, C. (1980, June). Domestic Savings and International Capital Flows. *The Economic Journal, 90*(358), 314–329.

Fukao, M. (1990, September). The Liberalization of Japanese Exchange Controls and Structural Changes in the Balance of Payments. *The Bank of Japan Monetary and Economic Studies, 8*(2), 101–165. Tokyo.

Fukuyama, F. (1989). The End of History. *National Interest*, Summer.

Goos, M., Manning, A., & Soloman, A. (2009). Job Polarization in Europe. *American Economic Review: Papers & Proceedings, 99*(2).

Goos, M., Manning, A., & Soloman, A. (2014). Explaining Job Polarisation: Routine Biased Technological Change and Offshoring. *American Economic Review, 104*(8), 2509–2526.

Helpman, E., Melitz, M. J., & Yeaple, S. R. (2004). Export Versus FDI with Heterogeneous Firms. *American Economic Review, 94*(1), 300–316.

Johnson, C. (1982). *MITI and the Japanese Miracle: The Growth of Industrial Policy, 1925–1975*. Stanford, CA: Stanford University Press.

Liu, L. (2005, March). Bidding Farewell to This Year's Laid off Workers. *China News Weekly*, Vol. 220.

Ma, G., Roberts, I., & Kelly, G. (2016). A Rebalancing Chinese Economy: Challenges and International Implications. In *Structural Change in China: Implications for Australia and the World*. Reserve Bank of Australia.

Ma, G., & Wang, Y. (2010, June). *China's High Saving Rate: Myth and Reality* (BIS Working Paper No. 312). Bank for International Settlements.

McKinnon, R. I. (1973). *Money and Capital in Economic Development*. Washington, DC: Brookings Institution.

Melitz, M. J., & Redding, S. J. (2012). *Heterogeneous Firms and Trade* (NBER Working Paper No. 18652). National Bureau of Economic Research.

OECD. (2002). *Forty Years' Experience with the OECD Codes of Liberalisation of Capital Movements*. Paris: OECD.

OECD. (2011). *Divided we Stand: Why Inequality Keeps Rising*. Paris: OECD.

OECD. (2015). *Business and Finance Outlook*. Paris: OECD.

OECD. (2017). *Business and Finance Outlook*. Paris: OECD.

Radelet, S., & Sachs, J. (1998). The East Asian Financial Crisis: Diagnosis, Remedies, Prospects. *Brookings Papers on Economic Activity, 1*, 1–90.

Rodrik, D. (2008). The Real Exchange Rate and Economic Growth. *Brookings Papers on Economic Activity, 39*(2) (Fall), 365–439.

Stiglitz, J., & Yusuf, S. (2001). *Rethinking the East Asian Miracle*. New York: Oxford University Press.

Tica, J., & Druzic, I. (2006). *The Harrod-Balassa-Samuelson Effect: A Survey of Empirical Evidence* (Working Paper Series No. 06-07). University of Zagreb.

United States Department of the Treasury. (2016, October). *Foreign Exchange Policies of Major Trading Partners of the United States. Semi-Annual Report to Congress.*

Williamson, J. (2004, September 24–25). *A Short History of the Washington Consensus.* Paper Commissioned by Fundación CIDOB for a Conference "From the Washington Consensus Towards a New Global Governance." Barcelona.

Wyplosz, C. (2001). *Exchange Rate Regimes: Some Lessons from Postwar Europe* (CEPR Discussion Paper No. 2723). Centre for Economic Policy Research.

2

Financial Innovation and Basel II

Introduction to Financial Deregulation and Innovation

At the same time that industrialisation and trade were taking off in Asia, with implications for global saving and investment and for pressures on living standards, financial deregulation and innovation were proceeding at a rapid pace in the west. These structural trends were on a collision course.

The Great Depression and wartime controls that followed led to extensive widespread regulation of the financial system, involving restrictions on international capital movements, interest-rate ceilings and various types of quantitative controls. In the USA, these included Regulation Q interest ceilings, federal insurance for bank deposits and, importantly, the Glass-Steagall Act that separated deposit-insured banking from securities-broking and insurance businesses. Europe never had this separation, and its universal banks have always mixed commercial, retail and investment banking. Major regulations on interest rates, capital controls and links between fiscal budgets and central bank funding began to be removed in the early 1980s. Bank capital adequacy rules

A. Blundell-Wignall et al., *Globalisation and Finance at the Crossroads*,
https://doi.org/10.1007/978-3-319-72676-2_2

were generally absent, and leverage was considered to be an indicator of risk rather than a minimum required ratio. The soundness of bank balance sheets relied more on informal bank supervision.

Much of this structure was intended to allow macroeconomic policies more supportive of employment without generating financial instability or pressures that could threaten the Bretton Woods par value system, which was designed to permit the progressive opening of the international trading system. Lack of international adjustment mechanisms and inflationary biases created tensions, such as those described in Box 1.2 in the previous chapter, with which the system could not cope and the par value system collapsed in the early 1970s. Soon afterwards, regulations on international capital movements began to be relaxed or abolished, and by the early 1980s, this applied to major controls on interest rates, bank lending and links between budget financing and central banking.

Bank failures and the savings and loan crisis turned regulatory attention in the USA during the 1980s to bank solvency. From 1981, the Fed and the Office of the Comptroller of the Currency announced a minimum 6% capital ratio versus total assets for community banks and 5% ratio for larger deposit-taking institutions. The FDIC announced a similar rule. At the international level, two sets of issues concentrated regulators' attention:

- The emerging market debt crisis, especially in Latin America (recounted in Chapter 1) was threatening the balance sheets of large internationally active banks in advanced countries, especially the USA; and
- The relentless rise of the Japanese yen after 1984 steadily strengthened the capital base of Japanese banks and encouraged aggressive competition which banks in other countries found difficult to resist.

By the late 1980s, the Basel Committee of Banking Supervisors (BCBS) had become the *de facto* global bank regulator and, after much consultation with banks, the Basel I Accord was announced (implemented in 1992). This imposed a simple risk-weighted capital rule. The concept, much loved by the banks, was that instead of holding capital against possible losses to the total balance sheet from wherever they might come, it would all be done the other way around. Regulators would know which assets were risky and which were not, so they could apply fixed weights—large for risky assets and smaller for less-risky ones. The added up risk-weighted assets' total was to be the base for a minimum capital ratio of 8%. The experience of Basel I revealed a number of flaws (see below), and this led to a process to replace it with what proved to be an even more flawed framework in Basel II.

The 1933 Glass-Steagall Act reflected the judgement that the mixing of more risky business models with traditional deposit banking was a significant contributor to the Great Depression. Citigroup led the lobbying to remove restrictions on these activities in 1999, and this was one of the key steps towards the 2007–08 crisis. In the preceding 50 years, major banking crises had been avoided. The repeal of Glass-Steagall in 1999, the agreement for Basel II to replace the flawed Basel I in 2004 and SEC rule changes in the same year that removed effective leverage constraints on broker-dealer activities together were to cause leverage and asset prices to explode upwards. In just a few years, the world was to be thrown into the greatest financial crisis since the Great Depression.

The problem with regulators, after consulting with banks, defining what is 'risky' in order to set risk weights is that there are too many moving parts: not least financial innovation to find new ways to game the regulatory rules and to take advantage of taxation structures to benefit clients and to generate fees and profit. What is 'risky' becomes dynamic, depending on what banks do in response to how rules are set. By studying the mistakes made in the lead up to the 2007–08 crisis, better insights can be obtained as to the sorts of regulations that might work.

This chapter sets out the capital and other rules changes in the first half of the 2000s that proved conducive to leverage, and outlines the endogenous financial innovations and instruments that enabled banks to expand leverage despite attempts to improve the regulatory system—undermining the latter completely. One cannot hope to understand the crisis without investing a little time into these basic components that conditioned what happened. Subsequent chapters then provide empirical evidence about the causes of the crisis and what sort of regulatory framework is essential.

Too often everyone has a view, and regulatory policy proceeds based on national interests and objectives other than the stability of the financial system—regulatory capture and what most benefits the '*national champions*' plays an important role. After a crisis, policy proceeds without the benefit of empirical evidence—by necessity of the urgent situation—making the process *ad hoc* and more subject to pressures from vested interests. But with time more evidence has become available, and this should be looked at with the aim of getting better bank business models and regulatory structures.

The Basel Accords I and II

Capital regulations under Basel I came into effect in December 1992 (after their development via consultations between members and with the banks since 1988). The aims were: first, to require banks to maintain enough capital to absorb losses without causing systemic problems; and second, to level the playing field internationally (to avoid competitiveness conflicts, especially by restraining Japanese banks).

The Basel Accords define Tier 1 capital, which is in principle of higher quality—and hence of best use in a crisis. In the view of the present authors, this should be equal to equity capital less goodwill and a few other deductions. Tier 2 capital is of lesser quality (certain subordinated debt, etc.) and was negotiated in the Committee because some countries had more lax definitions of capital than others, and they didn't want hardships imposed on their own banks.[1] A minimum ratio of 4% was required for Tier 1 capital versus risk-weighted assets (RWA), and 8% for Tier 1 and Tier 2 capital together. The Basel I risk weights for different loans are shown on the left side of Table 2.1. The securities listed on the far left are multiplied by the weights, and the total is added up.

---

[1]See Tarullo (2008). This kind of favouring of one's own banks in a 'competitiveness' sense, instead of consistent cross-country rules for stability, continues to this very day.

Table 2.1 Basel I and Basel II: Risk weights and summary

Risk weights under Basel I and Basel II (Pillar I), %							
Security	**BASEL I**	**BASEL II Simplified Standardised**	**BASEL II Standardised based on External Ratings**		**BASEL II Advanced: Internal Ratings Based (IRB)**		**Basel II Advanced IRB**
					2004–2005 QIS 4 Avg % Change vs Basel I MRC	**2004–2005 QIS 4 Median % Change vs Basel I MRC**	
Most Government/ central bank	0	0			0	0	Comes close to letting banks set their own **Pillar 1** capital, with supervisory oversight. Risk weights depend on internal estimates of a loan's probability of default; loss-given-default; exposure to loss. These are based on the banks' own complex risk models, relying on subjective inputs and often on unobservable (e.g. OTC illiquid securities) prices.
AAA to AA–			0				
A+ to A–			20				
BBB+ to BBB–			50				
BB+ to B– (& unrated)			100				
Below B–			150				
Other public (supervisors discretion)	0–50	0			0	0	
Claims on MDBs	20	0			–21.9	–29.7	
Most OECD Banks & Securities firms (1)	20	20	<90days	Other	–21.9	–29.7	
AAA to AA–			20	20			
A+ to A–			20	50			
BBB+ to BBB– (&unrated)			20	50			

(continued)

Table 2.1 (continued)

Risk weights under Basel I and Basel II (Pillar I), %							
Security	**BASEL I**	**BASEL II Simplified Standardised**	**BASEL II Standardised based on External Ratings**		**BASEL II Advanced: Internal Ratings Based (IRB)**		**Basel II Advanced IRB**
					2004–2005 QIS 4 Avg % Change vs Basel I MRC	**2004–2005 QIS 4 Median % Change vs Basel I MRC**	
BB+ to B–			50	100			**Pillar 2** provides for supervisory oversight. With stress testing, and guidance from supervisors, banks can be made to hold capital for risks not adequately captured under Pillar 1. **Pillar 3** is disclosure and market discipline which relies on some notion of market efficiency. Rational markets punish poor risk managers.
Below B–			150	150			
Residential Mortgages-fully secured	50	35	35		–61.4	–72.7	
Retail Lending (consumer)	100	75	75		(–6.5 to –74.3)	(–35.2 to –78.6)	
Corporate & Commercial RE	100	100			(–21.9 to –41.4)	(–29.7 to –52.5)	
AAA to AA–			20				
A+ to A–			50				
BBB+ to BB– (&unrated)			100				
Below BB–			150				

(1) Securities firms subject to risk-based capital requirements and consolidated regulation
Source BCBS (1988, 2004, 2006) and FDIC (2005); authors' commentary. QIS4 was a Quantitative Impact Study conducted by the BCBS to examine the impact of the proposed rules on bank portfolios

Experience showed, however, that banks had an incentive to pool the more risky loans, turn them into securities, and sell them off the balance sheet while retaining low-risk assets that didn't need much capital—a process of disintermediation that amounted to regulatory arbitrage. For example, consumer loans and commercial real estate with a 100% weight could be pooled, turned into securities (securitisation) and sold off. In this way, banks quickly accumulated capital well in excess of the regulatory minimum: i.e. the rule had no constraining impact on bank risk-taking, and leverage could be increased for the lower risk-weighted assets banks chose to retain.[2] For these reasons, the regulators decided to propose a new accord, and again in consultation with the banks.

The '*revised framework*' known as Basel II was released in June 2004. It was built around three 'Pillars':

- Rules to define capital and minimum requirements to buffer unexpected losses;
- Supervision; and
- Market discipline.

Pillar 1 required banks to hold a minimum of 8% of capital (Tier 1 and 2) versus RWA. Total RWA are based on a complex system of risk weighting that was simple under Basel I but became much more complex under Basel II. The weights are applied to all bank assets to calculate the 'credit' risk component. 'Market' (MR) and 'operational' risk (OR) are calculated separately and then added:

$$\text{RWA} = \{12.5(\text{OR} + \text{MR}) + 1.06 * \text{SUM}[w(i)A(i)]\} \quad (2.1)$$

where $w(i)$ is the risk weight for asset i; and $A(i)$ is asset i; OR and MR are directly measured exposures and grossed up by 12.5 (to make it

[2]Bank always want to increase leverage for profitability. A 1% spread on a \$100 loan with \$100 of equity gives rise to a 1% return on equity. Levered up 30 times gives a 30% return on equity. With fees for securitisation on top of this, the return on equity can be very large indeed. If banks are implicitly guaranteed by governments, perfect moneymaking machines are created—private gains for shareholders in the good times, and socialised losses if greed risks taking the bank down.

equivalent to an asset level to which the 8% ratio can apply), and credit risk is the sum of the various asset classes, each weighted by its appropriate risk weight.[3] Basel II was scheduled to begin in January 2008.

Banks were to be able to choose between: first, a simplified approach (for smaller institutions without the capacity to model their businesses in risk terms) by using the fixed weights shown in column two of Table 2.1; second, a 'standardized' approach based on external ratings (shown in the columns three and four in Table 2.1); and third, an internal ratings-based (IRB) approach for sophisticated banks, driven by their own value-at-risk (VaR) models (see the far right side of Table 2.1). The IRB approach required banks to specify the probability of default (PD) for each individual credit, its loss-given-default (LGD), and the expected exposure at default (EAD). To do this requires highly complex modelling and aggregation. These in turn offer banks with the necessary expertise the possibility of deriving lower weights on the basis that these are more risk-sensitive than the weights defined by the Basel Committee. This approach required the approval of the bank's supervisor.

The simplified system and the external rating-based approach retained the basic features of Basel I. It is striking (with the hindsight of the financial crisis) that all these approaches show the Basel Committee cutting the risk weight on mortgages by some 15 percentage points (from 50 to 35%), and by much more if the bank could use the IRB approach (by between 60 and 70%). The weight for lending between banks was only 20% under Basel 1, and this was kept the same under the simplified Basel II and for most categories above 'junk' in the external ratings approach. For banks using their own models, the indicative average cut was in the range of 20–30% below Basel I.

It is somewhat surprising that the regulators allowed large sophisticated banks to run their own internal models to define the riskiness of their assets for regulatory purposes. With a little creativity, banks would be able to hold as little capital as they liked—so needless to say it was strongly

---

[3]At the time, a scaling factor was applied to this latter term, estimated to be 1.06 on the basis of Quantitative Impact Studies (QIS), in order to preserve previous minimum capital over a transition period.

supported by them. There are in fact many problems with the Basel Accord framework, and these are set out for reference in Appendix to Chapter 2. It was left to Pillars 2 and 3 to ensure that any problems with Pillar 1 would be dealt with in a timely way (see Table 2.1).

The issues of regulatory arbitrage and problems with the Basel system will be returned to later in this chapter, after first introducing the financial innovations that were going on at the same time.

Financial Innovations: Securitisation and Derivatives

The regulatory system in the 60 years prior to the crisis provided a context for extensive trade liberalisation within Europe and globally under successive GATT rounds, a huge expansion of world trade and a growing world economy without repeating the banking crises of the 1930s. All this would come to an end by 2007. The innovations known as securitisation and derivatives eventually interacted with badly designed capital adequacy regulation and resulted in the world's greatest financial crisis since the Great Depression.

Support for Housing in the USA

The earliest roots of the crisis can be traced back to New Deal support given to the collapsing housing sector at the bottom of the Depression and never really withdrawn. The Home Owners Loan Act (1933), the National Housing Act (1934) and its amendment in 1938 created various financial vehicles to slow the wave of foreclosures. These vehicles offered government support for the mortgage market by providing liquidity and guarantees to banks offering mortgages. These efforts were generally successful, and two of the financial vehicles, the Federal Housing Administration (FHA) and the Federal National Mortgage Corporation (FNMC), continued to operate during the post-war boom that followed the Depression and the War. Favourable tax treatment, notably deductibility of interest payments, and interest-rate regulation that channelled funds to specialised housing finance providers (savings and loans, known as S&Ls or 'thrifts') reinforced the policy bias in favour of homeownership.

In 1965, the FHA was folded into the newly created Department of Housing and Urban Development, and, in 1968, the FNMC was split into two financial enterprises. One ('Ginnie Mae') bought government-guaranteed loans and remained part of the government. The other ('Fannie Mae') was a more ambiguous creature which could also buy ordinary (i.e. not guaranteed) mortgages under a social mandate from Congress to provide support for low- and middle-income housing. Fannie Mae was structured as a quoted company. Around the same time, Congress created a competitor for Fannie Mae, the Federal Home Loan Mortgage Corporation ('Freddie Mac'). This was owned by S&Ls until it also became a quoted company in 1989. Fannie and Freddie's Congressional origins together with their social mandates led them to be known as 'government-sponsored enterprises' (GSEs) that were widely perceived to have an implicit guarantee, notwithstanding that they were private quoted companies. This implicit guarantee would eventually play an important role in the 2007–08 crisis.

As long as the macroeconomic environment was stable, this framework supported robust residential construction and a strong expansion of homeownership throughout the middle and working classes. S&Ls provided low-risk long-term (typically 30 years) fixed-rate mortgages to homebuyers who provided 20% down payments while NHA and FNMC and its successors provided liquidity. As reported by Michael Lewis,[4] outstanding mortgages rose from $55bn in 1950 to $1200bn in 1980, exceeding all US stock markets combined in size.

[4]This account of the emergence of the securitised mortgage industry draws heavily from Michael Lewis (1989). Other sources are Bethany McLean and Joe Nocera (2011) *and* Barry Ritholtz, with Aaron Task (2009).

Packaging Mortgages

In 1970, Ginnie Mae decided to enhance its liquidity by pooling some of its mortgages, packaging them as bonds and selling them. Freddie Mac soon followed. A major problem with this approach is that US borrowers can repay mortgages ahead of time with no penalty. This insulates a fixed-rate mortgage from any rises in market rates but allows it to be refinanced at a lower rate if market conditions permit. In effect, a call option for the borrower is incorporated in the mortgage contract which is likely to be exercised if market rates fall. So the holder of mortgages, or any security containing them, has no idea what maturity his or her investment has. This is unattractive to an investor, and securitised mortgage bonds were not very successful during the 1970s. But two major forces emerged which, as Lewis recounts brilliantly in *Liar's Poker*, led to change.

One was the steady movement of economic activity and population in the USA towards the south and west and away from the north-east and heavy industrial region around the Great Lakes. This created a regional imbalance in the overall funding of home building since financing demands were high in the south and west, where most of the building took place, but the flow of deposits to the S&Ls in these regions was more limited. S&Ls, as secondary institutions, did not enjoy good access to the interbank market, which in any case deals in very short-term instruments, so equilibrating flows did not relieve this imbalance.

This appeared to offer an opportunity to a money trader in the US Treasury bonds department at Salomon Brothers, named Bob Dall, who occasionally also traded Ginnie Mae securities. Salomon Brothers could buy mortgages in the south, relieving the funds shortage at local S&Ls, package them as securities and sell them to S&Ls with an excess of deposits and limited investment outlets in the north and mid-west. This would effectively transfer surplus funds in the north and mid-west to the south where they were needed. Based on this idea, Dall persuaded Salomon's executive committee in mid-1978 to separate trading in Ginnie Maes from the US Treasury bonds department and to transfer it to a newly created mortgage department. He appointed 30-year-old Lewis Ranieri, an aggressive young bond dealer, to run it. As the department grew so did Ranieri's authority and Dall was squeezed out of the picture.

The second force was the loss of monetary discipline which led to the collapse of the Bretton Woods system and high and variable inflation during the 1970s. Soon after Ranieri took control of the mortgage department, US inflation rose above 10% and money market rates followed, varying between 10 and 20% for most of the next three to four years as the Volcker Fed got serious about bringing inflation down below 5%. While S&Ls enjoyed a regulatory advantage vis-à-vis commercial banks in attracting funds, deposit rates were capped below 6%. This was far below market rates.

The result was severe problems at all deposit-taking institutions in attracting and retaining deposits. Money drained into market instruments, notably money market mutual funds which were available in small amounts to retail investors. Inevitably, Congress moved to deregulate interest rates on deposits,[5] which could now rise to competitive levels so S&Ls could retain their funding. But with market rates far higher than they had been historically, this put them in the position of funding old fixed-rate mortgages earning between 5 and 10% with deposits costing in the 15 to 20% range. As a practical matter, nearly the whole sector was effectively bankrupt.

In this environment, there was little activity in the securitised mortgage sector. With the yield curve typically inverted during this period, even new mortgages yielded too little to cover their carrying costs. So S&Ls stopped originating new mortgages, which meant no raw material to securitise. At the same time, losses on carrying historical mortgages acquired when interest rates were much lower were consuming S&Ls' capital so buyers were scarce. Most mortgage departments on Wall Street closed. Only Lewis Ranieri's operation at Salomon Brothers expanded.

---

[5]The Depository Institutions Deregulation and Monetary Control Act of 1980.

Trading Mortgages Take off

On 30 September 1981, Congress came up with a solution to the S&Ls' problems. In effect, it allowed S&Ls to exchange similar or identical mortgages, record losses by booking their disposals at prices far below par, i.e. their acquisition price, and then recover back taxes for up to 10 years.[6] The prospect of recapitalising created by the tax break transformed the market overnight as S&Ls raced to churn their mortgage portfolios. Virtually, all spontaneous activity involved selling, as this was necessary to claim the tax break, and Ranieri's department was the only buyer. Salomon Brothers could not suddenly just add hundreds of billions in bad mortgages to its balance sheet, but it could act as a market maker by insisting that sellers replace their old mortgages with essentially identical mortgages provided by Salomon Brothers. Ranieri's department extracted large spreads on these deals but so long as the tax break was worth more to the S&Ls than the cash loss from the deal with Ranieri, the S&Ls agreed to terms. In 1982, his department made $150m, a very large sum in those days, and this is believed to have risen significantly during the following few years.

At the start, this flood of activity involved trading whole loans, i.e. individual mortgages. Salomon Brothers thus owned and sold large numbers of loans on property whose quality it was in no position to monitor. Administrative costs were high. This was an odd role for an investment bank whose business was trading in securities, especially given the poor reputation of the S&Ls that had originated the loans. All this made Salomon Brothers' management uneasy. In addition, the tax break which generated all this activity encouraged sellers but not buyers. Salomon Brothers sought ways to package the loans into securities that would appeal to a wider range of investors. This would have two major advantages: first, securitisation fees would become an important source of revenue; and second, the underlying assets would be off Salomon Brothers' balance sheet, conserving capital and providing a means of circumventing eventual rules on capital adequacy.

[6]Lewis reports that S&Ls were selling mortgages at 65 cents on the dollar around this time.

Securitisation Follows

Mortgage securities created during the 1970s and early 1980s, i.e. when Ranieri was establishing his operations, were simple pools of individual mortgages. The pools were divided into shares, eventually known as 'tranches', and the pools' cash flows were passed pro rata to the owners of the various tranches. They were structured as 'Grantor Trusts', which for tax purposes operated like a partnership. This structure, however, has important limitations.

One limitation of the Grantor Trust structure is that the cash flows from a mortgage pool are a mix of principal and interest which are passed through to investors. Principal receipts must be reinvested, and tax implications vary across different classes of investors (i.e. tax-exempt investors, financial businesses and individuals). Uncertainty about prepayments exacerbates this problem since the cash flows are unpredictable. Another limitation is that since the underlying securities entail risk, and will normally involve some defaults, the pools must include a 'residual interest', essentially an equity component. A third issue is that most underlying mortgages have a 30-year term at a fixed rate making the securities unattractive for many investors who prefer shorter maturities. Finally, unless the credit quality of the underlying mortgages can be made transparent, the riskiness of the securitised pool is difficult to assess.

The 'Waterfall'

In 1983, Ranieri's team, working with Larry Fink[7] at First Boston, tried to deal with these issues in a security package created for Freddie Mac. They allowed the tranches to be differentiated, essentially creating multiple classes of securities in a 'Collateralized Mortgage Obligation (CMO)'. Instead of passing the cash flows through to owners or tranches on a pro rata basis, the CMO ordered the tranches in terms

[7]Later co-founder and CEO of Blackrock.

of seniority and passed all cash flows to the most senior tranche until it was fully paid before moving on to the tranche next-in-line. Thus, no tranche received any money until all tranches senior to it had been fully serviced. This served to create a hierarchy of certainty about the cash flows and the creditworthiness of the various tranches. The most senior tranches would be fully serviced in almost any circumstances while the tranches last in line were unlikely to receive anything unless, very fortuitously, none of the underlying securities defaulted. In each time period, the cash flows would service some number of tranches fully and partially service a single tranche when the money ran out while leaving nothing for the remainder. When the money would run out in each period could not be known ahead of time. In all likelihood, the tranche first affected as the money ran out would move over time as the number of cumulative defaults in the pool rose.

The practical result was that the tranches could be loosely divided into three groups: first, a 'super senior' class of high instruments with predictable cash flows that could be marketed as a fixed instrument; second, a 'mezzanine' class covering the uncertain range of tranches where cash flows could be expected to run out; and third, a residual 'equity' class which would be first in line to absorb all losses on defaults by the underlying mortgages.

This structure had several favourable features. First, the most senior tranches could obtain high ratings from the rating agencies and be sold to a wide range of investors as high-quality fixed interest instruments. Second, investors in the most senior tranches would be isolated from the uncertainties arising from early repayments and defaults, which could be shifted to the lowest tranches. Third, maturities of these tranches could be fixed at shorter terms than those of the underlying mortgages, concentrating long-term interest-rate risk in the lower tranches. Fourth, tranches could be packaged into different types of securities that catered to different investor preferences, e.g. by splitting payments into interest-only and principal-only bonds. Such a structure allowed a large share of the package to be marketed to a wide range of investors paying interest rates that reflected the quality of the security and its repayment terms. If the residual (equity) interest is not marketable, it remains on the balance sheet of the investment bank doing the securitising. While high risk, because this is where most of the risk of the entire pool has been concentrated by design, it is not guaranteed to lose money, and if underlying mortgages perform better than anticipated when the loans were extended, it could prove to be lucrative.

The Mortgage Conduit (REMIC) and Structured Investment Vehicles (SIVs)

This CMO structure raised tax issues which resulted in a subsequent problem when Sears Mortgage Securities (SMS 1984-1) transaction was challenged by IRS on a regulatory basis. It was denied status as a Grantor Trust. IRS considered that there were two problems:

- Treating different tranches differently typically involves deferral of income that IRS considers unacceptable.
- An investor no longer holds a simple direct share in the trust, whose income can be passed through, since the ownership structure varies over time as principal repayments are allocated according to priority and not pro rata to owners.

The only solution to this, if the advantages of differentiating tranches were to be preserved, was new legislation that authorised a clear structure that would avoid double taxation of cash flows, i.e. at both entity and investor levels. Ranieri made common cause with Fannie Mae (David Maxwell), which recognised the potential advantages of securitising mortgages, and together they invested considerable time and energy lobbying Congress about the issue.

Ultimately, they were successful. The 1986 Tax Reform Act included the authorisation of the 'Real Estate Mortgage Investment Conduit' (REMIC). This accommodated multiple classes of ownership, i.e. differentiated tranches, while remaining exempt from taxation at the entity level, like a partnership. The REMIC structure shifts the basis for taxation from the principal and interest received by the REMIC to the form in which it is paid to investors. Notably, this can involve conversion of interest to principal, creating tax benefits which tend to be higher, the lower the quality of the underlying mortgages. A REMIC structure must also contain a residual interest, i.e. equity tranches, which passes the entity's profit or losses to its holder.

The REMIC structure greatly enlarged the potential market for securitised mortgages. But limitations remained. The underlying securities were confined to mortgages and their underwriting standards largely conformed to Fannie Mae and Freddie Mac's fairly high standards, given their central role in the market as middle-men between borrowers and the capital market. Over time, the development of Structured Investment Vehicles (SIVs) in tax havens provided a way around these limitations. It enlarged the potential market further by facilitating securitisation of non-conforming, i.e. larger or lower-quality mortgages and other types of credit (i.e. a collateralised 'debt' obligation, or CDO) within a corporate vehicle. Since the tax havens had no corporation tax, this replicated the tax advantages of a REMIC for a wider class of securities. Over time, as the share of securitised mortgages in private pools rose relative to federal pools packaged for Fannie and Freddie, more and more SIVs containing mortgages would be established in tax havens, notably the Cayman Islands (in Fig. 3.1 in the next chapter, these would be included in the private mortgage securities shown there).

The essence of the securitisation process is set out in Fig. 2.1. Banks make loans in the traditional way, but instead of keeping them all on the balance sheet they sell them for a fee to investors in the form of securities. This avoids any need for capital backing, due to either regulation or market discipline, and adds to profits notwithstanding low interest rates. The pooled loans pay interest which in turn pays the return on the securities. An investment bank might design the product and arrange custody and administrative servicing—ensuring the interest from the loans finds its way to the securities. The entity issuing the securitised product could be a SIV set up by the bank, or taken up by a government-sponsored agency like Fannie Mae and Freddie Mac. Credit ratings would be sought for the various tranches—senior tranches receiving AAA, AA, A ratings, etc., mezzanine tranches having higher risk (in the 'B' grades) while an equity tranche would absorb the

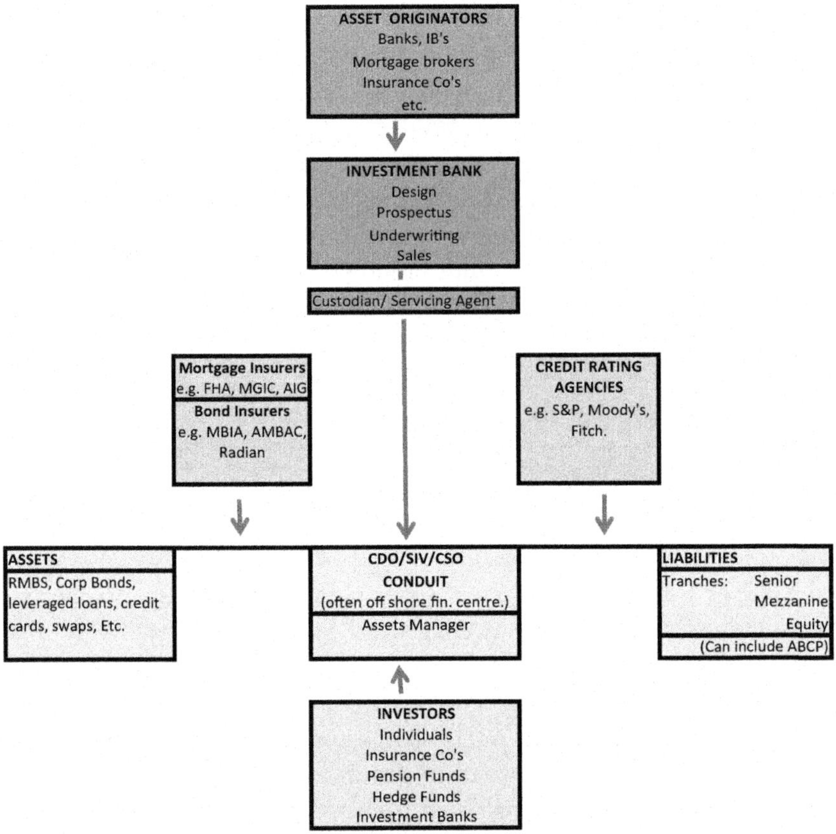

Fig. 2.1 CDO securitisation (*Source* Authors)

first loss in the event of defaults. This would protect the senior and mezzanine tranches.

Insurance for the underlying bonds and loans could be used to get better credit ratings. The bank may or may not have connections with the SIV. It might own some of it, or have a repurchase arrangement with the SIV, requiring the bank to buy back the securities under certain specified conditions.

Teaser Rates and On-Selling

To keep the pipeline going for the securitisation process, more and more loan origination was required from banks and S&Ls. The demand was insatiable, because adding fee-for-sale revenue to the profit line had a powerful effect on returns compared to interest-rate spreads. Finding more borrowers could be made easier by making them cheaper and more available and then essentially selling them to get rid of any responsibility for them. This was one of the accelerating factors in the subprime crisis. The strong incentive was to keep finding borrowers—no matter what their creditworthiness—to keep the pipeline going. Loan rates and 'teaser' deals were common—interest rates were very low rates for the first couple of years before a 'reset' occurred (reversion to a normal rate) that could trigger defaults of poorly informed consumers.

Derivatives

Derivatives play a critical role in the structuring of products discussed above, particularly interest rate and credit default swaps (CDS). These also play a key role in regulatory arbitrage that goes on to this day.

Derivatives are contracts between 2 parties the value of which derives from the price of the underlying reference asset, most commonly: commodities, stocks, indexes, interest rates, currencies and property. Specific conditions apply to the contract: a date for maturity; and the nature of outcomes, such as the strike price versus the underlying price at the time and the default status of a bond.

Derivatives Have a Long History[8]

Variants of forward contracts date back to ancient Mesopotamia and Athens to facilitate exchanges of perishable goods harvested at

[8]This Discussion Draws Heavily from William S. Mathis (2017), Kiernan (2015), and Abraham (2017). See also Moss and Kintgen (2010).

different times of the year and trade involving high-risk merchant voyages. Options may also date back to ancient Greece, as suggested by Aristotle's story of Thales of Miletus who became rich by buying options on the right to use olive presses during a strong harvest. Mediterranean traders in the middle ages also used option-type contracts as insurance vehicles.

A limitation of such instruments is that buyers and sellers have to find each other and then negotiate a contract, which are time-consuming. Another is that if prices fluctuate before settlement the loser has a strong incentive to back out, creating a significant counterparty risk. Indeed, with unstandardised and unregulated markets, fraud and counterparty risk limited the use of derivatives for centuries. Options were even outlawed at times in Europe.

Improvements in forward markets that evolved into futures exchanges emerged in feudal Japan during the eighteenth century (the Edo period). Taxes in many regions were levied in physical rice. This was stored by the authorities in cities and sold at auction. The winning bidder at the auctions would receive a voucher, rather than the physical rice itself, allowing them some flexibility in handling the rice. The vouchers eventually became transferable. In 1697, the Dojima Rice Exchange was established in Osaka, and, following a collapse in rice prices in 1729, changes were introduced to make the process more efficient. Physical rice could be traded at the *shomai*, where vouchers were issued to allow short-term flexibility but had to be settled within four days. A second venue, the *choaimai*, was also established to permit contracts to be signed for future delivery of various types of rice up to four months before they were harvested. No trading took place, but all relevant information was recorded at a clearinghouse. To participate, traders had to establish a line of credit at the clearinghouse and the clearinghouse assumed responsibility for payment in the event of default, effectively eliminating counterparty risk. This was effectively the first futures exchange and it operated until 1937.

Further development along these lines followed the repeal in 1846 of the Corn Laws in the UK. This stimulated the internationalisation of trade in grain at a time when the American mid-west was being settled. Around the same time, the Illinois and Michigan Canal was completed, linking the Great Lakes to the Mississippi River and the Gulf of Mexico; the telegraph was introduced, transforming communications between Europe and North America; and the railroad boom gathered pace in that region. These forces would soon turn the small town of Chicago into a major metropolis with a central role in the world's grain markets.

In 1848, the Chicago Board of Trade (CBOT) was created to oversee the expansion of trade in commodities that was already getting underway. The Board evolved much as the Dojima Exchange had evolved in Japan leading to the development of formal future markets but on a much larger scale. The CBOT moved quickly to develop rules and product standards to facilitate more efficient trading and, over time, the range of commodities that could be traded increased.

The evolution of options markets was much slower, given the difficulty of negotiating prices in the absence of standardised contracts and the counterparty risks options entailed. First steps in providing methodologies for pricing were developed by New York-based Russell Sage in the late nineteenth century, and a key figure in the development of an organised market for options was Jesse Livermore, who operated out of 'bucket shops' in New York early in the twentieth century. He was essentially a bookie making a market for people who wanted to bet on equity prices. These activities remained on the fringe, however, until a period of grain market turbulence during the 1960s led the CBOT to extend trading to include options for both some commodities and quoted equities. It then established the Chicago Board of Options Exchange (CBOE) which it soon spun off as a separate exchange. The CBOE quickly moved to standardise contracts and establish clearing and settlement processes with trades guaranteed by the Options Clearing Corporation. Nevertheless, as late as 1973 options activity was quite limited with equity option trading only available for calls in just 16 stocks.

But the Huge Expansion of Derivative Activity Is Recent

During the 1970s this changed dramatically, driven by three forces:

- Macroeconomic instability involving high and variable inflation and deregulation of prices and controls in many individual markets. This led to widespread demand for ways to both hedge and to gamble on a broader range of risks, notably in financial markets relating to interest rates and exchange rates, generated by this instability.
- Advancing computer technology made a large increase in trading activity feasible. It permitted complex and tedious calculations needed to apply tools of statistical inference to future price movements on a large scale. It also allowed much more rapid processing of transactions, accommodating the vast expansion of trading volumes.
- The Black–Scholes theorem, which established a better methodology for pricing options than existing alternatives. Black and Scholes also demonstrated how options could be used to hedge equity positions in a portfolio, much as they were used in commodity markets.

The result has been a rapid and enormous expansion of derivatives activity, which today mainly relates to futures, options, forwards and swaps. As innovation has proceeded rapidly in the main financial centres (the largest of which is London), various hybrid contract have emerged: for example, 'swaptions' are options on the swap market useful for trading based on interest-rate expectations. Many derivatives are still traded on exchanges and have a clearing house that guarantees to make good payments in the event of a default by one of the parties—such as with future markets. However, the bulk of derivatives are still traded 'over the counter' (OTC) due to their specificity (they are unlike other contracts and don't have the uniformity and depth to be exchange traded). For the securitisation market and structured products, the derivatives that are of most interest concern interest-rate swaps and CDS set out more fully in Box 2.1.

Regulating OTC Derivatives in the Run-up to the Crisis[9]

A basic regulatory authority for future markets in agricultural commodity markets in the USA was established as early as 1922 by the Grain Futures Act. The Securities Exchange Act of 1934 was part of the New Deal trend to regulating financial markets and led to the CBOT registering as a securities exchange, bringing it under the auspices of the Securities and Exchange Commission, and the Commodities Exchange Act (CEA) of 1936 required all futures and commodity options to take place on organised exchanges. Significantly, in the light of the subsequent evolution of the markets, this left treatment of non-commodity options and derivatives that were not 'futures' undefined. The establishment of the Commodity Futures Trading Commission (CFTC) in 1974 to regulate commodity futures and options did nothing to clarify the treatment of other types of derivatives.

The rapid growth of interest-rate and currency swaps during the 1980s attracted increasing attention to derivatives from regulators as concerns were voiced that exposure to risk was being shifted from individual institutions to the system as a whole. To counter calls for regulation, the large banks active in derivatives markets formed a lobby group now known as the Independent Swaps and Derivatives Association (ISDA) in 1985. Mark Brickell, from JP Morgan, joined in 1986 and emerged as its chief spokesman, becoming Chairman in 1988. Around the same time, the CFTC published a notice saying that it planned to examine whether derivatives fell under the rubric of 'futures', in which case they came under the CFTC's regulatory authority.

This issue had significant implications for derivatives markets given that, under the CEA, all futures activity had to be on organised exchanges. OTC activity would be illegal, and contracts not traded on exchanges would not be recognised by the courts. Brickell and the ISDA prevailed on this issue when Wendy Gramm, Chair of the CFTC, ruled in 1989 that derivatives were not futures.

---

[9] This account draws heavily on Barry Ritholtz, with Aaron Task (2009) and, especially, Bethany McLean and Joe Nocera (2011).

Discussion about regulating derivatives in Washington continued throughout the 1990s. In March 1998, under Brooksley Born, a successor to Gramm, the CFTC circulated a draft 'concept' paper to other regulators, industry representatives, legislators and the Treasury for 'feedback' before circulating it more widely. It posed a variety of questions suggesting reassessment of the CFTC's approach to derivatives, arguing that OTC derivatives functioned essentially as futures that needed functional supervision. It reasserted the CFTC's jurisdictional claim in the area.

The negative reaction was intense, with a group of bankers threatening to move their derivatives business to London if the CFTC pursued the ideas set out in the paper. The President's Working Group of regulators, led by Fed Chairman Greenspan and Treasury Secretary Rubin, met in April to pressure Born to abandon her initiative. There seems to have been some difference of interpretation between Born and Rubin as to what had been agreed. In May, the CFTC published a revised version of the paper which immediately led Greenspan, Rubin and SEC Chairman Levitt to send a letter to Congress asking it to block the CFTC's request for comments. Many hearings took place during the remainder of 1998, during which Long-Term Capital Markets (a highly leveraged hedge fund using derivatives) collapsed with \$129bn of counterparty exposure. This seriously disturbed financial markets and the New York Fed organised a rescue plan, financed by large Wall Street banks. But no action was taken as regards derivatives.

These events left the regulatory status of OTC derivatives open. This was fixed by the Commodity Futures Modernisation Act (CFMA), introduced on the last working day before the Christmas recess in 2000, never debated and attached as a rider to an 11,000-page Omnibus Budget bill signed by outgoing President Clinton on 21 December. The sponsor of the CFMA was Senator Phil Gramm, Wendy Gramm's husband. He had also sponsored the Gramm–Leach–Bliley Act, more formally known as the Financial Services Modernisation Act, that had abolished the Glass-Steagall Act (discussed earlier) in 1999. The gist of the 2000 law,[10] made

[10]As an aside, the exemption of energy, oil markets and the trading of such on electronic exchanges would not be subject to functional supervision. This suited Enron, who reportedly

explicit, was that OTC derivative products, including CDSs, between 'sophisticated parties' would not be regulated as 'futures' under the CEA. Nor would they be subject to any other federal or state regulation. This meant in effect that the CFTC would be able to supervise activity at the 'entities' level, but not as a setter of the rules about the functioning of the market. In effect, the combination of the 1999 and 2000 Acts meant that banks could involve themselves in all securities-broking businesses and that they would not be regulated in OTC derivatives markets. This opened the door for unregulated CDS trading as a part of the structured products businesses getting underway. Notional amounts outstanding rose from less than $100bn when the law was signed to more than $50tn by 2007.

The Demand for Securitisation and Derivatives

Basic Bank Balance Sheet Arithmetic

Low interest rates discussed in the context of globalisation in Chapter 1 reduced the ability of banks to make profits because margins are squeezed. This occurred at the time when deregulation, securitisation and increasing derivatives activity opened new ways for banks to increase their return on equity (ROE). Two channels were particularly important: first, securitisation. This allowed assets to be sold for a fee which goes through to the profit bottom line without affecting the balance sheet, facilitating indefinite repetition of such fee-for-sale activities. Second, derivatives and banks' own VaR models can be used to minimise the amount of costly equity banks are required to hold. The first mechanism raises the numerator of the ROE (the profit line), while the second can reduce the denominator (the bank's equity capital).

If loans are kept on balance sheet, then profits depend on the interest-rate spread and the ability to grow loans and deposits. A simple bank balance sheet is shown on the left side of Fig. 2.2.

---

lobbied heavily to influence the bill and where Gramm's wife Wendy was a member of the Board, very well.

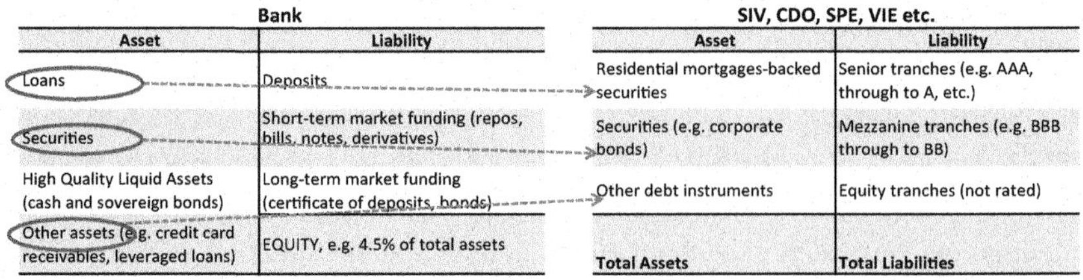

Fig. 2.2 Basic bank balance sheet and securitisation (*Source* Authors)

Let: $A =$ Total assets;
$F =$ fees earned from securitization;
$r_1 =$ yield on loans and securities;
$r_2 =$ yield on high quality liquid assets;
$r_3 =$ interest paid on deposits;
$\lambda =$ equity as a share of total assets;
$\alpha =$ high quality liquid assets as a share of A;
$c =$ operating costs as a percentage of A;
$l =$ default rate on A; and
$\pi =$ profits.
If we assume, for simplicity, that

$$r_1 > r_2 > r_3 \text{ and}$$

that the bank operates to ensure that α and c are held constant, then:

$$\pi = [r_1(1-\alpha) + r_2\alpha - r_d(1-\lambda) - c - l] * A + F. \qquad (2.2)$$

The return on equity (ROE) becomes:

$$\pi/\lambda A = [r_1(1-\alpha) + r_2\alpha - r_d(1-\lambda) - c - l]/\lambda + F/\lambda A. \qquad (2.3)$$

It can be seen immediately that low interest rates are bad for bank profits and, as market rates are reduced, the bank's normal trading profits are squeezed. Choosing a high ratio of high-quality liquid assets (α) also reduces profits (as the return is less than for loans and securities) and obviously higher bank costs and/or greater loan losses are also bad for profits.

In the emerging low-interest-rate environment, the growth of derivatives and securitisation could not have come at a better moment. Securitisation allows a bank to hold down the size of its balance sheet (as in the left side of Fig. 2.2), even as it originates more loans by shifting them through securitisation to the (off-balance sheet) structured investment vehicle (follow the arrows from the bank to the SIV on the right side of Fig. 2.2). The fees earned by securitisation add directly to profits, at least while it goes on. Derivatives and IRB models could also be used to reduce required equity holdings and hence the capital ratio λ, thereby raising leverage and the return on equity, by lowering the ratio of RWA to total assets.

The Boom in Derivatives

Figures 2.3 and 2.4 shows the notional value of derivatives as a multiple of GDP and in nominal terms, respectively. There has been spectacular growth: rising from \$80tn in 1998, less than 3-times world GDP; to \$670tn (around 11-times world GDP) by 2008; to a peak of \$700tn by 2013, after which regulatory reform began to cut in. On the eve of the crisis, interest-rate derivatives were about 80% of the total, 9% related

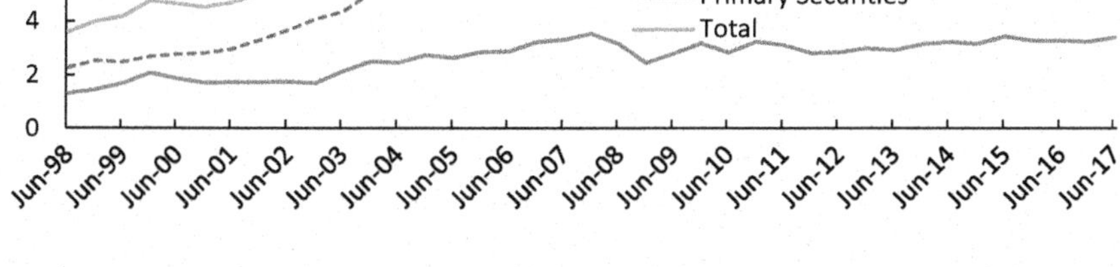

Fig. 2.3 Global notional derivatives versus primary securities as a multiple of world GDP (*Source* Bank for International Settlements; authors)

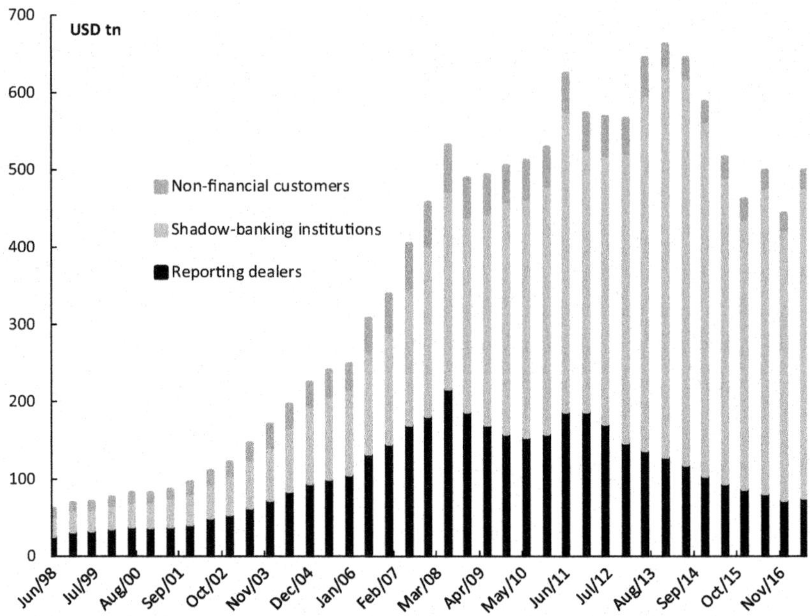

Fig. 2.4 Notional value of derivatives by sector (*Source* Bank for International Settlements and World Federation of Stock Exchanges; authors)

to exchange rates, CDSs accounted for 5%, 5% related to commodities and 1% were equity-linked. Most of the derivatives are still traded over-the-counter (OTC), despite progress with those traded on exchanges in recent years following regulatory reform.

These are enormous sums, and it is on these notional amounts that fees are set. Gross market values (GMV) of outstanding contracts shown in Fig. 2.5 are much lower than notional. The GMV refer to the net amounts that would have to be settled if all derivatives had to be replaced at the prices prevailing at the time. The GMV rose to over \$20tn at the start of 2008, but the veritable explosion of volatility following the failure of Lehman Brothers and the freezing of financial markets at the end of the year caused the GMV to rise further. Increased attempts to hedge risk at high costs (option values change with volatility), and rising default probabilities for CDS's (see Box 2.1), caused the GMV essentially to double between 2007 to 2008.

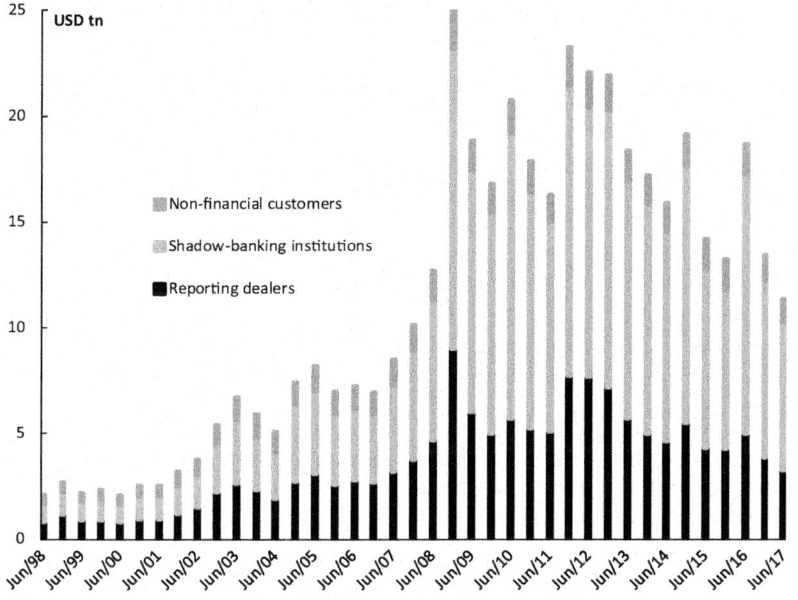

Fig. 2.5 Gross market value of derivatives by sector (*Source* Bank for International Settlements; authors)

Some derivatives are more dangerous than others—interest-rate swaps are the largest component, but are relatively low risk. CDS, on the other hand, are the potential 'nuclear bombs' of the derivatives market, and these played an important role in the crisis. Some of the basics of derivatives are set out in Box 2.1.

Some of the growth of derivatives is associated with legitimate hedging, even if the share of derivatives activity involving non-financial customers is striking. The world is changing all of the time, particularly in taxation and regulation, which gives rise to enormous arbitrage opportunities for large global banks. They leverage arbitrage opportunities to make profits. They also pursue tail risk opportunities, using derivatives, and are incentivised to do so as regulations change and threaten profitability. Corporate client hedging and other activities involving derivatives in 1998 amounted to a total of around 2.5-times world GDP. But while the primary assets base has remained relatively stable, the exponential growth of derivatives as a share of GDP to 2008 suggests a very strong role for bank arbitrage and speculative activities, both for their own account and for other investors, such as hedge funds, insurance companies and mutual funds.

Box 2.1: Derivatives

Notional versus Gross Market Value: The notional value of a derivative contract is an exposure measure calculated as the number of contracts multiplied by the price of a contract at the start date. This amount is the basis on which fees are set. The GMV is the dollar value of the cost of replacing the derivatives at current prices.

Interest-Rate Swap Example

Interest-rate swaps are by far the biggest component of the derivative market. Two parties agree to exchange interest-rate cash flows—typically fixed versus floating rates. These can give exposure at a better price than the underlying reference assets and/or allow for management of the volatility of flows according to product/client needs. Their prices vary with movements of the fixed interest rate. The following example shows the flows and what happens to exposure when the fixed interest-rate shifts (Fig. 2.6).

Notional Value: $100m (price times the number of contracts).

Time Period and Rates: 5-year dollar interest-rate swap, where counterparty D pays fixed rates of 5% per annum against receipt of floating rate Libor. Counterparty C undertakes the reverse transaction. C and D deal with their investment banks. So D enters into the swap with Broker-Dealer B, while C enters into its swap with Broker-Dealer A. The 2 banks match their books.

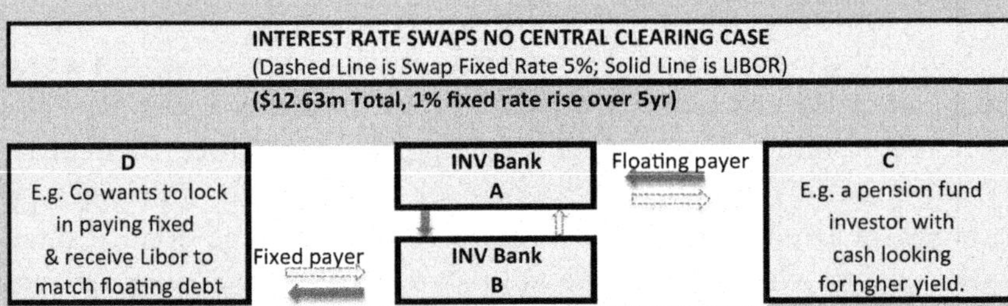

Fig. 2.6 Interest-rate swaps (*Source* Authors)

A Bond Sell-off: The market value of these contracts at the time they are signed should be zero because they can be closed out at no cost. But derivative prices change with those of the underlying securities (the delta). If the market rate on which the swap-fixed rate is based rises by 1% p.a., then the market value of each of these \$100mn swap contracts rises to \$4.21m, equivalent to 1% p.a. present-valued over five years, i.e.

$$[1/1.06 + 1/\mathrm{POWER}(1.06,2) + 1/\mathrm{POWER}(1.06,3) \\ +1/\mathrm{POWER}(1.06,4) + 1/\mathrm{POWER}(1.06,5)] * \$100\mathrm{m}$$

Thus, D now has a claim on B, hence a counterparty risk, of \$4.21m; B has a similar claim on A worth the same amount—as does A vis-à-vis C. So the aggregate GMV of these contracts, hence total counterparty risk, is \$12.63m.

Clearing Reduces Risk: With a clearing house exposure to risks falls. The banks' books are both matched so they remain hedged. The fixed-rate payer (D) is in the money, since his obligations have fallen in value while his LIBOR claims remain at market. Provided positions can be netted in the event of default, only the LIBOR payer (C) creates a risk for the clearing house. So total counterparty risk is only \$4.21m. This all assumes the clearing house itself is solvent—well-capitalised and not likely itself to default.

Credit Default Swaps—Potentially the Most Dangerous Derivative

The buyer of the CDS pays a premium, and the seller insures the security against default according to contractual terms for an agreed notional amount (net of the recovery value of assets following a default). In the absence of default, the CDS expires worthless to the buyer. The securities can be traded at prices that depend on the probability of default, a discount rate and the period of time for the contract. They are dangerous because the seller can be exposed to the full notional amount (less any recovery value).

The following example assumes the contract is over-the-counter for 4 years. For simplicity, the probability of survival each period is assumed to be the same. The value is calculated as the sum of the present discounted expected value of the notional less the recovery value each period: where expected values come from the cumulative probability of default (allowing for the probability of survival in previous periods). The value is lower, the higher the premium charged (a per cent of the notional) and the higher the discount rate. Thus:

$$\begin{aligned} PV = {} & (1-p1)N(1-R)d1 + p1(1-p2)[N(1-R)d2 - (Nc/4)d1] \\ & + p1p2(1-p3)[N(1-R)d3 - (Nc/4)(d1+d2)] \\ & + \ldots p1p2p3(1-p4)[N(1-R)d4 - (Nc/4)(d1+d2+d3)] \\ & - p1p2p3p4(d1+d2+d3+d4)Nc/4 \end{aligned}$$

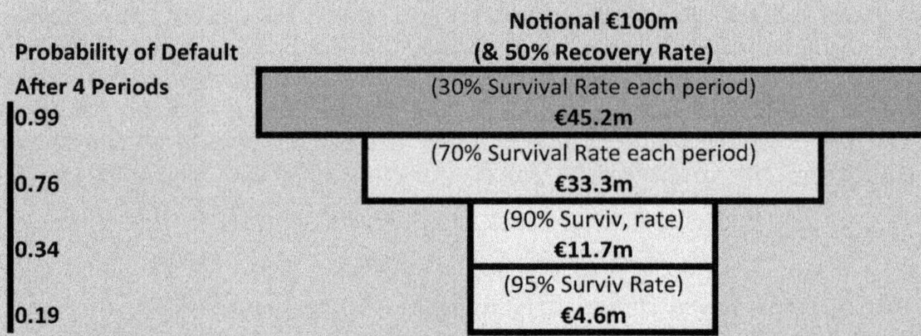

Fig. 2.7 Credit default swaps (*Source* Authors)

Where: *N* is the notional, \$100m; *R* is the recovery rate, 50%; *p* is the probability of survival; $d(i)$ is the discount factor each period, 6%;($d1 = 1/1.06$; $d2 = 1/(1.06)^2$... etc., and *c* is the premium as a % of *N*, at 4%. The top rung of Fig. 2.7 uses a 30% survival rate to illustrate very high risk (like a subprime mortgage bond). In this case, the contract for the buyer is worth a very high €45.2m.

More generally, Fig. 2.7 shows a number of cases, with the cumulative probability of their defaults shown on the far left. At the top is the high-risk case with the 30% chance of survival in each period, just mentioned, and which has a 99% chance of default after 4 periods. The case of a safe security, like an investment grade corporate bond, is shown at the bottom, with a 95% chance of survival each period. The value to the buyer is only \$4.6m. Like an atomic bomb, as the probability of default rises, so too does the risk to the seller insuring the bond.

Regulatory and Tax Arbitrage with Complete Markets in Credit

While securitisation, SIVs and the like helped the profit line of banks, the second complementary way to improve the rate of return on equity for the bank is to reduce the effective capital ratio (λ in Equations 2.2 and 2.3). The Basel risk-weighting approach proved a bonanza for banks wishing to do this, an issue that remains to this very day.

The growth of and innovations in derivatives were in essence a movement towards '*complete markets*' in credit (the ability to buy and sell all

Table 2.2 Promises treated differently

Basel II Promise Transformations	Bond Face Value	Bank A 100% Cap Weight 8% Required K	Bank A 20% Cap Weight 8% Required K	Bank B Regulatory adjustment 50% Off B/sheet Wt. 1.5% surcharge coef & 8% Req K.
Bank A				
Face value BBB bond	1000	80		
Buy CDS on BBB bond from bank B			16	
Bank B				
Underwrites to Re-insurqnce $50 prem.				2.6
Total Banking Capital		80	16	2.6
Reinsurer		?	?	?

Source Authors representation, taken from Box 2 French Ministry (2009)

assets in all states)—and particularly the ability to go short bank credit. Complete markets make it difficult to specify the risk of a security in the Basel system when derivatives can transform and shift risks (see, e.g. Table 2.2). Differential regulatory capital weights, the tax status of investment products, and the tax rates faced by investors are fixed parameters and cannot be arbitraged away by trading—the tax and regulatory 'wedges' being exploited do not disappear with increased trading because they are policy parameters. These fixed policy parameters that cannot be arbitraged away are an open invitation to the innovative minds of traders to find ways to minimise regulatory and tax costs. There is an incentive in financial markets to use the completeness of markets to reconfigure credits and capital market instruments in ways to minimise capital charges and reduce tax burdens for clients.

The example in Table 2.2 illustrates the point in a simple fashion.

- Bank A lends $1000 to a BB-rated bond issuer, 100% risk weighted under Basel II; in buying the bond it would have to hold $80 capital (8% capital ratio weighted at 100%). Bank A holds a promise by the company to pay a coupon and redeem at maturity. But it might default.
- Bank A buys a CDS from Bank B on the bond, thereby passing the promise to redeem from the company to Bank B. Because B is a bank, which carries a 20% capital weight, Bank A reduces its required capital to 20% of $80, or $16.

- One would think that Bank B would have to carry the promise and 100% risk weight the exposure—but instead it underwrites the risk with a reinsurance company outside of the banking system—the promise to redeem is now outside the banks, and the BIS capital rules don't follow it there. Under Basel II, Bank B's capital required for counterparty risk is only 8% of an amount determined as follows: the CDS spread price of say \$50 (500bps), plus a regulatory surcharge coefficient of 1.5% of the face value of the bond (i.e. \$15), all multiplied by the 50% weighting for off-balance-sheet commitments. That is, \$2.60 (i.e. 0.08*\$65*0.5).
- So jointly the banks have managed to reduce their capital required from \$80 to \$18.60 (\$16 plus \$2.60)—a 70.6% fall. In effect, in this example, the CDS contracts make it possible to reduce risky debt to some combination of the lower bank risk weight and a small weight that applies to moving the risk outside of the bank sector—so there is little point in defining an ex-ante risk bucket for the BB-bond as 100% risk weighted in the first place.

The simple transaction described above allows the banks to raise the leverage ratio on the transaction from 12.5 (the Basel 8% minimum requirement) to 53.8. The Basel II risk-weighting approach has allowed banks to expand their leverage in this example by almost 400%. In a global crisis, all three of these players may fail, and losses could be huge, but no one is holding much capital. It will be important to bear this example in mind later in this book where the case is made for a simple unweighted leverage ratio—losses may come from unexpected events and a bank can't predict what these will be with its risk-weighting models.

A Basic Regulatory Principle

The financial system is a system of promises. A basic problem with the Basel system is that it cannot deliver a regulatory ideal of treating the same promises in the financial system in the same way wherever they are passed in the regulatory and tax arbitrage process. The same promises should be treated in the same way, regardless of where they sit in the financial system. In the above example, this is problematic as shown in Table 2.2. Without further regulatory intervention, the banks manage to reduce the overall capital in the banking system to $18.6, instead of $80, by passing the promise to a sector that lies beyond the banking regulator. The model multipliers can be adjusted somewhat by regulators so that counterparty risk is penalised by more—but a one-size-fits-all model adjustment will take no account of the actual situation of the reinsurer in another jurisdiction and which possibly holds insufficient capital. Banks A and B are not treated equally, and the reinsurer is out of the regulatory picture.

Banks, Implicit Government Guarantees and Shadow Banks

Banks have their own separate regulators. But they deal with insurance companies in various jurisdictions which are not regulated in the same way so financial promises can be shifted there. Some hedge funds issue securities in their own name and take deposits of investors and invest with leverage on their behalf—they act like capital market-oriented banks. They are lightly regulated, but market discipline in the absence of any implicit public guarantees for hedge funds gives rise to a higher cost of capital that is more likely to correspond to the risks that are being taken. Typical hedge funds have leverage ratios in the 4 to 5 range. Banks on the other hand are highly regulated, and deposits are widely perceived to be publicly guaranteed. This has allowed leverage of some bank institutions to be in the 30–75 range. Even if the guarantee is not a formal one, the fact of being regulated acts as a 'stamp of approval' helping to reduce funding costs. It is from the regulated sector that the crisis arose. Going forward, as will be argued in later chapters, as regulations on banks are stepped up, there is a corresponding shift in the amount and nature of business conducted in the shadow banking system, i.e. an evolution not unlike that witnessed in the lead up to the crisis.

Where regulatory lines should be drawn is a very difficult subject on which to obtain a consensus—but as noted earlier the one guiding principle is that similar promises should be treated in similar ways—wherever the promise sits. Lobbying and regulatory capture have made sure that this does not happen.

Tax Arbitrage

Counterparty risk arising from the use of OTC derivatives was one of the key hallmarks of the crisis. Regulatory arbitrage and shifting promises were an important contributor to the explosion in CDS use. Tax arbitrage too allows promises to be transformed with strong implications for bank on- and off-balance-sheet activity.

Consider two bonds H (high) at a 10% coupon and L (low) at an 8% coupon. One investor is tax exempt while the other investor is subject to a 15% tax rate on bond L and a 40% tax rate on bond H[11] (e.g. municipal bonds held from another state and federal bonds held in a taxable account). The non-taxable investor can buy bond H with the proceeds of shorting bond L and capture 2% of the face value traded, per year, with no initial investment. The taxable investor can buy bond L with the proceeds of shorting bond H and capture a 1% spread after-tax with no investment. The simple arithmetic is set out in Table 2.3.

Both traders gain as long as the taxable investor can utilise the tax deductions. Neither partner needs to know that the other even exists—the broker does the securities lending to the respective parties. Tax disparities signal the opportunity. The combined profits realised by both trading partners, after-tax, come at the expense of reduced government tax revenue (by the deductibles of the 'short' exposure 40% of $6, or $2.4). These sorts of transaction using CDS complete-market techniques give strong incentives to banks with investment-banking arms to create structured notes that are very interesting to investors—giving rise to returns and risk profiles that they might not otherwise be able to achieve. Banks arbitrage tax parameters that are never closed by their actions, providing new businesses and revenues—but at the same time

[11]For example, municipal bonds held from another state and federal bonds both held in a taxable account.

Table 2.3 Tax arbitrage

Investors X & Y Create Opportunities for Broker Dealers				
Lower Yield Bond L @ 8% and Higher Bond Yield H @ 10%				
Non-Taxable Investor X	Asset		Liability	
Buy H with proceeds of Shorting L	H +100		L −100	
Income	10		−8	
Net Income (spread)	2			
Taxable Investor Y (Tax 15% on L & 40% on H), Net of Tax				
Buy L with the proceeds of shorting H	L +100		H −100	
Income	6.8	i.e. 100*0.08*(1−0.15)	6	i.e. 100*0.1*(1−0.4)
Net Income (spread)	0.8			

Note These spreads can be levered up with derivative trades as much as the client wants
Source Authors

risking a build-up of counterparty risk and leverage. Without a properly binding constraint on the ability of banks to expand leverage through capital arbitrage, the incentive to build attractive businesses on the basis of these incentives—continually expanding counterparty risks—may become excessive.

Targeting the Ratio of Risk Weighted to Total Assets to Maximise the Return on Equity

If the Basel system has nothing to say about the ratio of RWA to total assets (A), then banks that have not already pushed this to the limit can adjust to a target for RWA through regulatory arbitrage to achieve a complementary target for the ROE.

From Equation (2.1) and focusing on the Basel II objective for core Tier 1 capital plus buffer of 8% then, with the ROE defined as profit (π) divided by capital, it follows that capital can be defined as[12]:

[12]Ignoring the temporary transition scalar 1.06 that is not relevant.

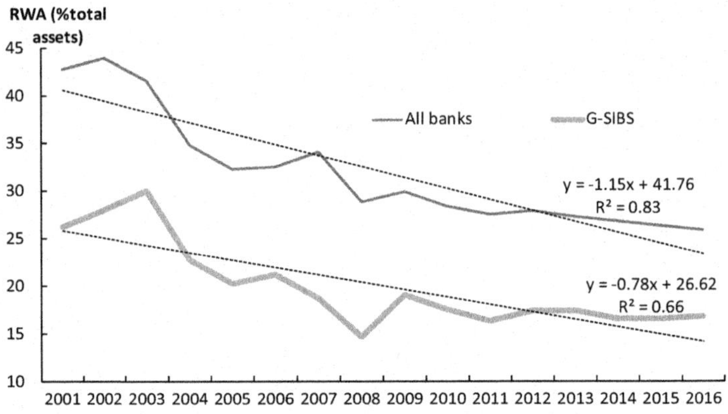

Fig. 2.8 Ratio of risk-weighted assets to total assets: GSIBs versus the full universe of large banks, 2003–2016 (risk-weighted assets as a percentage of total assets). *Notes* The sample includes 129 large global banks over the period 2003–2016. All systemically important banks (GSIBs) listed by the Financial Stability Board (2017) are included. Based on Sarin and Summers (2016), the six US GSIBs, the fifty largest US banks by 2016 assets, the fifty-five largest banks in the world ranked by market capitalisation (including European, Japanese and Australian GSIBs) and eighteen listed domestic systemically important European banks identified by the European Banking Authority. Following Ayadi et al. (2015), banks considered as systemic in this paper are the ones identifiable in the list of banks which are directly supervised by the ECB, non-euro area EBA stress tested and Swiss banks with more than €30bn. Chinese banks are excluded from the sample as state ownership involves different issues than for the ones relevant for the other banks considered here. Financial statement data are collected from SNL Financials. For consistency purposes, financial statements reported under GAAP accounting standards are adjusted to be comparable with IFRS basis (*Source* SNL Financials, author calculations)

$$0.08\left\{12.5(\mathrm{OR}+\mathrm{MR})+\sum w_iA_i\right\}=\pi/\mathrm{ROE} \tag{2.4}$$

The bank would use regulatory arbitrage (choosing weights, w_i) to achieve the weighted portfolio of assets such that the targeted ROE* is achieved:

$$\left(\sum {}_iw_iA_i\right)=\pi/(\mathrm{ROE}*.08)-12.5\,(\mathrm{OR}+\mathrm{MR}) \tag{2.5}$$

Banks choose their ROE target and then (large banks) use IRB modelling to optimise the weights (w_i) to achieve ROE*. The RWA feature has been criticised by the OECD since the beginning of the crisis.[13] Global systemically important banks (GSIBs) have an incentive to use their internal models to minimise the holding of costly capital. Figure 2.8 shows the ratio of RWA to TA. A large sample of banks is used, consisting of GSIBs and other large national banks. A fall in the ratio of RWA/TA permits a rise in leverage, which is always the most attractive means for a bank to gear up its spreads (including synthetically via derivatives) for increasing profits. The GSIBs in particular have targeted a reduction in this ratio (from 50% on average in 2003 to 34% by the time of the 2007–08 crisis, and much more extreme examples can be found on an individual bank basis). Non-GSIB banks are less able to use internal models (the systems require sophisticated processes and derivatives for shifting exposures and 'netting risks') but may shift risks around with derivatives. Quantitative impact studies have shown that each bank can have very different capital levels to support identical asset portfolios (all of their models differ, are used differently and can't easily be verified and changed by supervisors).[14]

Summary

The ability of banks to transform risk with complete markets in credit allows them to shift promises around according to their different regulatory and tax treatment and basically to avoid the proper intent of the Basel risk-weighting approach and thereby expand leverage in a relatively unchecked manner. Basel risk weighting was associated with a perverse outcome in the crisis—those that looked best on the Tier 1 capital adequacy ratio, the greater the losses and in some cases bankruptcy of the banks concerned—because:

[13]See Blundell-Wignall and Atkinson (2008, 2009).

[14]See Bank for International Settlements (2013). An identical set of assets required some 300% more capital at the most demanding bank than at the least demanding one.

- Capital arbitrage under the Basel weighting of assets precisely permits higher leverage (economising on capital while expanding the balance sheet as shown in the above example) which is more risky.
- A low amount of capital versus the un-weighted balance sheet is symptomatic of a banking culture with a greater willingness to take on more risk with taxpayer's money—a culture of privatising gains and socialising losses. This is where the 'too big to fail' incentive comes for policy makers that banks and investors know is there—an implicit guarantee.

With these basic concepts and tools in hand, the following chapters will use them to analyse the crisis in more detail.

Appendix to Chapter 2: Problems with Pillar 1

There are a large number of technical problems with the Basel risk-weighting approach, most of which have been carried over into Basel III.

Portfolio invariance: The risk-weighting formulas in the Basel capital regulations are based on a specific mathematical model, developed by the BCBS, which is subject to the restriction that it be 'portfolio invariant', i.e. the capital required to back loans should depend only on the risk of that loan, not on the portfolio to which it is added (Gordy 2003). This is convenient for additivity and application across countries. But it has an important disadvantage: it does not reflect the importance of diversification as an influence on portfolio risk. Thus, the minimum capital requirements associated with any type of loan due to credit risk simply rise linearly with the holding of that asset type regardless of the size of the exposure (appropriate diversification is simply assumed). This means that Pillar 1 does not penalise portfolio concentration (as might occur, e.g. under a quadratic rule applied to deviations from a diversified benchmark). Dealing with concentration issues are left to supervisors in Pillar 2.

Single global risk factor: For the mathematical model underlying the Basel approach (I or II), each exposure's contribution to value-at-risk is portfolio invariant only if: (a) dependence across exposures is driven by a single systemic risk factor—a global risk factor, since it is supposed to apply to global banks operating across jurisdictions; and (b) each exposure is small (Gordy 2003). What we know of the subprime crisis (discussed later) is that it originated in the US housing market (a regional-sector risk) and exposures were quite large. Of the two conditions for invariance, by far the most important is the requirement of a single risk factor that applies to all participants. Almost prophetically, Gordy states: *'A single factor model cannot capture any clustering of firm defaults due to common sensitivity to these smaller scale components of the global business cycle. Holding fixed the state of the global economy, local events in, for example, France are permitted to contribute nothing to the default rate of French obligors. If there are indeed pockets of risk, then calibrating a single factor model to a broadly diversified international credit index may significantly understate the capital needed to support a regional or specialized lender'.*

Different treatment of 'financial promises': Securities are essentially financial *promises*—e.g. to pay income and repay credits. If regulations treat promises differently for different instruments and in different jurisdictions, then financial markets will innovate to find ways to exploit these differences. This is made very easy with modern derivatives (CDS in particular). Promises of one sort can be transformed into those to which the lowest capital charges apply and ownership can be moved around easily. The Basel IRB-weighting approach encourages innovations like this on a quite massive scale.

Bank capital market activities: In many ways, the main hallmarks of the global financial crisis were the contagion risks between counterparties. This came about with banks involving themselves in capital market activities for which they did not carry sufficient capital. Examples include: securitisation and its warehousing and the option rights of structured product vehicles; and the massive industry of regulatory and tax arbitrage.

Pro-cyclicality: The Basel system is known to be pro-cyclical. There are many reasons for this. The most basic reason is that judgments tend to underestimate risks in good times and overestimate them in bad times. More specific factors include:

- The modelled quality of assets varies over the cycle—risk spreads are narrower in good times possibly understating risks and vice versa;
- While some recent new regulations try to address this, banks' risk measurements tend to be point-in-time and not holistic measures over the whole cycle;
- Counterparty credit policies are easy in good times and tougher in the bad;
- Profit recognition and compensation schemes encourage short-term risk-taking, but are not adjusted for risk over the business cycle (e.g. high dividends and buybacks in the good times and vice versa); and
- The external ratings-based approach uses credit ratings, which are notoriously pro-cyclical.

Subjective inputs: The IRB approach of the revised framework actually exacerbates subjectivity by making banks themselves responsible for estimating probability of default, loss given default and exposure at default. Private bankers cannot predict future asset prices and future volatility events better than anyone else. Unobservable securities prices (e.g. those not traded on exchanges) rely on pricing to models which are particularly subjective.

Unclear and inconsistent definitions: The main problems here have been the definition of capital.

- Regulatory adjustments for goodwill and other deduction are not treated in the same way in all jurisdictions. They should apply to common equity, and not to Tier 1 and/or a combination of Tier 1 and Tier 2 capital.
- Banks do not provide clear and consistent data about their capital.

This means that in a crisis the ability of banks to absorb losses will differ between banks and jurisdictions.

Problems with Pillars 2 and 3

Pillar 2 relates to the supervisory review process: With stress testing and guidance from supervisors, banks can be made to hold capital for risks not appropriately captured under Pillar 1. Building buffers in this way requires supervisors to be forward-looking, that is: to keep up with changes in market structure, practices and complexity. This is inherently difficult. Supervisors may be less likely to be able to predict future risk events than private bankers—as the 2007–08 crisis illustrates so well. Supervisors have smaller staff (per regulated entity) and are mostly less well paid. If supervisory practices lag, the risk cycle policy makers will be ineffective in countering the defects in Pillar 1.

In this respect, it is worth noting (see below) that the former UK Financial Services Authority (FSA), which was one of the best staffed and most sophisticated of supervisors, signed off on Northern Rock to be one of the first banks to go to the Basel II IRB approach, understanding fully that this would reduce their capital significantly, immediately prior to the subprime crisis. Later, the Lehman use of repo 105 to disguise leverage in its accounts was not hidden from supervisors—it appears they did not fully appreciate what they were looking at (Sorkin 2010).

Pillar 3 relies on disclosure and market discipline: Markets will supposedly punish banks with poor risk-management practices. Underlying this is an efficient markets notion that agents all act in a fully rational way as market discipline is allowed to work. Unfortunately, the consequences of allowing the financial system to collapse are so severe that this threat is not credible, creating the perception, often called 'implicit', of a government guarantee that the most severe developments will not be permitted.

References

Abraham, S. (2017). *The History of Options Contracts*. https://www.investopedia.com/articles/optioninvestor/10/history-options-futures.asp.

Ayadi, R., De Groen, W. P., Sassi, I., Mathlouthi, W., Rey, H., & Aubry, O. (2015). *Banking Business Models Monitor 2015, Europe*. Montreal: HEC Montreal.

Basel Committee on Banking Supervision. (1988, July). *International Convergence of Capital Measurement and Capital Standards*.

Basel Committee on Banking Supervision. (2004, June). *International Convergence of Capital Measurement and Capital Standards: A Revised Framework*.

Basel Committee on Banking Supervision. (2006, June). *International Convergence of Capital Measurement and Capital Standards: A Revised Framework*—Comprehensive Version.

Basel Committee on Banking Supervision. (2013, January). Regulatory Consistency Assessment Program (RCAP). *Analysis of Risk Weighted Assets for Market Risk*.

Blundell-Wignall, A., & Atkinson, P. E. (2008). The Subprime Crisis: Causal Distortions and Regulatory Reform. In Kent & Bloxham (Eds.), *Lessons from the Financial Turmoil of 2007 and 2008*. Reserve Bank of Australia. http://www.rba.gov.au/PublicationsAndResearch/Conferences/2008/Blundell-Wignall_Atkinson.pdf.

Blundell-Wignall, A., & Atkinson, P. E. (2009). Origins of the Financial Crisis and Requirements for Reform. *Journal of Asian Economics*. https://doi.org/10.1016/j.asieco.07.009.

FDIC. (2005). Capital and Accounting News: Basel II and the Potential Effects on Insured Institutions in the United States: Results of the Fourth Quantitative Impact Study (QIS4). *Supervisory Insights* (Winter): 27–32.

Financial Stability Board. (2017, November 21). *2017 List of Global Sytemically Important Banks (GSIBs)*. Basel.

French Ministry for the Economy, Industry and Employment. (2009, February). The Credit Default Swap (CDS) Market. *Trésor-Economics*, No. 52. Available at: https://www.tresor.economie.gouv.fr/Ressources/file/327008.

Gordy, M. D. (2003). A Risk-Factor Model Foundation for Ratings-Based Bank Capital Rules. *Journal of Financial Intermediation, 12*(3), 199–232.

Kiernan, K. (2015, May 20). *From Ancient Greece to Wall Street: A Brief History of the Options Market*. FINRA (https://www.FINRA.org).

Lewis, M. (1989). *Liar's Poker*. New York: W. W. Norton.

Mathis, W. S. (2017). *A Brief History of Derivatives*. http://www.realmarkits.com/derivatives/3.0history.php.

McLean, B., & Nocera, J. (2011). *All the Devils Are Here*. New York: Penguin.
Moss, D., & Kintgen, E. (2010, November 10). *The Dojima Rice Market and the Origins of Futures Trading*. Harvard Business School, revised.
Ritholtz, B. (with Aaron Task). (2009). *Bailout Nation*. Hoboken, NJ: Wiley.
Sarin, N., & Summers. (2016, September). *Have Big Banks Gotten Safer*. Brookings Papers on Economic Activity, Conference Draft.
Sorkin, A. R. (2010, March 15). At Lehman, Watchdogs Saw It All. *New York Times*. Available at: http://www.nytimes.com/2010/03/16/business/16sorkin.html.
Tarullo, D. K. (2008). *Banking on Basel: The Future on International Bank Regulation*. Washington: Peterson Institute for International Economics.

3

The Watershed Year of 2004: Origins and Causes of the Crisis

Introduction

The financial crisis was caused and facilitated at a number of different levels. Chapter 1 discussed globalisation in the context of two very different and inconsistent economic systems butting up against each other: one leading to a savings glut, excess capacity and downward pressure on jobs, wages, inflation, company returns and interest rates; and the other responding at the company level by digitalisation, technical innovations and restructuring, which added to the pressure on the middle class already dealing with import penetration effects. The build-up of foreign exchange reserves invested heavily in US treasuries—and ultimately the Fed's own purchases—resulted in lower interest rates. Occurring as it did at a time of financial innovation, use of derivatives and deregulation an equity culture became a feature of the banking industry—to develop new business models for banks that would turn them into growth stocks and reward executives driving the process. There was a growing pressure to take on leverage and sell new products in order to grow earnings.

A first line of defence for the financial system in the face of growing pressure to take on risk is to have sound institutions supported by

A. Blundell-Wignall et al., *Globalisation and Finance at the Crossroads*,
https://doi.org/10.1007/978-3-319-72676-2_3

strong micro-prudential regulations. Both of these were absent in the lead up to the 2007 crisis. The first objective of this chapter is to analyse the main local (as opposed to global) causal factors that directed these pressures into subprime mortgages and securitisation from 2004 within the USA. Understanding why this happened is an important prerequisite for developing prudential policies and institutions to protect the financial system.

Global Competition and the Equity Culture for Banking

Securitisation discussed in Chapter 2 was most easily executed by an investment bank (IB). US banks felt that European banks had a competitive advantage with their universal banking corporate structure. US lobbyists pointed to the 'unfairness' of three important sets of regulations: the Glass-Steagall Act; Securities and Exchange Commission (SEC) rules for IBs that were too restrictive; and the FDIC Act of 1991 that required US commercial banks to adhere to a leverage ratio. On these grounds, US banks lobbied the US authorities first to remove Glass-Steagall in 1999; and then to change the SEC rules and to adopt Basel II as soon as possible.[1]

During the lead up to the 1999 Gramm-Leach-Bliley Act and its aftermath, there was a rush to buy IBs, broker-dealers and credit card businesses in order to turn banks into '*financial supermarkets*'. The aim of CEOs such as Sandy Weill of what became Citigroup in pushing for the removal of restrictive regulations was, after all, to achieve earnings expansion and share price appreciation—to become '*growth stocks*'. The model of separated institutions, with bank businesses based on balance sheets and interest rate spreads on loans, was thought not conducive

[1]See, for example, the letter by Davis C. Bushnell, senior risk officer of Citigroup to the Federal Reserve, FDIC, Controller of the Currency and the Office of Thrift Supervision. As late as the 17th of March 2007, just before the crisis, Bushnell argued against leverage ratios that would require more capital, and strongly supported the push to Basel II.

to this growth strategy. The removal of Glass-Steagall and the series of innovations that resulted in the ability to buy and sell bank-related securities on capital markets required an aggressive culture on the part of institutional sales, origination and trading staff to book more revenue through the new products coming on stream. This brought the '*equity culture*' of investment banking into institutions that might otherwise have run more conservative businesses.

From the late 1990s, a consolidation wave swept through banking to create financial supermarkets where cross-selling and global expansion were perceived to be the keys to success. Chemical Bank merged with Chase Manhattan in 1996, and this group in turn merged with JP Morgan in 2000. JP Morgan Chase bought Bank One in 2004. Bank of America was acquired by Nations Bank in 1998; this group in turn bought Fleet Boston Financial in 2004 and the MBNA credit card company in 2005. Continental Europe always had universal banking, but fear of competition from the USA saw their banks join the merger trend and global expansion through foreign branching strategies, particularly with respect to the lucrative New York and London markets. Thus, while Sandy Weill was busy tying up Travellers Group (Primerica, Smith Barney, etc.) with Citibank in the late 1990s, Union des Banques Suisses amalgamated with the Bank of Switzerland and bought Paine Webber, while Deutsche Bank bought the UK's Morgan Grenfell and Bankers Trust Corporation. Banque National de Paris bought the IB Paribas in 1999; Societe Generale bought into TCW asset management group in 2001; and Barclays bought the US credit card company Juniper Bank in 2003 and the Home Equity Servicing Corporation in 2006.

These and other bank mega-groups that formed at the time found themselves in a competitive environment that required new ways to make money. The benefit for earnings growth of switching more heavily towards fixed-income businesses with upfront recognition of fees for securitisation saw the 'early movers' race ahead in market share and earnings. Those that delayed suffered in the league tables (see the UBS discussion below). Originate-to-distribute businesses would also be able to benefit from economising on capital by gaming the Basel system. This all became a key part of the process to drive revenue, the return on capital and the share price in a globally competitive marketplace.

Remuneration

In order for executives and sales staff at all levels to benefit from the 'equity culture' compensation, schemes designed to reward revenue growth were important (see the corporate governance section below). Bonuses were based on upfront revenue generation. To keep valued employees stock purchase plans were widespread prior to the crisis, sometimes with free option features, and they were seen as 'key' for achieving growth and earnings targets. This was argued to be in shareholders' interest—the common philosophy being that: '*if you pay peanuts you get monkeys*'. In one such plan, employees could buy a lot of stock and hand it back to the bank at cost price if the market price fell over the following 2 years.[2]

The culture of pushing the envelope with remuneration incentive in mind has not changed even a decade after the crisis. To illustrate this, one need not look beyond the fines for misconduct over numerous money making issues in recent years (such as rigging interest rate markets, misleading customers, creating fake accounts and breaking money laundering and terrorist financing laws). The incentives of the equity culture are strong, and management seems unable to control it—if anything the data on fines shows that things may have become worse.[3] The need to develop a better path to reform that does not rely on 'sensible management' but instead limits risk-taking via leverage controls, and sensible legal corporate structures are dealt with later in this book. A first step in understanding why this is needed is informed by understanding why leverage and securitisation got out of hand in the USA from 2004.

[2]The Citi Stock Purchase Plan in 2000 let employees buy Citi shares at the July 31 closing price, allowing them the option to return the stock if the price had fallen. Each bank had its own scheme in the market for attracting and holding staff.

[3]See Resti (2017), and CCP data.

Causality

Low interest rates were a global phenomenon, and so too was the rise in mergers between banks and branching to gain global access. Pressures to grow businesses were building as mergers were being completed: while business structures may become more concentrated, this doesn't matter to shareholder unless earnings grow at a faster rate as a consequence. Merger trends were already accelerating in the 1990s, as it became clear that regulatory change sought in the USA was gaining in Congressional and Senate support. But these factors do not explain why the securitisation business took off from 2004 in the USA and not elsewhere.

When economists talk about 'causality' they usually have some notion of exogeneity in mind; that relatively independent factors changed and caused endogenous things to happen—in this case the biggest financial crisis since the Great Depression. With respect to subprime securitisation in the USA, there were local causal factors concentrated in 2004. Why this relatively small part of the world financial system contributed to a global financial crisis on a much larger scale—issues related to the business models of large banks and their interconnectedness through derivatives—will be examined in detail in subsequent chapters.

Institutional and Regulatory Issues

Why Subprime Securitisation Was Concentrated in the USA

Many of the background factors discussed earlier such as low interest rates and the agreement of the Basel rules were common to all countries, so the initial pressures bursting through in subprime securitisation in the USA deserves an explanation. There are in fact many reasons for this, all relating to facilitating factors some of which had been set in train before 2004.

- First was the greater reliance on capital markets relative to banks in the USA, which contributed to an overall dominance of an investment banking culture. This 'equity culture' was to be a key feature of the new business model for banks and proved to be critical in the speed with which new opportunities would be taken advantage of.
- Second, while interest rates were low in most advanced countries, mortgage interest for homeowners is deductible in the USA whereas this is not the case in most other countries.
- Third, as noted in Chapter 2, the 1986 Tax Reform Act included the Real Estate Mortgage Investment Conduit (REMIC) rules, which can issue multiple-class pass-through securities without an entity-level tax. This greatly enhanced the attractiveness of mortgage securitisation. It also meant that investors in other countries could also take advantage of US innovations in this area.
- Fourth, the 1997 Taxpayer Relief Act substantially exempted sales of personal residences from capital gains tax (which did not apply to financial assets like stocks).[4]
- Fifth, the USA Government Sponsored Enterprises (Fannie Mae and Freddie Mac) play a crucial role in absorbing mortgage risk and facilitating their securitisation. This implicit government guarantee for mortgage risk is not present in any other country.
- Sixth, the regulator of Fannie/Freddie at the time, the Office of Federal Housing Enterprise Oversight (OFHEO), was separate from the bank regulators (the Federal Reserve, the Office of the Comptroller of the Currency and the FDIC), so that policies of bank regulators had little jurisdiction over this large part of the intermediation process.
- Finally, the Bush Administration 'American Dream' policy that tried to spread home ownership to lower income groups through zero equity lending greatly facilitated the origination of new mortgages which are the key raw materials for the securitisation process.

[4]More precisely, the Act exempted from taxation the capital gains on the sale of a personal residence of up to $500,000 for married couples filing jointly and $250,000 for those filing as singles.

A lot of the discussion about the causes of the crisis has focused on processes, corporate governance and the role of institutions. For example: that securitisation was the problem; that the operation of credit rating agencies (CRAs) was flawed; that risk modelling and underwriting standards in banks were not adequate; and that there were corporate governance lapses. While these all had a role to play, they are not causal with respect to time and place: why the USA and why in 2004? After all, securitisation is present in a number of countries, and both CRAs and large global banks operate their processes across multiple countries—not just the USA. For the most part these processes were aspects of the financial system that accommodated the equity culture in banking in its drive to benefit from incentives that had been created over a longer period of time, and they do not explain why the rapid acceleration in residential mortgage-backed securities (RMBS) from 2004 occurred in the USA. To be causal in the exogeneity sense would require that these processes and roles became subject to independent behavioural changes. For example, CRA practices would be 'causal' if in 2004, they had developed new inferior practices that triggered events. In fact, they were only accommodating banks' drive for profit as the banking system responded to other exogenous factors.

Why US Subprime Securitisation Accelerated from 2004

In 2004, four time-specific factors came into play that unleashed the sudden surge in RMBS:

- First, the Bush Administration 'American Dream' zero equity mortgage proposals became operative, helping low-income families to obtain mortgages[5];
- From early 2004, the then regulator of Fannie Mae and Freddie Mac OFHEO imposed an ongoing requirement on each enterprise to maintain a capital level at least 30% above the statutory minimum

[5]See the White House (2004).

requirement due to past problems associated with operational control and audited financial statements. Balance-sheet caps were subsequently imposed.[6] These constraints created the incentive for banks to accelerate private label RMBS;

- The Basel II accord on international bank regulation was finalised and published. It opened an arbitrage opportunity for banks that caused them to accelerate off-balance-sheet activity; and
- The SEC agreed to allow IBs voluntarily to benefit from regulation changes to manage their risk using capital calculations under the '*consolidated supervised entities program*'.

The appendix to this chapter reports econometric analysis presented to the annual Reserve Bank of Australia International Conference at Kirribilli in 2008 supporting the view that these changes caused the building pressures to break out in the form of banks accelerating their off-balance-sheet mortgage securitisations.

The American Dream Act

The American Dream Downpayment Act was signed into law in December 2003, and in June 2004 the Department of Housing and Urban Development announced $160m for implementation. It provided funds for assisting very low-income households with upfront down payment and closing costs. Perhaps more important than the financial support was the signal this provided to both regulators and the banking industry that Congress and the Administration were positively supportive of home purchases by people providing no capital themselves. The availability of down payment funds, supported by political endorsement of subprime mortgage at a time when interest rates were

[6]For Freddie Mac, the cap was set at ½% per quarter growth above the mid-2006 level. For Fannie Mae, the cap was the end of 2005 balance-sheet level, with any increase to be approved by OFHEO. These were to remain in place until the GAAP audit issues were solved. These were removed in March 2008 (to help alleviate recession pressures from the subprime crisis), as OFHEO was replaced by the Federal Finance Housing Agency (FHFA).

relatively low and S&Ls and banks were offering encouragement with 'teaser rates' (discussed in Chapter 2), worked to accelerate originations.

The Fannie and Freddie Caps

When OFHEO imposed greater capital requirements and balance-sheet controls on Fannie and Freddie, it caused the contraction and subsequent 'hobbling' of these two major players in securitised mortgages, which had always been operating with the unfair advantage of perceived government guarantees. Banks that had been selling mortgages to them faced revenue gaps and an interruption to their earnings. Their solution was to create their own Fannie and Freddie 'look-alikes': the structured investment vehicles (SIVs) and collateralised debt obligation (CDOs) based on mortgages discussed in Chapter 2.

The influence of the controls affecting federal mortgage pools and the corresponding response in private label RMBS can be seen in Fig. 3.1,

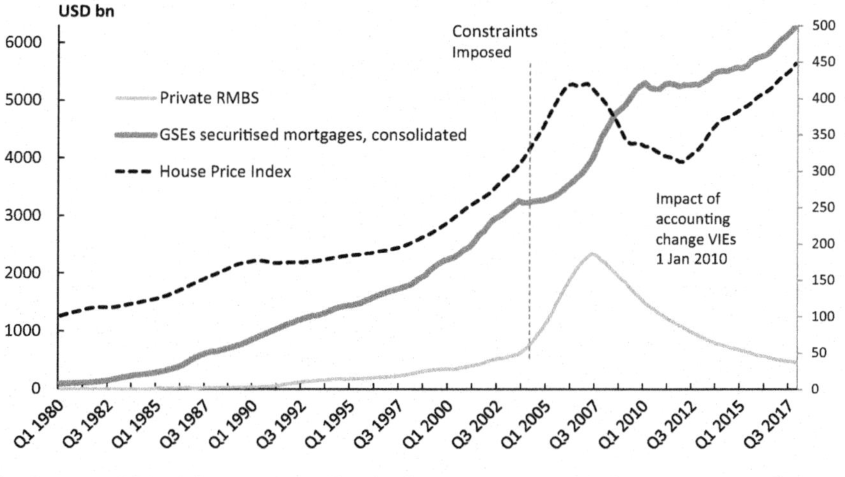

Fig. 3.1 Residential mortgage-backed securities and house prices (*Source* Thomson Reuters, US Federal Reserve and author's calculations. GSE securitisations and home mortgage pools)

together with house prices. House prices had been rising for some time, creating expectations of capital gains and resulting in rising equity for homeowners. The GSE balance sheets and trusts had been rising in line with house prices, but when the constraints were imposed, and this momentum faltered, private RMBS accelerated sharply. The big difference of course is that this was occurring in institutions that were not sponsored by governments and where there were no guarantees of any kind.

The Announcement of Basel II

There has never been agreement with the view of the current authors with respect to the idea that the transition from Basel I to Basel II was a 'co-sponsor' of the added pressure to originate mortgages and issue RMBS.[7] This arbitrage opportunity and its implementation illustrate well the equity culture issues discussed earlier whereby the pushing of the envelope to enhance returns is a permanent feature of the corporate culture of IBs.

Smart traders will always take advantage of any anomalies in the financial system regulation very quickly. When Basel II was published in 2004 banks were informed that the capital weight given to mortgages would fall from 50% (under Basel I) to 35% under the simplified Basel II, and to as little as 15–20% depending on whether and how a bank would use the sophisticated internal ratings-based (IRB) version. A lower capital weight raises the return on capital for a given mortgage asset, and the corollary of this is that greater concentration in low-capital-weighted mortgages improves the overall bank return.

One of the '*gob-smacking*' assumptions of basic capital regulation under the Basel system is something called 'portfolio invariance'.[8] In simple terms, the riskiness of an asset like a mortgage is independent of how much of the asset is added to the portfolio. Banks appear to

---

[7]This issue was discussed at length in the OECD Committee on Financial Markets and at Financial Stability Board (FSB) meetings.

[8]See the appendix to Chapter 2.

have believed this, judging by the way they responded to the arbitrage opportunity that arose in the transition from Basel I to II. Banks moved quickly to take advantage of it, and regulators did not see what was going on.

If mortgage securitisation could be accelerated and pushed into off-balance-sheet vehicles, banks could raise the return on capital right away in 2004 without waiting for the new regime to come into effect. It would be quite rational to do this to the point where the proportion of on-balance-sheet mortgages (with a 50% capital weight) and off-balance-sheet mortgages (with a zero capital weight) equated the (higher) return likely to emerge for a Basel II mortgage (where capital weightings would apply regardless of whether assets were on or off the balance sheet).

When this point was made at a policy seminar at the European Parliament in 2009, a very senior representative from the Bank of England replied: '*I agree with you up to a point, but there is one problem with your argument. Basel II might have been announced in 2004, but it was not due to take effect until 2008*'.

The implication, of course, is that bank management is so blinkered that it takes no account of known future changes in the regulatory environment even as they apply to portfolio assets with a thirty-year term. The light only seemed to come on in the Bank of England delegate's eyes when an example was given from Citigroup's balance sheet.

Citigroup chose to move towards using the IRB Basel II option, where FDIC data on the Quantitative Impact Study Number 4 (QIS4) showed that such banks expected the capital weight on mortgages to fall by 2/3, say from 50% under Basel I to 15–20% under Basel II, for example say 17%.[9] With securitised off-balance-sheet mortgages not attracting a capital charge under Basel I, this presented a straightforward arbitrage: what percentage of on- and off-balance-sheet mortgages would allow the increased return on capital for mortgages now (from 2004) without causing a

[9]See FDIC (2005).

shortage of capital later when Basel II became fully operational? The arbitrage in the perfect case would be:

$$\begin{aligned} &0.33 * (50\%\ \text{On} - \text{Bal. Sheet Cap. wt. Basel I}) + 67\% * (0\%\ \text{Off} - \text{Bal Sheet Basel I}) \\ &\quad = 17\%\ \text{Basel II Equivalent Overall Capital Requirement for Mortgages} \end{aligned}$$

At the end of 2007, Citi 10K filings show \$313.5bn on-balance-sheet mortgages and \$600.9bn Qualifying Special Purpose Entities (QSPEs) in mortgages, almost exactly the 33 and 67% split.

The SEC Rule Changes in 2004

Prior to 2004, the SEC was responsible for broker-dealer subsidiaries of IBs, where stringent rules (permitting a maximum 15:1 debt to equity ratio) applied, but no provision was made for compulsory consolidated supervision of IBs, even if they had banking affiliates. This posed a problem for internationally active securities firms since operating in Europe required consolidated supervision to comply with the EU's Financial Conglomerate Directive.[10]

To deal with this situation, the SEC adopted a purely voluntary 'Consolidated Supervised Entities' (CSE) programme in 2004. This was recognised by the Financial Services Authority (FSA) in the UK as 'equivalent' to other internationally recognised supervisors, providing supervision similar, although hardly identical, to Federal Reserve oversight of bank holding companies. It proved to be inadequate.[11]

[10]For IBs with no US banking affiliate, the law does provide for voluntary supervision of the holding company. Only Lazard Ltd opted for this arrangement. The 5 (former) major IBs all had some US banking affiliates and hence were uncovered until the Consolidated Supervised Entity program described in the main text was created.For discussion by the SEC director, Division of Trading and Markets, see Erik Sirri (2008).

[11]A report by the Inspector General of the SEC in September 2008 on the Bear Stearns collapse was very critical of the CSE program and SEC supervision: '…we have identified serious deficiencies in the CSE program that warrant improvements. Overall, we found that there are significant questions about the adequacy of a number of program requirements, as Bear Stearns was compliant with several of these requirements, but nonetheless collapsed. In addition, the audit found that [the SEC] became aware of numerous potential red flags prior to Bear Stearns' collapse, but did not take actions to limit these factors'. See SEC (2008).

Table 3.1 US and European bank leverage ratios. The leverage of global systemically important banks is compared by converting the US banks and one Swiss bank from GAAP to IFRS for comparability. The ratios are total assets divided by core Tier 1 common equity (IFRS basis, total assets divided by core equity)

Year	6 US Global Banks	9 EU Global Banks	4 UK Global Banks	2 Swiss Global Banks
2005	26.7	39.9	32.8	75.4
2006	25.1	42.1	31.7	71.8
2007	29.5	40.1	39.0	81.2
2008	34.2	45.9	47.2	89.3
2009	22.6	37.7	27.2	61.8
2010	21.8	36.0	26.3	52.1

Source Bank reports, authors

Furthermore, even if the SEC had been well-equipped to carry out supervisory responsibilities beyond the activities of broker-dealer subsidiaries, the scope for different approaches to enforcement noted by the General Accounting Office (GAO) would have remained as a potential distortion to competition.[12]

These new arrangements permitted a sharp rise in the leverage ratio of US GSIB's towards 34.2 on average in 2008 (on a comparable IFRS basis, see Table 3.1). Still constrained by FDIC rules, the increase due to the SEC rule change did not see the US banks catch up to the high and rising levels of leverage applying in European banks. This quantum shift in leverage was a great enabling factor for banks to take advantage of the arbitrage possibilities in bank capital requirement and tax regulations. From 2004, there was a material acceleration in off-balance-sheet mortgage securitisation and the use of derivatives (particularly CDS) to create synthetic bonds as key avenues to drive the revenue and the share price of banks.

[12]In 2007, the GAO reported to Congress that the Federal Reserve, the Office of Thrift Supervision (OTS) and the SEC 'employ somewhat different policies and approaches to their consolidated supervision programs' and reiterated a recommendation that Congress modernise or consolidate the regulatory system. See GAO (2007).

Corporate Governance

It was noted earlier that an equity culture in banking and remuneration practices played a role in the crisis as traders exploited opportunities created by poor regulatory structures. At OECD and FSB meetings, the question was often asked as to why company executives weren't able to play a greater role in controlling the risks. This question seemed to imply some moral aspect to bank governance—that if there were poor regulations that could be exploited, companies should not take advantage of them.

The most basic principle of the 'equity culture' is to make money. CEOs, traders and sales staff have insecure jobs, and their objective is to maximise their benefits while they are still sitting in the relevant chair. Poor regulations will always be exploited, and in this respect, the Basel II rules announcement in 2004 was a clear opportunity to be taken advantage of. Mounting excess leverage via the gaming of the Basel system became a phenomenon in all jurisdictions, as temptation to grow quickly via securitisation spread globally. The example of Northern Rock in the UK is a useful '*smoking gun*' example of how Basel II came to be used to bloat leverage (see Box 3.1). It did not seem to occur to the CEO of Northern Rock not to take advantage, even as profit warnings came into play—an example of poor corporate governance.

Box 3.1: The Northern Rock Example

Liquidity problems can easily arise when bank liabilities are not matched to the duration of their assets. This is well-illustrated by Northern Rock in the UK which rapidly added mortgage products to its balance sheet in anticipation of Basel II. Mortgages products had been made so attractive under the IRB regime due to come into effect under Basel II that there was an incentive to grow them more quickly than could be funded by deposits. Northern Rock increased its assets at a rate of over 25% per annum in the few years preceding its collapse in 2007, funded by borrowing heavily in wholesale markets. Assets were concentrated in mortgage products (75% of the total) which would reduce capital requirements once their Basel II application came into force. When equity culture was mixed in with credit culture, the attraction for management was to expand businesses with more profitable mortgage products driving earnings and (therefore) the share price; or they could return excess capital to shareholders, with an equally beneficial impact on the share price.

Here is an exchange between the Northern Rock CEO and the UK Parliamentary Treasury Committee taking evidence about the crisis[13]:

Mr. Fallon:	"Mr. Applegarth, why was it decided a month after the first profit warning, as late as the end of July, to increase the dividend at the expense of the balance sheet?"
Mr. Applegarth:	"Because we had just completed our Basel II two and a half year process and under that, and in consultation with the FSA, it meant that we had surplus capital and therefore that could be repatriated to shareholders through increasing the dividend."

By June 2007, just as the crisis was to break and liquidity was to dry up, Northern Rock had total assets of £113bn and shareholders' equity of £2.2bn. Thus, their capital had been leveraged by a factor of more than 50. Their RWA under Basel II had been reduced to a mere £19bn (16.7% of total assets), compared to £34bn under Basel I (30% of assets). Under Basel II Tier 1 capital was a 'healthy' 11.3% of RWA, but only 2% of total assets. When concerns about asset values and loan soundness emerged in the markets liquidity dried up and Northern Rock suffered the first run on a British bank since 1866. Their regulatory capital was less than 10% of the £23bn that the authorities used to support the bank.

The other crucial financial stability issue concerns high-risk investment banking activities, losses within which led to contagion of more stable traditional business segments in bank holding companies that were not formally separated from each other. In this respect, sound corporate governance can and should make a difference. But boards seemed unable to understand and/or to act in a timely way. In this respect, the UBS example discussed in Box 3.2 is instructive.

[13]See Treasury Committee (2007); *Evidence* 47.

Box 3.2: The UBS Example of Investment Banking Culture and Governance[14]

UBS management saw Citigroup and others rapidly growing their fixed-income business in investment banking through securitisation. An external consultant was also appointed to recommend strategy. This consultant pointed out that of all the businesses, fixed income was the area where the UBS investment bank lagged its three leading competitors the most. The IB had its biggest product gaps in the Credit, Securitised Products and Commodities businesses—those in credit, interest rates, mortgage-backed securities (MBS), subprime and adjustable rate mortgages (ARMs) were singled out. In March 2006, UBS presented its conclusions and key initiatives to close revenue gaps. These included expanding: its securitised products via a new Securitised Products Group; its Global Structured Finance and High Yield Loan Business; Structured Credit; and the development of trading strategies for these products.

The three biggest players in fixed-income revenue in 2005 and 2006 were Goldman Sachs (about $8.75bn and rising to $10.4bn in 2006), Citigroup (about $9.25bn and rising to $10.5bn in 2006); and Deutsche Bank (about $9bn and rising to $11.5bn in 2006). These numbers were presented by the UBS head of fixed income in March 2007 as the 'gap' that had to be closed—UBS was a mere ninth at around $6bn in 2005 and about $6.2bn in 2006. UBS developed a revenue gaps strategy—a 'growth at any cost' mentality—at exactly the wrong time from a macro-prudential risk perspective.[15] This is classic investment banking (from the Latin American debt crisis to subprime, the modern bankers continued a long tradition). Market share, revenue gaps and beating the key competition are the topic of every morning meeting at all levels in the bank, and for senior management, it can be a question of holding your job.

The corporate governance and risk control functions in many firms will adjust to accommodate strategy when an equity culture is mixed in with a banking credit culture. In UBS departing top risk managers were replaced by people from a sales background (consistent with growth) not a risk-management background.

UBS has a centralised Treasury able to raise funds efficiently in the open market. It chose to charge recipients of funds distributed internally within (i.e. lower than) the normal external spread:

---

[14]This section is based on UBS (2008).

[15]A UBS strategist identified a $4.3bn revenue gap to the top 3 competitors of UBS, and saw this as the most significant revenue opportunity.

...i.e. internal bid price bids were always higher than the relevant LIBID and the internal offer prices were always lower than LIBOR.[16]

The businesses were able to fund themselves at prices better than in the market. No attempt was made to take account of liquidity in this process (to match term funding to liquidity). A stricter funding model was seen as a '*constraint on the growth strategy*'.

There was strong resistance from the IB management to hard limits on the balance sheet. Such limits were quickly installed in Q3 and Q4 2007, only once the crisis was under way.

Staff compensation incentives did not differentiate between the creation of genuine 'alpha' versus the creation of returns based on low-cost funding, nor the quality (risk attributes) of staff earnings for the company. The relatively high yield from subprime made this an attractive candidate for long position carry trades (even with thin margins) via leverage (and using derivatives). This encouraged concentration in the higher carry mezzanine tranches of CDOs. It also encouraged minimal hedging of super senior positions (in order to be more profitable).

Notwithstanding the fact that the senior management and the board identified the subprime issue as a major risk in September 2006, the IB management did not adjust until July 2007. The Board did not feel strongly enough about the risk. Growth and revenue are in the interests of the shareholders, and the Board would not have been able to act forcefully. This was in complete contrast to their actions once the crisis became clear and more weight had to be assigned to a negative view. IB management held sway, and senior management and the Board went along with it. The Shareholder Report (April 2008) states that senior management took comfort from the main exposures being AAA CDO's, and that they were prepared to rely on IB assurances that the risk was well managed. Revenue growth and catching up to competitors were central to the dominant corporate culture. All management focus within the IB on 'processes' for new business initiatives and prior approval of transactions were:

'...on speeding up approvals as opposed to ensuring that the process achieved the goal of delivering substantive and holistic risk assessment of the proposals presented'.[17]

---

[16]UBS (2008), p. 25.

[17]UBS (2008), p. 41.

The report also states that internal reporting of risk positions was complex, even across the 'silos' within a business line. A holistic picture of the risk situation within IB business lines was not presented to management or the board, and there was no serious internal challenge to the overall strategy.

The UBS example illustrates that poor corporate governance, too, played a role in the crisis.

There are perhaps four hypotheses about why poor corporate governance failed to counter the worst excesses of banks in the lead up to the crisis.

- One is that the culture of investment banking is much harder to control from the boardroom.
- Another is that the business is more complex, and the products are inherently more difficult to understand than simple banking products so that risk control practices are much more difficult.
- Another is the extent of ownership of risks associated with bank strategy in the longer run, perhaps associated with board structure and the independence of directors.
- Still another concerns remuneration incentives that became such a clear part of the business model drivers, with bonuses linked to up-front revenue and the current share price.

However, an examination of some crude indicators of corporate governance in Table 3.2 suggests that there are no simple answers. The US banks' governance characteristics were surveyed in mid-2007 just prior to the crisis, and are arranged from left to right in terms of their known subsequent share price declines—from the worst to the best. All of the above banks had a majority of so-called *independent directors* and this line was excluded from the table. When the corporate governance indicator shown in the left column applies, it is marked with an X. While the sample is small, a few interesting observations emerge:

Table 3.2 Corporate governance features in June 2007 (prior to crisis M&A)

Company	Washington Mutual Inc.	Lehman Brothers Holdings Inc.	National City Corp.	Wachovia Corporation	Citigroup Inc.	Merrill Lynch & Co.	Fifth third bancorp	Regions Financial Corp.	Morgan Stanley	Bank of America Corp.	Suntrust	Goldman Sachs Group Inc.	JPMorgan Chase & Co.	U.S. Bancorp	BB&T	PNC Financial Group	Wells Fargo & Company
Ticker	@WAMUQ	@LEHMQ	NCC	WB	C	MER	@FITB	RF	MS	BAC	STI	GS	JPM	USB	BBT	PNC	WFC
% Stock price over the period 2007-2009	-100.0%	-100.0%	-95.0%	-90.3%	-88.0%	-87.5%	-79.8%	-78.7%	-76.3%	-73.6%	-65.0%	-57.7%	-34.7%	-30.9%	-37.5%	-33.8%	-17.1%
Board characteristics (as of June 2007)																	
Investment banking segment	-	x	-	x	x	x	-	-	x	-	-	x	x	-	-	-	-
Consumer/Regional bank	x	-	x	-	-	-	x	x	-	-	x	-	-	x	x	x	x
Family or partnership control	-	-	-	-	-	-	-	-	-	-	-	x	-	-	-	-	-
Chairman and CEO same	x	x	x	x	x	x	x	x	x	x	x	x	x	-	x	x	x
Risk committee chair not on Board	x	x	-	-	-	x	-	-	x	-	-	x	-	-	-	-	-
Risk committee chair on board	-	-	-	x	x	-	-	-	-	x	-	-	x	x	-	-	x
Staff compensation																	
Employee compensation (%revenues > avg. of 20%)	-	-	x	x	x	x	-	x	-	-	x	x	-	-	-	x	x
Employee compensation (%revenues ≤ avg. of 20%)	x	x	-	-	-	-	x	-	x	x	-	-	x	x	x	-	-
Executive Compensation																	
Top 5 compensations / salaries and benefits < avg. 78%	n/a	-	-	x	x	x	-	-	x	x	x	-	x	x	-	-	x
Top 5 compensations / revenue > industry avg. of 16%	n/a	-	x	-	-	-	x	x	-	-	-	x	-	-	-	x	-
Stock based comp. / total comp. > industry. avg of 51%	n/a	x	-	x	-	x	-	-	-	-	-	x	x	x	-	x	-
Stock based compensation / revenue > industry. avg. of 8%	n/a	x	-	-	-	x	x	-	-	-	-	x	-	-	-	x	-

Source Survey by authors. (1) Source is Thomson Reuters; (2) Sources are proxy statements; (3) Majority shares owned by or stable and long-term management established by insiders, e.g. partners or family members; (4) Includes banks where the Board does not have a subcommittee primarily responsible for the company's risk policy

- *Investment banking segment*: arguably a complex and high-risk activity that is difficult to govern. Of the six worst banks on the left, four are IB operations. This seems to have some validity.
- *Consumer/regional banks*: on the right, four of the six best banks are regional consumer type banks. This is consistent with the above IB comment and suggests that business models (to be discussed in Chapter 4) have quite a lot to with good or bad outcomes in the crisis.
- *Partnerships*: Goldman Sachs sits towards the right side of the table (for good performance), suggesting it is not impossible to manage high-risk businesses. A key feature in Table 3.2 is that it is the only one with a partnership-like corporate structure. At the time, 88% of the shares were held by insiders or those with a greater than a 5% stake. This arguably gives the partners '*skin in the game*'—a positive feature. No other bank surveyed comes close to this concentration of ownership, all of the others having very dispersed share ownership.[18]
- *Chairman and CEO the same person*: this raises lack-of-accountability issues, but it seems common to all the banks other than (the less crisis-affected) US Bancorp.
- *Employee compensation greater than 20% of revenue*: arguably good, if it attracts and maintains quality staff. However, Wachovia, Merrill Lynch, National City, and Citigroup all paid well, but were in the 6 worst performers.
- *Risk committee chair not on the board*: arguably a bad thing, if the risk team reports only to the CEO and not to the full board. However, this seems not to be a factor. On the far right, most of the regional consumer banks did not have a risk subcommittee, and yet

[18]A key member of Santander's Board told one of the present authors back in 2010 that the main reason why that bank avoided the subprime crisis was because the Botin family has run the bank since the beginning (140 years) and care about losing money—instilling a strong risk culture and controls. This once more is the '*skin in the game*' issue.

performed well. This suggests once again that it is what banks actually do—investment banking or consumer banking—that is a more important determinant of good and bad outcomes than anything internal risk managers are able to influence.

- *Staff compensation*: above-average general staff compensation is not obviously linked with better or worse outcomes for banks. Four of the six worst banks paid well, and three of the six best also did so.
- *Executive compensation*: paying high for the best executives is arguably a good thing, because they are incentivised to drive the business. In the table, executive compensation is divided between base remuneration and that related to stocks. Focusing on the IBs in Table 3.2, a few interesting observations emerge. Lehman Brothers, whose failure was to be a key '*moment*' in the crisis, has the feature that its executives had relatively low base remuneration but well above-average stock compensation. The question arises as to whether this causes the 'envelope' to be pushed too hard to benefit from stock price appre-caiation. Goldman Sachs differs from Lehman Brothers as it pays its executives well right across the board—in terms of their base compensation and stock rewards. This presumably links up with their near-partnership financial structure, as noted earlier. Amongst the regional consumer banks, PNC Financial is the second best performer (according to the narrow criteria used here) and its compensation structure at the time looked exactly like that of Goldman Sachs.
- *Wells Fargo*: this bank has not been mentioned so far, and as this book was being written they were caught up in a scandal with respect to cross-selling and fake accounts. However, as diversified large national banks at the time of this survey, they were widely regarded as one of the best-managed banks in the USA. They went through the crisis unscathed and were able to absorb the troubled Wachovia Corporation at the peak of the crisis. It is interesting to note that this well-run bank did not pay its executives above-average base compensation or stock programme awards compared to its peers.

These observations suggest that there is no simple way to summarise good corporate governance. Good governance is likely to be complex and idiosyncratic to the firm. It is not high pay or moderate pay, but whether executives are involved with the firm with *skin in the game*—as with family-run or partnership structures. Managers' interests must be aligned with those of shareholders so that they share any negative consequences of their decisions with the ultimate owners. In this way, long-term thinking about downside consequences is built into decision making. Bringing long-term value comes first for banks run this way, with financial rewards following through in due course to those with ownership and control. Unfortunately, very few banks have this type of structure. Most of the banks considered in this book have widely dispersed share ownership, usually in the hands of institutional investors or mutual fund managers. Typically these agents of owners do not play a significant role in corporate governance.

One of the best papers explaining and providing empirical support for these difficulties can be found in Isaksson and Celik (2013). Institutional investors are a highly heterogeneous group, and their willingness and ability to engage in corporate governance depend on the incentives between chains of agents (ultimate owners, agency managers, proxy advisors, security lending agents and asset consultants) as opposed to skin-in-the-game owners. The ultimate owners of shares are very far away from the company, and their agents operate according to different business models, investment strategies and trading practices. While it is always desirable to work to improve governance via regulatory initiatives to increase shareholder engagement, these are shown by the authors to have unintended consequences. The diversity and complexity of the investment chain can render general policies or regulation ineffective. This set of issues is particularly relevant for financial firms, as some of the above examples have shown.

Even within the firm, control and effective governance becomes a part of the degrees of separation in the governance chain. For example, discussions with senior bank management post the crisis suggested to the present authors that when remuneration incentives are based on deal flow with upfront recognition of fee-for sale revenue, loan officers often presented to the risk officers simply to get the deal approved—with the equity culture pressuring them to comply. The very same loan officers then took comfort from the approval they received from the risk officer. The loan officers did not own the risk assessment process in a traditional credit risk culture way.

The Crisis Hits, the Lehman Moment

The first wobbles in the crisis happened in 2007 when house price began to fall (see Fig. 3.1). Countrywide Financial and New Century Financial stopped taking applications for loans because their funding was drying up. Two hedge funds owned by Bear Stearns went bankrupt in July. Liquidity was becoming an issue. In August, BNP Paribas froze withdrawals on funds that had invested in subprime mortgages that were falling in value and suffering rising redemptions. The run on Northern Rock occurred a month later. Still, policymakers didn't catch on to what was happening to liquidity—the subprime market was thought to be small in the world financial system. In March 2008, subprime securities issued by Bear Stearns were downgraded, and at this point, the Fed began to understand that liquidity was an issue—they launched the lending facility programme for banks in trouble. Investors too began to understand something was amiss. Bear Stearns was quickly sold for $2 a share to JP Morgan (a week earlier it had been at $65 on the stock exchange), in the hope that would put an end to the crisis. It did not.

Fannie and Freddie, the two mortgage monoliths began to collapse, forcing the government to guarantee them formally in early September—underlining that these huge mortgage securitisation agencies were too big to fail (TBTF). Even more that 10 years after the 2008 crisis, the Fannie and Freddie issues, and the quality of the securities held in conservatorship, are not resolved. But the big test arose the following week: Lehman Brothers.

Lehman Brothers was one of the biggest underwriters of MBS. It succumbed to the falling value of subprime mortgages and filed for bankruptcy in September 2008. Its capital was not nearly enough to absorb the massive losses, and the immediate issue was that no one would lend to it to fund its activities. Tim Geithner president of the FRBNY decided not to lend to Lehman, and called a meeting to sell it in pieces to other banks. This was the greatest bankruptcy filing in US history, and it was to be a test that led to all the emergency measure that followed. The bankruptcy set off contagion losses in all of the Lehman Brothers counterparties. The Fed and the US banks had gotten together over the weekend to work through the exposures, by netting them—cancelling offsetting trades to reduce the problem to the smallest net exposure. But the net exposure caused losses for those who had Lehman positions in derivatives, particularly Credit Default Swaps (CDS).

US officials felt that drawing the line at Lehman Brothers, by not to supporting its sale with guarantees, would send a good message to the financial markets in terms of the moral hazard issues. Even with hindsight, there is no way to know what would have happened if Lehman had been saved, and whether letting it go was the right decision. But what is clear is that the 'Lehman moment' happened at a point in time when the global systemic nature of the crisis was about to unfold.

The decision to let Lehman fail, and to go into close-out netting, led to a freezing up of the financial system. Merrill Lynch came into the gunsights at the Lehman moment, and Bank of America was essentially forced to absorb it for an all-stock deal of $50bn. Then AIG, which had guaranteed vast amounts of bonds, and had written cheap CDS contracts for gaming the Basel system, to all intents and purposes failed. On the verge of its collapse, and after the experience with Lehman Brothers, the government decided it could not allow AIG to fail too.

This chapter has explained the immediate causes of the crisis in the few short years following poor regulatory decisions made in 2004. The following Chapter 4 will focus on the business models of banks and just why global contagion became the key issue—and why saving AIG was so essential.

Appendix to Chapter 3: Modelling the Acceleration of US RMBS from 2004

In a paper presented to the 2008 Reserve Bank conference at Kirribilli, two of the authors modelled the evolution of the stock of RMBS outstanding using the following explanatory variables: GDP; the mortgage rate; the mortgage spread to Fed funds; 12-month house price inflation;

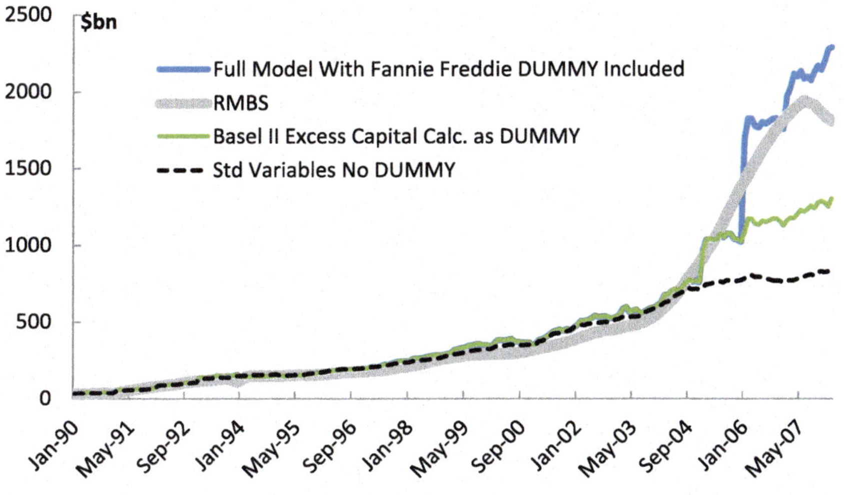

Fig. 3.2 Model of RMBS and the 2004 acceleration (*Source* Blundell-Wignall and Atkinson (2008))

aggregate excess bank capital under Basel; and an allowance (via a dummy variable) for the impact of the S&L crisis at the end of the 1980s. With these standard variables, the model worked well for sample periods prior to 2004, but broke down afterwards. The parabolic jump after 2004 shown by the full-model line in Fig. 3.2 cannot be explained without reference to the four causal regulatory/structural shifts noted earlier which occurred around that time.

The authors then calculated the likely freeing up of capital under the full Basel II system for sophisticated adherents as was known to banks through their participation in the QIS4 simulations. This would be an additional capital saving of $220bn by the end of 2007 (in addition to existing Basel 1 excess capital). When included in the model, this variable adds a jump of around $500bn in private label RMBS. When a dummy variable is included for the Fannie and Freddie controls (and doubling for the SEC rule change in 2004) a further $800bn is added.[19]

[19] This corresponds also with the period of the 2004 SEC rule change, and it is impossible to separate this effect from the Fannie and Freddie effect—clearly greater leverage possibilities for IBs greatly helped the response to compensating for Fannie and Freddie constraints.

This full model result is shown in the thick line. Once these two dummy variables are added, the coefficients on all the standard variables return to their pre-2004 values (see Blundell-Wignall and Atkinson (2008) in the Reserve Bank Conference volume). This suggests that the period in which Basel II was anticipated and arbitraged (as in the Citigroup example) and the Fannie and Freddie controls were in play, banks were able to accelerate RMBS using lower quality mortgages (and supported by 'American Dream' policies) by some $1.3tn. Much of the problems now known as the subprime crisis can be traced to these securities.

References

Blundell-Wignall, A., & Atkinson, P. E. (2008). The Subprime Crisis: Causal Distortions and Regulatory Reform. In Kent & Bloxham (Eds.), *Lessons from the Financial Turmoil of 2007 and 2008.* Reserve Bank of Australia. http://www.rba.gov.au/PublicationsAndResearch/Conferences/2008/Blundell-Wignall_Atkinson.pdf.

FDIC. (2005, Winter). Capital and Accounting News: Basel II and the Potential Effects on Insured Institutions in the United States: Results of the Fourth Quantitative Impact Study (QIS4). *Supervisory Insights, 2*(2), 27–32.

General Accounting Office. (2007, March). *Agencies Engaged in Consolidated Supervision can Strengthen Performance Measurement and Consolidation*, GA-07-154. Washington, DC, p. i.

Isaksson, M., & Celik, S. (2013). *Who Cares? Corporate Governance in Today's Equity Markets* (OECD Corporate Governance Working Paper No. 8).

Resti, A. (2017, March). Fines for Misconduct in the Banking Sector: What Is the Situation in Europe. *In Depth Analysis*. European Parliament.

SEC. (2008, September 25). *SEC's Oversight of Bear Stearns and Related Entities: The CSE Program* (Report No. 446-A), pp. viii–ix.

Sirri, E. (2008, May 7). Testimony Concerning the Turmoil in Credit Markets: Examining the Regulation of Investment Banks by the Securities and Exchange Commission, Before the Subcommittee on Securities, Insurance and Investment. United States Senate.

The White House. (2004, September 2). President George W. Bush, "Increasing Affordable Housing and Expanding Home Ownership", Press Release.

Treasury Committee. (2007). *The Run on The Rock: Fifth Report, Session 2007–08*, Vol. 2: Oral, EV. 47.

UBS. (2008, April). *Shareholder Report on UBS Write-Downs*. UBS AG.

4

Business Models of Banks and Global Contagion

Introduction

In the preceding chapter, it was noted that the corporate governance of banks had no clear correlation with banks that succeeded or failed. Once regulations constraining the 'equity culture' were removed, and the flawed Basel II rules were announced, the floodgates opened to give full force to regulatory arbitrage and the use of high-risk subprime securitisation. One of the obvious puzzles was that all banks faced:

- The same global regulatory and capital rules.
- The same listing rules on stock exchanges bearing on boards and corporate governance.
- Similar senior staff bonus mechanisms.
- The same accounting firms and credit rating agencies (CRAs) institutions and processes.
- Tax distortions everywhere that give rise to arbitrage opportunities.
- The same availability of OTC derivatives, securitisation and structured products.

A. Blundell-Wignall et al., *Globalisation and Finance at the Crossroads*,
https://doi.org/10.1007/978-3-319-72676-2_4

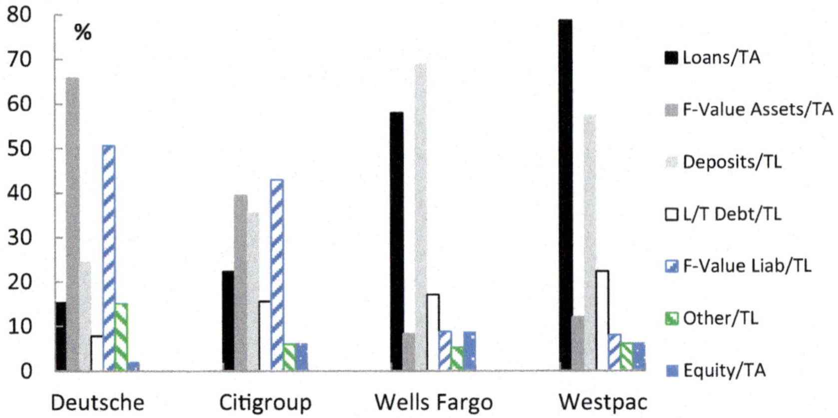

Fig. 4.1 Consolidated balance sheet structure of conglomerates: % of assets, June 2009 (*Source* Company reports)

But all banks did not have the same crisis outcomes. In this chapter, it is shown that it is the business models of banks—what they actually do—that really explain which banks succeeded and which failed, and the contagion effects to which they give rise. To this day, regulatory capture and political connections have prevented anything meaningful being done about this critical issue.

Contrasting Banking Conglomerate Asset and Liability Composition

This chapter focuses on the balance sheet structures of banks and how these (more than anything else) determined outcomes in the crisis.[1] To illustrate the issues, it uses examples and numbers that are easy to follow, setting the scene for more formal evidence later on.

Figure 4.1 shows main components of the balance sheets of four banking conglomerates in 2009, two of which needed support in the crisis and two which did not. The contrasts in asset composition are

[1]It draws heavily on the 'Elephant in the Room' paper by Blundell-Wignall et al. (2010).

striking. Citigroup and Deutsche Bank belong to countries that figured prominently in the crisis. These banks are widely acknowledged to be '*too big to fail*' (TBTF). Wells Fargo and Westpac required no support during the crisis. The salient features of the balance sheet composition of all four banks in 2009 (at the height of the crisis) are as follows:

- '*Loans*': to businesses (that produce real things) and to households (for housing and consumption) are shown in the first set of bars on the left. Loans generate more reliable cash flows, and amortised cost accounting applies. For the safer banks, loans were 58% of assets for Wells Fargo and 79% for Westpac. In the case of Deutsche and Citi, loans were only 15 and 22%, respectively.
- *Securities at fair value through profit* or loss (including derivatives): These assets (the second set of bars) accounted with fair value are held in the '*Trading Book*'.[2] For the two banks needing support, these assets were in the 40–60% range, in contrast to Wells Fargo and Westpac, where this component was in the 8–12% range. Broad differences of this kind are common for traditional deposit-taking banks compared to those encompassing vast investment bank (IB) activities. Fair value assets including derivatives were inside a 10–15% range in a wide range of safer banks during the crisis.
- *Deposits*: Activities on the asset side of the balance sheet are funded out of deposits and wholesale borrowing (including via derivative sales). Deposits tend to be more stable ('sticky' with predictable cash flows), which reduces the risk of liquidity crises. Low deposits, implying higher wholesale funding, appeared to be a strong feature of the German and US banks containing investment banks (IBs). Wells Fargo and Westpac have a strong deposit base.
- *Long-term Debt funding*: Bond funding is longer duration and requires the maintenance of a strong credit rating to be cost-effective—acting as a discipline on banks. Deutsche Bank is very low in long-term bonds.

[2]The trading assets are consolidated with other assets at fair value through profit or loss. See the Glossary for definitions of Banking and Trading Books.

- *Other liabilities*: are highest in the German bank.
- '*Equity*': This critical balance sheet item—the object of regulatory capital rules—appeared to be small in 2009, and particularly so in Deutsche Bank, at 2%. Wells Fargo easily had the largest capital base.

Some greater details for the four banks are shown in Table 4.1. If Wells Fargo and Westpac conformed to the structure of a 'bank', as it is thought of by politicians and the public at large (i.e. an institution that funds mainly via deposits and longer-term borrowing and lends to households and to companies that do real things), this cannot be said to be the case for Citigroup and Deutsche Bank in 2009.[3] On a consolidated basis, these latter institutions looked much more like large highly levered hedge funds—though no hedge fund running these sorts of structured products would dream of having a leverage ratio of almost 50 (assets versus equity), as was the case of Deutsche Bank.[4]

Synthetic CDO Issuance by Banks

In Chapter 2, the basics of 'waterfall' cash-flow CDOs were explained and the use of off-balance-sheet special purpose vehicles (SPVs) to avoid capital regulations was set out. Tax arbitrage incentives were also explained. Synthetic CDOs are of two basic types:

- *Balance sheet synthetic securitisation*: Banks keep the assets on balance sheet, but transfer the credit risk to the CDO SPV by buying credit default swap (CDS) protection. The investors (insurance companies, hedge funds, etc.) are sellers of protection and get the spread premium synthetically. The CDO is tranched as with the cash CDO, but the underlying assets remain with the originating bank. How the CDS transfers risk in this way is set out in Table 2.2. The investor (as with AIG) is exposed to defaults of the originating bank assets. The

[3] Deutsche Bank is typical of other large French, German, Swiss and UK banks.

[4] A typical hedge fund has a leverage of 4 or 5 times equity.

Table 4.1 Key balance sheet and off-balance-sheet ratios: Deutsche, Citi, Wells Fargo, Westpac

In millions of local currency	Deutschebank €m	Citi $m (converted to IFRS)	Wells Fargo $m (converted to IFRS)	Wespac in A$m
	Jun 30, 2009	Dec 31, 2009	Dec 31, 2009	Sep 30, 2009
Assets	1,732,873	2,500,986	1,309,572	589,587
Cash like	108,315	414,908	67,965	21,581
Fair value securities	1,140,525	987,113	108,965	71,029
of which derivatives	769,678	703,219	89,484	na
Financial assets available for sale	19,960	306,119	217,537	1630
Loans	264,485	555,471	758,254	463,459
Other	199,588	237,375	156,851	31,888
Liabilities	1,732,873	2,346,013	1,195,213	589,587
Cash like (non-int.)	57,698	116,229	181,356	9235
Deposits (Int. bearing)	368,532	719,674	642,662	329,456
Fair value liabilities (incl. S/T repos)	875,115	1,005,012	104,892	47,326
Long-term debt	134,811	364,019	203,861	131,353
Other	261,277	141,079	62,442	35,646
Equity	35,440	154,973	114,359	36,571
Memo: MAX LOSS EXP. TO SPEs	23,900	106,405	95,240	0
Key Ratios	%	%	%	%
Loans/assets (%)	15.3	22.2	57.9	78.6
Fair value assets/ total assets (%)	65.8	39.5	8.3	12.0
Deposits/liabilities (%)	24.6	35.6	68.9	57.4
L-T Debt/liabilities (%)	7.8	15.5	17.1	22.3
Fair value liabilities/ total liabilities (%)	50.5	42.8	8.8	8.0
Other debt/liabilities	15.1	6.0	5.2	6.0
Equity/assets (%)	2.0	6.2	8.7	6.2

Source Company reports. VIEs (Variable Interest Entities) are special purpose entities (SPEs) which must be consolidated on the balance sheet if losses arise. QSPEs (Qualifying Special Purpose Entities) are where risks have been fully transferred to a third party

bank has counterparty risk as the protection seller in a credit event may default (as with AIG). Often the main point of this transaction was to expand leverage by the bank, by reducing capital requirements (as noted in the previous chapter). The investor is motivated by achieving a risk and return profile for their portfolio.

- *Arbitrage collateralised synthetic obligation* (*CSO*): These are a means to undertake market risk transactions via products that arbitrage spreads using purpose-built indices. These indices (like CDX and iTRAXX) are portfolios of single name CDS which contain typically 125 fixed names. New versions of the index (the *on-the-run* index) are launched periodically as the CDS in the previous index begin to mature. They can be CDS related to underlying RMBS names, but also government securities and other debt. The mechanics are that an SPV is created, and the investors pay in par amounts to establish the collateral pool. The SPV invests in the collateral required. It then sells CDS protection on the index pools set up by the bank dealer, and these pay the associated CDS spread to the SPV (related to the credit risk in the pool). The investor receives the spread premium through the SPV and any income from the collateral. The par principle is paid at the end of the maturity of the CSO (net of any payments for defaults). The bank setting up the structure will offer different tranches related to seniority—but often sells a *single tranche* (typically mezzanine). With 'single tranche CSOs', the arranger sells a 'bespoke' tranche to the investor and the payment structure does not depend on that for any other tranches (as in the cash waterfall model of the standard CDO). These products became very popular and accelerated after 2004.

In the CSO case, the credit institution is the credit protection buyer (a direct counterparty) in the tranche sold to the investor; they pay the premiums and hence are exposed to the volatility risk of credit spreads in the portfolio (market risk) and to the risk of default of the investors. Banks work with investors like hedge funds and pension funds to achieve specific outcomes—but single tranche CSOs can be highly illiquid. Like cash CDOs, the SPV would normally set up a CSO in a low-tax jurisdiction. CSOs may also be unfunded (which was quite common in the run-up to the crisis).

Each tranche has a notional value and is defined by lower and upper loss points. The objective for a tranche might be to achieve Libor plus X%, with a certain maturity, but with loss points defined (attachment points). For example, the BBB-rated tranche might be defined by a 5 and 10% loss range. When the synthetic CDO is 'unfunded' (meaning there is no upfront cash investment), payments are required on a regular basis or at the end of the maturity period. In this example, if the losses are less than 5%, then no payment is required for the 5–10% loss tranche; if it moves into the 5–10% range, payments are required; and at 10%, the tranche value goes to zero.

It is important to note the '*atomic bomb*' nature of investing in unfunded CSOs. An investor buying the underlying bond would lose 10% in the above example of 10% losses. But the buyer of the BBB tranche is completely wiped out. This sort of thing was to play a big role in the global crisis. CRAs were under pressure to underprice the risk of CDOs and CSOs to help IBs transfer the risk to investors more easily. As noted earlier, they played a facilitating role in the crisis. This issue of the role of CRAs and what should have been done to improve their processes are set out in Appendix A to this chapter.

Issuance of Credit Derivative Structured Products

Credit derivative products are exposed to two sorts of risks: defaults (as discussed above) and spread movements, so that the value of an index tranche depends on price movement of underlying names and the correlation assumptions used to value the issue. The 'delta-adjusted' value is roughly the price at which a tranche could be traded at any time prior to maturity on the open market.[5]

Figure 4.2 shows the issuance by major banks of standardised structured credit products (index-based tranches). Both notional and delta-adjusted values are shown.[6] Just prior to the crisis, this was

[5]More specifically, delta-adjusted means the sensitivity of the tranche based on derivatives to changes in the price of the underlying names that are referenced.

[6]This is a highly standardised single tranche CDO, with (say) iTraxx Europe or CDX NA IG as its reference portfolio. Besides using standard portfolios, the attachment and detachment points, maturity and documentation of index tranches are also standardised, ensuring that these products are much more liquid than bespoke synthetic CDOs. Structured equity products are not included. These Credit Flux data do not include CSOs based purely on CDS instead of the underlying credit instruments.

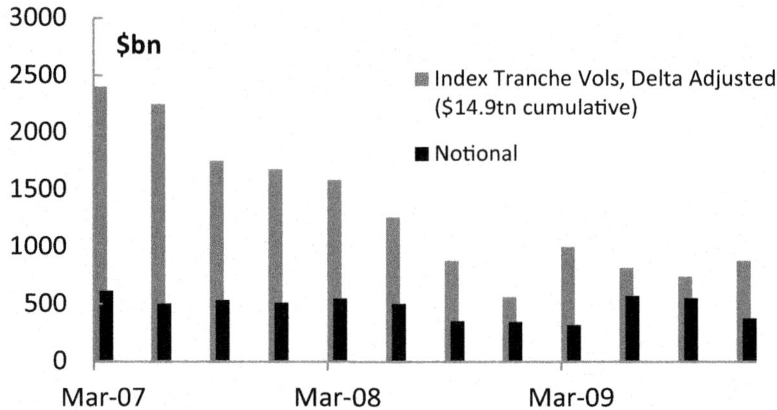

Fig. 4.2 Issuance of CDO index tranche volumes (Delta-adjusted, quarterly) (*Source* Credit Flux, authors)

running at $500bn notional and $2.4tn per quarter delta-adjusted. It fell away sharply during the crisis—particularly in the last quarter of 2008. However, the policies for recovery—including zero rates in some countries and massive liquidity support—saw values pick up again somewhat in 2009, as volatility normalised (i.e. as the market rallied, volatility fell and spreads narrowed somewhat). The effect of these value shifts (that must be accounted for at fair value) contributed to the losses and write-downs in banks, a phenomenon that made the 2008 crisis so different from previous ones. The biggest issuers (in order) were JP Morgan, Deutsche Bank, Citigroup, UBS, BNP Paribas, Lehman Brothers, Merrill Lynch, Morgan Stanley, Barclays, Societe Generale and Calyon.

These banks were responsible for $508bn dollars of the $1.1tn losses admitted to by banks by mid-2009, some 46% of the total. If the ultimate losses resulting from the total collapse of Lehman Brothers were included (rather than the write-downs before the collapse), the total would be much higher, and these banks would be responsible for 2/3 of the higher total losses. Similarly, losses of Bear Stearns absorbed by JP Morgan are not included because they would not be apparent for some years after the takeover (being held as collateral by the Fed in exchange for a loan of $30bn).

Figure 4.3 shows CDS contracts in notional outstanding amounts and their net value on the RHS scale. The explosive growth in CDS from 2004 to 2007 is explained by regulatory factors noted earlier, which permitted a leap in leverage with the expansion of the CDO market, as well as the growing use of CDS in 'reducing risk' on risk-weighted assets for taking advantage of Basel weighting procedures.

Bank Losses at the Time of the Crisis

Figure 4.4 shows the losses from all sources (including from CDOs and CSOs) of: banks (most of which can be described as having participated in the '*equity culture*' in banking discussed in Chapter 3); the insurance companies like AIG that wrote CDS contracts; and Fannie and Freddie (that were the mill for the mortgage securitisation process).

These losses admitted to at the time (and excluding the payouts to AIG counterparties and the losses of the Lehman balance sheet after it collapsed) sum to $1.6tn, but may actually understate the true situation. This is because banks shifted products from their trading book to their banking book when it proved convenient to do so, and held them there for long periods (particularly longer-run cash CDOs rather than synthetic products which were shorter term in nature). When institutions hold products in their banking book, they are not marked to market. Accounting standard issues related to this are discussed in Appendix B to this chapter.

The AIG Payouts

Table 4.2 shows the amounts US authorities paid out to settle bank exposures to the single counterparty AIG during the crisis.

AIG was the biggest writer of CDS through its London financial products arm. Given what happened, it is now clear that the CDS was written in a way that was underpricing risk. In many ways, AIG was underpinning the entire house of cards. In August 2008, it reported $441bn in 'super senior' CDS exposure alone, $307bn of which was: '*written to facilitate regulatory capital relief for financial institutions*

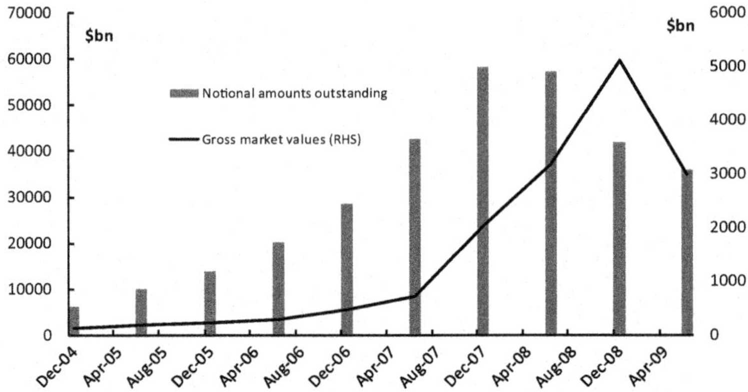

Fig. 4.3 Credit default swaps outstanding (*Source* BIS, authors. Notional amounts are all the debt exposure covered. Gross market values on the RHS refer to how much money would actually change hands after netting if derivatives were sold on the reporting date at prevailing market prices)

primarily in Europe'. By early September, on the eve of its collapse, 12,000 individual derivative contracts reportedly amounted to $2.7tn, of which $1tn with just 12 counterparties.[7] Had the USA allowed AIG to fail, it is not at all clear how well any of the banks in the table would have withstood the additional losses. The drain on their capital and the indirect effects of the turmoil that would have followed in the markets to which they were exposed would likely have increased losses.

Too Big to Fail, Contagion and Counterparty Risk

The 'too big to fail' (TBTF) problem (where the market knows the government will have to save institutions that might otherwise take the whole system down) seems to have been a feature of underpricing risk in the 2008 crisis. Banks carry relatively small amounts of capital.

[7] The quotation is from AIG's August 2008 10Q filing as reported by Sorkin (2009). The comment about 12 counterparties is attributed by Sorkin to a confidential source. See p. 236 and the endnotes to Chapter 16, p. 395.

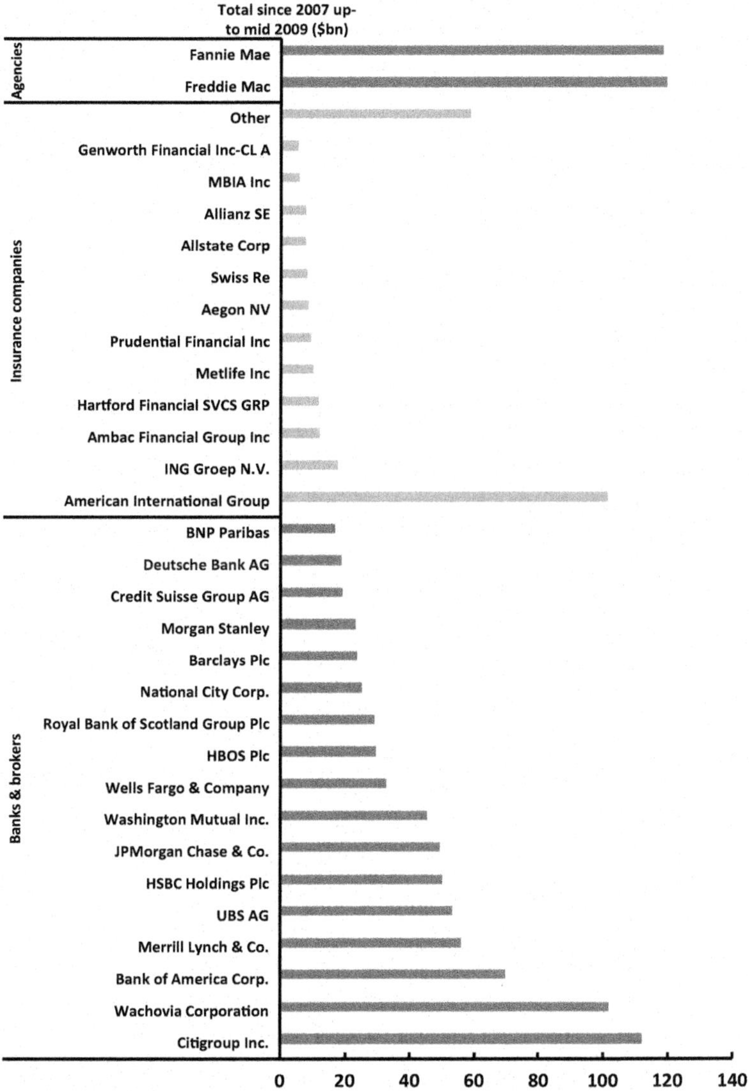

Fig. 4.4 Major financial institutions' write-downs and credit losses to mid-2009 (*Source* Proxy statements. Totals for 2007 to mid-2009, $bn)

Table 4.2 US payments to settle AIG obligations to prevent its failure

In $bn				
Institution	Collateral postings for credit default swaps[a]	Payments to securities lending counterpaties[b]	Total	As a share of capital[c] at end-2008 (%)
Goldman Sachs	8.1	4.8	12.9	29.1
Société Générale	11	0.9	11.9	28.9
Deutsche Bank	5.4	6.4	11.9	37.4
Barclays	1.5	7	8.5	20.0
Merrill Lynch	4.9	1.9	6.8	77.4
Bank of America	0.7	4.5	5.2	9.1
UBS	3.3	1.7	5	25.2
BNP Paribas	...	4.9	4.9	8.3
HSBC	0.2	3.3	3.5	5.3
(*memo: Bank of America after its merger with Merrill Lynch*)			12	[*18.1*]

[a]Direct payments from AIG through end-2008 plus payments by Maiden Lane III, a financing entity established by AIG and the New York Federal Reserve Bank to purchase underlying securities
[b]September 18 to December 12, 2008
[c]Common equity net of goodwill; net of all intangible assets for Merrill Lynch and HSBC
Source AIG; company reports for capital data

Assets valued at fair value through profit or loss on both side of the balance sheet may be extremely volatile in a crisis, particularly where liquidity issues arise, and these movements can wipe out the capital very quickly (if properly accounted for). If the conglomerate includes a commercial bank alongside other subsidiaries, it may also be wiped out (in the absence of a rescue), i.e. because of 'contagion risk' arising from the activities of other members of the banking group. This is because the (highly volatile) securities businesses (based on fair value through profit or loss accounting) share the bank's capital with the less volatile commercial banking business where cost amortisation accounting applies and volatility is much lower. Where insured deposits are involved, it is all the more likely that the group will be supported in a crisis, which in turn encourages greater risk taking by the higher-risk segment.

The use of counterparties in derivatives transactions to structure products and minimise capital requirements adds a further source of risk (in addition to leverage and risky trading). This is the potential failure of the counterparty to the derivatives transaction (another bank, an insurer, a pension fund, a hedge fund). The failure of a large counterparty like AIG may impact upon many banks at the same time. No matter how well hedged a bank may be in a technical sense, a counterparty failure can be devastating, as the AIG example in Table 4.2 shows. One senior banker at a conference where one of the present authors was speaking said that for them the possibility of AIG failing wasn't a material risk, because they had bought puts on AIG itself. But of course this misses the interconnectedness point: that the contract would have likely been held with another bank which is shown in Table 4.2 list.

In the case of all these institutions, the rescue of AIG (a single counterparty) resulted in a payout by the US Federal Reserve equal to enormous percentages of their capital at the time. Regulatory rules normally do not allow such large exposures to single entities, so the question arises as to how this could have happened. The answer is that the value of the position on the balance sheet reflects the exposure to immediate counterparty risk but not to the underlying exposure to future market risk. A sudden rise in volatility and collapse of liquidity in a crisis can result in levered derivative positions moving sharply and delta-hedging the portfolio to keep the exposure limited is not possible, as no one will trade. Prior to the crisis, limits were no doubt respected. Exposure limits based on current market valuations work well enough in normal periods, but they may break down with speed when they are most needed in a crisis.

Commercial Versus Investment Banking

Commercial banking has experienced large losses in previous crises. The fact that the unique feature of this crisis was business models based on securities and derivatives that are prone to contagion and counterparty risk does not mean that less volatile commercial banking is 'safe' for all states of the world:

- Commercial banks that are small and concentrated on assets in a particular region can have major problems if that region suffers idiosyncratic recessions and asset price falls—for example, a sharp fall in oil prices in an oil kingdom or state.
- Excessive concentration on specific assets such as mortgages or commercial real estate can also lead to major problems (the S&L crisis; Australian banks in the early 90s etc.).
- Related party transactions with industrial companies, as in Japan and Korea in the Asia crisis, can be very problematic, as can such transactions in family-owned banks.
- Borrowing in foreign currency within countries that run current account deficits has been a major issue (such as the Latin American debt crisis).
- In the aftermath of 2008, hundreds of small regional banks focused or mortgages failed or were merged with other banks.[8]

Nevertheless, a credit culture combined with the right degree of concentration in banking has one great advantage over investment banking securities businesses: the flows on incoming and outgoing cash flows are reasonably predictable and may be accounted for with amortised cost accounting. Securities prices, particularly those embedded with derivatives, are accounted for at fair value, and losses may arise with volatility and/or the failure of counterparties.

External Cost of Crises and Resolution Credibility

Some idea of the risks and costs of this crisis that were borne by the taxpayer globally are given in Table 4.3, which shows capital injections and emergency loans in the first column ($1.5tn), asset purchases and guarantees in the second ($5.2tn), and debt guarantees in the third

[8]See old press releases in www.FDIC.gov. One hundred and forty-six banks failed in the 2 years after 2008, almost all in the small specialised category. Local savings banks in Spain are also got into trouble and the so-called dynamic provisioning (counter cyclical) capital rules did not seem able to prevent this at the time.

Table 4.3 Official support for financial institutions following the crisis (2007–2010)

	Capital injection/ emergency loans		Asset purchase/ guarantees		Debt guarantees [a,b]	
	€bn	$bn	€bn	$bn	€bn	$bn
Australia	0	0	5	7	amount not specified	amount not specified
Austria	15	22	0	0	10	15
Belgium	21	31	39	57	91	134
Brazil	0	0	0	0	0	1
Canada	0	0	80	119	amount not specified	amount not specified
China	13	19	0	0	0	1
Denmark	13	20	0	0	81	119
Finland	4	6	0	0	50	74
France	27	40	4	6	320	474
Germany	80	119	480	711	450	667
Greece	5	7	0	0	15	22
Hong-Kong SAR	0	0	0	0	0	0
India	0	0	0	0	0	0
Ireland	10	15	77	114	amount not specified	amount not specified
Italy	0	0	0	0	amount not specified	amount not specified
Japan	97	144	202	299	0	1
Korea	11	17	0	0	67	100
Luxembourg	3	4	0	0	5	7
Mexico	0	0	0	0	0	1
Netherlands	42	62	58	86	200	296
New Zealand	0	0	0	0	amount not specified	amount not specified
Norway	6	9	6	9	0	1
Portugal	4	6	0	0	20	30

(continued)

Table 4.3 (continued)

	Capital injection/ emergency loans		Asset purchase/ guarantees		Debt guarantees [a,b]	
Singapore	0	0	0	0	0	1
Spain	90	133	133	197	100	148
Sweden	7	10	0	0	145	216
Switzerland	4	6	26	39	amount not specified	amount not specified
UK	55	81	164	243	24	36
USA	544	806	2242	3322	1552	2300
Total	1051	1557	3516	5209	3130	4644
Europe	*385*	*571*	*987*	*1463*	*1510*	*2239*
United States	*544*	*806*	*2242*	*3322*	*1552*	*2300*
Other	*122*	*180*	*287*	*424*	*68*	*105*

[a]Excludes deposit insurance

[b]Amount not specified is a transparency issue, not absence of the item

Source Authors compilation from multiple sources

($4.6tn).[9] This was well in excess of the capital of the banking system. In the US case, as Thomas Hoenig (2016) points out, US bank losses and the Troubled Assets Relief Program together summed to be 6% of total assets of the US banks concerned, about double the size of bank capital. No doubt the extremely large support numbers were justified to forestall the onset of an even greater crisis. These measures may have arrested the crisis, but in recent years complacency seems to have crept back in, with banks once more pushing for some roll-back of regulations.

The credit and derivative markets are inherently volatile and interconnected globally, so contagion and counterparty risk loom large. The following chapter will focus on what was done by way of reform after 2008, and whether this will prove to be enough to forestall future crises. Indeed, this will be the theme of much of the rest of this book, where more detailed evidence on risks and what causes them are presented.

Appendix A to Chapter 4: The Role of Credit Rating Agencies in the Crisis

History

CRAs began in 1909 with Moody's. CRAs are an '*experience business*' based on trust and past performance. The CRAs create public information on ratings to allow the trading of securities on public exchanges. This essential service assesses the credit risk of the issuer and the specific credit risk of the securities concerned. This helps to set a common standard for contracts, investment benchmarks and regulations. In short, they provide a means of comparison that is essential everywhere.

In the early days, rating agencies used an 'investor pays' business model. But a very high public demand for ratings emerged after the Penn Central/commercial paper market collapse in 1970. The old

[9] Estimates of losses looking forward are provided in Blundell-Wignall and Atkinson (2009).

model could not work anymore due to the '*free rider*' problem. So the entire payer basis changed from the 'investor' to the 'issuer' of a bond or structured security tranche. The issuer pays model was simply more convenient.

However, the rating agencies developed cosy relationships with issuers and particularly with IB underwriters. In the lead up to the crisis, senior tranches of CDOs were often classified as AAA, even though they were made up of highly correlated subprime mortgages, where 'pooling' could not eliminate the risks.

This conflict of interest is often referred to as a moral hazard problem—helping IBs sell poor-quality products to increase their revenue. There is no doubt in the view of the present authors that this played a role in facilitating the crisis. Things were changing quickly, and if a bond was guaranteed by a bond insurer, or because there was CDS insurance, much more digging needed to be done. What was the riskiness of the underlying mortgage pool? What was the nature of the legal covenants for the tranches? Did the insurers or counterparties have the capital or sufficient reinsurance to make good on their implicit promises if a worst-case scenario unfolded? Unfortunately, the aftermath of the crisis suggests this wasn't done.

Reforming Credit Rating Agencies in Light of the Crisis

The agencies came under huge criticism after the crisis, due to the conflict of interest issues. Now, either by regulation or on a voluntarily basis, most CRAs observe firewalls; i.e. the 'Ratings' and 'Advisory' and 'ancillary services' of CRAs can't talk to each other. This is a step forward. But the problems are deeper than that because methodology issues were and are still present.

First, it is the question of due diligence on the viability of insurers of the products. Presumably, steps have been taken, but it is not clear who supervises this process.

Second, it is the problem of '*linearity bias*'. CRAs use a scoring system based on dozens of categories with linear mostly equal weights. The problem here is that one single risk factor could become the dominating risk factor, but its influence will be lost amongst all the other variables. CRAs have claimed to the authors that they are on to this, and they have manual override processes where this is deemed to be the case. This introduces judgement—which depends on the experience and quality of staff (which takes the subject back to CRAs being an experience business).

Third, the industry is an oligopoly, which is underpinned by the use of external ratings in official regulations and in benchmark indexes for fund managers. Local presence rules also act as a barrier to entry to smaller entrants (they can't have offices in all capitals because of cost, which protects large incumbents). Cosy relationships are likely to build up in oligopolistic markets—as CRAs want to keep their clients and this can result in the underpricing of risk.

Finally, and related to all the above, it is the issue of pro-cyclicality observed during the crisis, where strong ratings are given in the boom times, which are followed by *cliff effects*, where a sharp drop in asset values results in a downgrade across multiple rating categories. Since Basel II, such a downgrading can result in very large and sudden increases in capital requirements.

Fundamental reforms could fix most of these issues but, like banks, the ability of these firms to push back on suggested changes is very strong—as there are few alternatives. The main reforms the current authors believe essential include:

- *Transparency*: The CRA ratings history must be publicly available.
- *Separation*: The ratings function and consulting functions must be separated formally and conflicts of interest prohibited.
- *Official support*: Remove ratings from regulations where possible (Dodd Frank proposes this).
- *Local presence endorsement rules*: These should be removed to encourage entry of smaller players (the EU does the opposite of this).
- *Recourse*: Negligence should result in recourse paths to third-party supervisors with the ability to impose penalties.
- *The platform-pays model*: In essence, a regulating entity with strong governance would be a buffer between the rating agency and the

issuer. The platform would direct the issuer to a ratings firm based on expertise and past performance (so issuers don't choose their own CRA). The choice would be broader than the current big three rating firms (S&P, Moody's and Fitch). The buffer would stop cosy relationships from developing, and business could be reallocated when performance is poor.

- *Encourage entry*: Plausible new entrants with experience (e.g. a Morningstar has a lot of relevant experience) could be encouraged to enter.

Appendix B to Chapter 4: Accounting Standard Controversy Around the Crisis and IFRS9

Prior to the crisis, banks (and regulators) did not complain about mark-to-market accounting for complex products with embedded derivatives, as markets rose, volatility declined, spreads narrowed and profits were booked. Problems arose immediately after the crisis, once the process reversed and asset impairment had to be taken as losses (large enough to overwhelm the capital of some financial conglomerates). At the heart of this matter lies the issue of how to value complex financial assets. As the crisis deepened, the applicability of 'fair value' or 'mark-to-market' accounting to assets for which no liquid markets exist was reviewed by IASB and in the USA by the FASB.

Accounting standards are set to ensure that investors and creditors of firms have clear information. Financial reports need to be reliable, understandable and comparable between companies and across jurisdictions. This includes all off-balance-sheet entities for which banks are exposed to loss, and the correct accounting for securities valued at fair value through profit or loss versus those to which amortised cost accounting might apply. This is important to maintain the confidence of investors in public markets and to help reinforce shareholder discipline on management. The manipulation of earnings by allowing firms to book mark-to-market gains in the good times but to hide losses when things go wrong is inconsistent with these goals. IASB has reviewed the liquidity issue extensively and IFRS 9 made some basic changes:

- Debt instruments that are not held for trading purposes may be measured at amortised cost (even if listed).
- Equity instruments only have to be measured at fair value through profit or loss if they are to be traded. If they are not, the firm has a choice between the fair value approach and a method that does not require impairment charges to be taken to profit or loss.

Similarly, FSP FAS 157-e applies since June 2009, allowing banks more judgement in determining whether a market is not active and a transaction is not distressed when discounting future cash flows of assets held to maturity (as opposed to the fair market price at the time).

The above changes allowed banks to reclassify some loans, essentially when the intrinsic value of assets is judged by management to exceed their estimated fair values, due to significantly reduced liquidity, and returns would be optimised by holding them as hold-to-maturity investments—essentially reclassifying from financial assets at fair value through profit or loss to loans where amortised cost methods would apply. Allowing firms too much scope to switch impaired fair value assets to amortised cost accounting categories—reclassifying a complex structured product with imbedded derivatives as a loan for example—because it suits the bank in the short run is inconsistent with sound long-run objectives. Transparency is very important.

Policy makers from some countries in Europe and the European Commission suggested at the time that the above changes didn't go far enough—they were concerned that applying the rules would make French and German Landesbanks look worse. Jörgen Holmquist, director general of Internal Markets at the European Commission, argued in a letter to IFRS that more assets might be marked to market under the new system than even under existing rules. He urged the IASB 'urgently' to consider further changes. A letter to Commissioner McCreevy from Ernst and Young, 9 November 2009, refers to an internal French report that suggests Europe may need to establish its own standard setter if demands for even further changes than in IFRS9 are not met. Markets require transparent and material information, so that the discipline on management can be maintained. Furthermore, accounting standard setters need to be free from this sort of pressure as they continue to work on bringing about the much needed convergence of FASB and IFRS.

References

Blundell-Wignall, A., & Atkinson, P. E. (2009). Origins of the Financial Crisis and Requirements for Reform. *Journal of Asian Economics*. https://doi.org/10.1016/j.asieco.07.009.

Blundell-Wignall, A., Wehinger, G., and Slovik, P. (2010). The Elephant in the Room: The Need to Focus on What Banks Do. *OECD Journal, Financial Market Trends, 2*, 1–27.

Hoenig, T. (2016, November 9). *Strengthening Global Capital: An Opportunity Not To Be Lost*—Remarks by FDIC Vice Chairman Thomas M. Hoenig to the 22nd Annual Risk US Conference, New York.

Sorkin, R. (2009). *Too Big to Fail*. London: Allen Lane.

5

Managing the Crisis, Exit and Requirements of Reform

Introduction

The Great Depression was caused by a system-wide debt deflation problem—a balance sheet recession. This occurs, when high levels of private sector debt build up, driving real estate or equity prices in a pro-cyclical manner. When the bubble bursts, negative equity often emerges among asset owners. Asset values go down but debt does not. Households may then save to hoard cash while paying down debt and to restore their equity. A recession or worse may follow that can cause even the general level of prices to fall, causing real debt burdens to rise. On the side of the banks, negative equity may emerge because loans go bad and wipe out bank capital. Defensive behaviour by banks trying to hide problems and protect their balance sheets may exacerbate deflationary pressures. The possibility of such a scenario was very real in 2008 and, in the end, policy makers moved forcefully to avoid it.

The quickest road to a bank shutting their doors is illiquidity which makes it impossible to operate, whatever their underlying solvency. A liquidity crisis arises because bank funding is typically short-term and doesn't match its longer-term assets. In normal times, this is a part of

A. Blundell-Wignall et al., *Globalisation and Finance at the Crossroads*,
https://doi.org/10.1007/978-3-319-72676-2_5

the maturity transformation role of banks. But in crisis conditions, when uncertainty about asset quality and survival of counterparties tends to increase, it can be lethal. Lenders seeking safety feel less inclined to roll over their loans or deposits with the bank concerned. At this point, banks become dependent on central banks for liquidity (the lender-of-last-resort) and sensible policy makers respond with adequate amounts quickly.

But when the market value of the bank's assets threatens to fall below the book value of its liabilities (deposits, interbank loans, certificates of deposit, bank bills, notes and derivatives), which would result in negative equity, solvency issues arise. In this circumstance, it is difficult, if not impossible, to raise capital in the market place. There may be some scope for regulatory forbearance while waiting for trading profits, not distributed as dividends, to rebuild capital via retained earnings. But this requires banks to retain enough confidence in the markets to ensure that funding withdrawals do not compromise its ability to operate. Central bank liquidity support cannot be allowed to turn into open-ended coverage of losses without measures to stabilise the situation and restore solvency.

Liquidity crises in individual banks can easily spread, especially where solvency is in question. If the problem becomes systemic, severe macroeconomic consequences in the form of a balance sheet recession can emerge. It is for this reason that governments were forced into the emergency role of becoming new owners of banks (via equity injections), owners of distressed financial assets, guarantors of loans and owners of poor quality collateral on loans from central banks, as shown in Table 4.3. They also had to make regulatory adjustments on the run, without the benefit of empirical research, to deal with the clearly failing Basel II regime.[1] This chapter looks at what was done in the emergency and raises hypotheses about what a safer baking system might look like in the longer run—setting the scene for testing some of these hypotheses in subsequent chapters.

---

[1]If they had strong empirical research on the determinants of bank risk, authorities would not have announced a system like Basel II.

Crisis Management

With respect to crisis management, four basic emergency measures are normally required[2]:

- *Provide liquidity to banks*: this is the lender-of-last-resort function of central banking that goes back to Bagehot (1873).
- *Guarantee deposit liabilities*: to stop bank runs. All deposits need to be covered to avoid creating runs between covered and non-covered institutions.
- *Identify the bad assets and separate them from the good ones*: to get the bad assets off bank balance sheets so that the cleaned-up bank can function.
- *Recapitalise the asset-cleansed banks*: by finding new equity holders. This can be via selling common shares or preference shares (that provide a higher yield to the owner) to private entities or to governments.

Longer-term reform requires the regulatory rules to be decided in a manner that does not give rise to excess leverage and the arbitrage opportunities discussed in earlier chapters. It also requires the business models of banks to be addressed for two reasons: first, to deal with contagion risk within and between banks; second, to remove the too-big-to-fail (TBTF) problem that subsidises risk-taking through an implicit guarantee from the taxpayer.

Provision of Liquidity

As noted in the introduction of this book, officials had very little idea about the risks with structured products in early 2007. This may have made them a little slow to respond to the liquidity crisis in 2007.

[2]See the Statement by Mr. Angel Gurría (2008), Secretary General of the OECD.

Shigehara and Atkinson (2011) reviewed official surveillance at the international level in the period preceding the crisis, concluding (on p. 23) that '*…the reports produced by the IMF, the OECD and the BIS in the month preceding the collapse of the two Bear Stearns hedge funds in July 2007 and subsequent disturbances in the money markets were notable for either their complacency or their obliviousness to the dangers as regards the financial system*'. They also noted that in the US Article IV consultation at that time the Fund staff argued (IMF (2007), paragraph 23)[3] that '*Core commercial and investment banks are in a sound financial position, and systemic risks appear low. Profitability and capital adequacy of the banking system are high by international standards*'.

US officials were no better. In the August 7 minutes of the Federal Open Market Committee (FOMC), the focus was mixed, with members talking about a reasonable outlook for the economy, and some believing the markets were '*skittish*', subject to '*choppiness*' and that long-term investors were on the sidelines waiting to buy. William Poole one-time president of the St. Louis Fed stated: '*My own bet is that the financial market upset is not going to change fundamentally what's going on in the real economy. First of all, bank capital is not impaired. So unlike in some past cases, when losses on real estate impaired bank capital… affected the lending in areas that had nothing to do with real estate, I don't think that's the case this time*'.[4] This contrasted with the views of the New York Fed, and particularly William Dudley, who felt the CDOs, and credit derivatives were in a more dangerous phase, where liquidity risked drying up and firms failing.

Four days before this FOMC meeting, CNBC's Jim Cramer made his famous meltdown utterance on the Fed's failure to open the discount window as the Bear Stearns situation was deteriorating: '*Bernanke has to open the discount window. That's how bad things are out there.… I have talked to the heads of almost every single one of these firms in the last 72 hours and he has no idea what is like out there. None! And Bill Poole has no idea what it's like out there. My people have been in this game for*

---

[3]IMF, *US Article IV Staff Report* (2007).

[4]Federal Open Market Committee (2007).

25 years and they're losing their jobs and these firms are gonna go out of business, and he's nuts.... They know nothing!'.[5]

Two days after the August 7 FOMC meeting, BNP Paribas could not value three of its credit-focused hedge funds and suspended redemptions. The liquidity crisis got under way in earnest. The Fed moved to stem the problem with an increasing sense of urgency as things worsened over the next year.

Open market operations began in October 2007 but, as Cramer said, the FOMC members didn't appreciate how bad the problem was and the government had to become a major lender to the financial system. In December, the Term Auction Facility (TAF) followed, which auctioned loans to depository institutions (at times reaching $100bn a month). Swap lines were opened with the European Central Bank and the Swiss National Bank. In 2008, the Primary Dealer Credit Facility (PDCF) was launched following the collapse of Bear Stearns, whereby the collateral conditions for repurchase agreements for prime dealers were loosened. The Commercial Paper Funding Facility (CPFF) was announced, where commercial paper was added to eligible collateral for Fed loans, in order to get the market moving: the Federal Reserve became the buyer-of-last-resort for the $1.6 trillion commercial paper market. In March, the Term Securities Lending Facility (TSLF) was launched, auctioning Treasury securities to primary dealers against eligible collateral in order to keep the market for government securities operating. Discount window lending was extended.

Then, on September 15 Lehman Brothers failed. There was a run against money market mutual funds (MMMFs) as the buck was broken (values fell below a $1 invested). Hence, on 18 September the asset-backed commercial paper Money Market Mutual Fund Liquidity Facility (AMLF) was launched, providing loans to depository institutions to buy high-quality asset-backed commercial paper (ABCP) from MMMFs that needed cash to meet redemptions. Loans to SPVs followed and, on November 25, the Term Asset-Backed Securities Loan Facility (TALF), which consisted of collateralised loans to eligible

[5]See CNBC television footage. Cramer's meltdown was mentioned at the August 7 FOMC meeting, with members laughing.

investors to buy ABS from entities (i.e. asset-backed security owners) in autos, credit cards, education, etc., that were suffering liquidity issues (redemptions and the need for cash). In addition, the Fed lent directly to institutions to fund mergers and to help banks in difficulty.

To help liquidity, the FDIC was charged (to 30 June 2009) with guaranteeing new debt issues for 3 years (the *Debt Guarantee Program*), capped at 125% of the debt outstanding at 30 September 2008, so potentially worth up to about $1500bn; and non-interest bearing deposit accounts used in business working capital around $500bn (*the Transactions Account Guarantee Program*). The ECB also eased collateral conditions and provided liquidity during the first phase of the crisis.

Through 2009, the Fed then began quantitative easing, taking onto its balance sheet a wide variety of assets.

Deposit Guarantees (and the Covered Bond Fallacy)

Most governments had some form of explicit or implicit deposit insurance before the crisis. But as the situation deteriorated the US government guaranteed bank deposits from October 2008 for up to $250,000 per bank per customer.[6] In a crisis, this is necessary, and most governments understand this, though it has to be said that in the European phase of the crisis in 2013 the authorities there did not. The 'troika' (consisting of the EU Commission, the European Central Bank and the IMF), overseeing the Greek crisis, proposed to tax Cypriot bank deposits in order to raise capital to deal with solvency problems. Amounting to the confiscation of deposits as it did, this led to turmoil that in the end forced the policy makers to back down.[7]

More generally, there is a problem with deposit insurance when it applies to conglomerates with 'Mum-and-Dad' depositors combined with investment banking businesses. In essence, the high-risk part of the business receives a subsidy from the fact that all traders know their money is safe. This is because it will always be cheaper to inject capital

---

[6]Other countries followed, with Europe at mostly around €100,000, Australia moved to cover all deposits (subsequently increased to a maximum of A$1 million per customer).

[7]See Blundell-Wignall (2013).

into the bank than to pay out the large insured deposit base amounts. This goes to the heart of the issue of implicit guarantees and the TBTF problem which will be discussed again in subsequent chapters.[8]

Furthermore, the presence of high-risk business segments results in the need for wholesale funding which is unstable (may be withdrawn in a crisis). Attempts to deal with this problem result in others. For example, use of 'covered bonds' has been expanded strongly in Europe. Covered bonds partition the best assets of the bank with what is known as a 'dynamic cover pool' to guarantee the bond holders with the best collateral. These are believed to be a low-cost and stable source of funding that make universal banks safer.[9] This is something of a fallacy, since covered bonds result in uncompensated risk transfer to depositors. In the event this isn't enough, they have recourse to the issuer bank as well (dual recourse). This means that in a solvency crisis the depositors, guaranteed up to €100,000 only in Europe, are at greater risk the more covered bonds a bank issues. The ordinary depositor is not compensated for this risk in the form of higher-risk bond yields. Perhaps more realistically, the risk to the taxpayer is increased. Credit risk is never destroyed; it is always shifted to another holder. The best way to deal with this is not to mix deposit banking with this sort of activity.[10]

Separation of Bad Assets

An inventory, or preferably an audit, of the assets on the balance sheet allows identification of the bad ones which can then be written down to realistic values or separated from the rest.[11] This makes transparent

---

[8]It is worth noting at this stage that a resolution regime needs to be in place that has some credibility to help avoid this—i.e. that the external costs of allowing a firm to fail are sufficiently small that it will not cause major systemic problems. The USA, where many banks fail, has proved better at this issue than Europe, in the opinion of the current authors.

[9]See EBA (2016) for a summary of the structure of covered bonds in different countries, especially Annex 2.

[10]Restrictive caps to such bonds could also be imposed, but banks that find covered bonds an attractive cheap source of funding lobby against this.

[11]Without this, uncertainty about asset quality can make it impossible to value the portfolio. This creates major difficulties in attracting the capital needed to allow it either to operate on a standalone basis or to be taken over by an existing bank.

the amount of capital needed to absorb losses and evaluate a portfolio to operate as a bank on a stand-alone basis. It takes time, however, and events during the crisis forced governments to take action to guarantee or inject their own capital to support the system without distinguishing good assets from bad. To the degree that bad assets were allowed to fester on the balance sheet, banks were encouraged to behave defensively while needed adjustments in the wider economy were postponed, prolonging the adjustment process with macroeconomic consequences (see Box 5.1 for the case of Japan since its asset bubble). By and large, the USA did a better job of addressing these problems than did the Europeans.

In the USA, the decision to guarantee Fannie and Freddie credibly achieved this step for mortgages, via the formation of the FHFA and its conservatorship role with the two GSEs. Guaranteeing the $5.5 trillion Fannie and Freddie portfolios for up to $200bn in losses clarified an ambiguity that had come to worry the market—i.e. was the paper issued by the two mortgage giants guaranteed by the US taxpayer or not? As the mortgage losses mounted, there was a risk that mortgage bond refinancing would not happen as maturities fell due—including those held by sovereign entities abroad. The bottom line of the Treasury action is that the market now regards Fannie and Freddie paper as essentially equivalent to Treasury securities. The collapse of numerous small lenders specializing in subprime and other low-quality mortgages worked to isolate many remaining problems from the system. In addition, the government guaranteed $306bn in dubious Citigroup loans and securities; $29bn Bear Stearns assets (to support the JPMorgan Chase takeover); and $9bn for Morgan Stanley. The Federal Reserve guaranteed money market funds to around $600bn.

Much of various governments' relief efforts, however, failed to target the problem assets. There was an initial thought in the USA to use the $700bn Troubled Asset Relief Program (TARP) for buying toxic assets. Indeed, Congress had approved their use either for such an asset management approach, or to invest directly in banks. But on the weekend of 11–12 October 2008 the UK Prime Minister Gordon Brown decided to inject new money directly into banks without necessarily separating bad assets in all cases—though assets were also purchased, as with the Royal Bank of Scotland, for example. Europe, following a summit led by France and Germany, also decided to inject money directly and to guarantee loans as part of the coordinated action plan, though again assets were bought in specific cases. Immediately after the UK decision (Monday 13 October), the US Treasury Secretary Hank Paulson decided to put to one side the original decision to buy bank assets with the TARP money. He used it in the main to invest directly in sound as well as troubled large institutions.

Overall by mid-2009, the USA had purchased or guaranteed debt equal to $5622bn (see Table 4.3). In Europe (excluding the UK and Switzerland) the analogous amount was $3382bn, in the United Kingdom $279bn and in Switzerland $39bn (excluding debt guarantees, which were not clearly specified). The USA moved to put the bad assets problem largely behind it. At this writing, the financial sector is functioning normally and the exceptional crisis macro-policy measures are being reversed. Europe's problems with bad assets dogging the ability of banks to lend continue into early 2018. In fact, non-performing loans have risen every year as a share of the balance sheet of banks and sluggish economic activity has been the result.

Box 5.1: Lessons of the Japan Banking Crisis

The Japan banking crisis led to repeated policy rescue packages from 1996 to 2004.[12] The failure systematically to take step three above, i.e. removing the bad loans from the banks as a precondition for recapitalisation, prolonged the crisis. There was a strong desire to keep (what came to be called) '*zombie companies*' alive, either as a decision of bank management due to strong past relationships with the companies, or because of official encouragement to avoid unemployment. If bad loans are not removed from the balance sheet, the potential for further asset deterioration in a period of recessed activity will require more capital and/or will result in greater deleveraging. It is this 'slippage' that caused the crisis to be dragged out for a longer period of time. The failure of the banks Asahi and Daiwa provides a good example. The two banks were merged into Resona Bank, and further injections of capital failed to save

[12]See Lumpkin (2008).

it as the bad loans were not dealt with. The decision to bypass step three in favour of direct capital injections (jumping straight to step four) makes recapitalisation a moving target; if loan problems worsen, leading to more write-downs of asset values, further injections are required to avoid bank failures and/or a credit crunch.

Recapitalisation of the Banks

To mid-2009, the US government invested \$806bn in banks compared to \$484bn in Europe (excluding the UK and Switzerland), \$81bn in the UK and \$6bn in Switzerland (Table 4.3). All other regions together invested around \$122bn. Hank Paulson moved very quickly with the eight most systemically important large banks, which received \$125bn in capital injections (Bank of America/Merrill Lynch, Bank of New York Mellon, Citi, Goldman Sachs, JPMorgan Chase, Morgan Stanley, Wells Fargo/Wachovia and State Street). These capital injections were in exchange for preferred shares (5% dividend for 5 years and 9% thereafter) and warrants equal to 15% of the equity infusion value, with a strike price equal to the average of the 20 days preceding the infusion (See Box 5.2). The Federal Reserve also bought MBS from Fannie and Freddie (around \$600bn). Importantly, the government nationalised AIG for \$53bn.

The swiftness and magnitude with which the USA responded in these areas is in contrast to Europe, which remained in denial about the extent of banking system problems—the capital injection was less, while the size of the banks and their non-performing loans were larger. Time and again in these early years of the crisis, European delegates to OECD and FSB meetings stated that the crisis was mainly a US problem. The full extent of the EU crisis was to follow a few years later.

Box 5.2: What Are Warrants and Why Were They Used?

- A warrant is like a call (or put) option, the right to buy (sell) a quantity of stock at a strike price any time prior to expiry of the contract (up to 15 years in the US case). Warrants are usually attached to preferred stocks. In the USA, warrants are tradeable (they are only exercised at expiry in Europe). Warrants are issued by the company (so they are essentially OTC instruments), not exchange-based as with standardised call or put options.

- A warrant, if exercised, dilutes the shares—whereas an option doesn't. With the exercise of options, existing shares are purchased from the writer of the option.
- The concept of gearing is relevant for a warrant: gearing = stock price/(warrant price). An example helps: suppose the price of the stock is \$1.50 and the price of 1 warrant is \$0.50. The gearing is 3.0 times. Suppose the strike is such that on fixed dates one can buy the shares for \$1. Then if things go well and the price of the shares moves up by \$0.50, to \$2, the warrant holder can still buy it at \$1. So the share price has risen by 33%. Since the warrant holders can buy at \$1, they also realise the \$0.50 gain by doing so (\$2.00 less \$0.50 of the warrant value less the \$1 cost of the shares). So the value of the warrant rises by \$0.50, which is a 100% rise in its value. (Of course, any fall in the share price would also be 'exaggerated' in its effect on the warrant.)
- The US capital injections took advantage of this structure—took preference shares and warrants. When the strategy of rescuing the banks worked, the taxpayer in the end made a profit. (Recall: in the USA, rescue warrants equal to 15% of the equity infusion value were issued, with a strike price equal to the average of the 20 days preceding the infusion—the stock holders paid dearly via the dilution of their shares.)

Exit from Emergency Measures

The exit from emergency measures even 10 years after 2007–2008 is still in its early stages—underlining just how grave the crisis was. While the USA has exited from being an owner of banks, selling most bank shares in 2009 and its Citigroup shares later in 2010, this has not been the case for purchased assets and guarantees. Fannie and Freddie, still in conservator status with the FHFA, had \$200bn of capital put at their disposal. Preventing the failure of these two monoliths of mortgage securities was essential, as was avoiding the huge social cost of foreclosures on subprime and Alt-A mortgages (achieved via the renegotiation of the terms of mortgages). But the situation is by no means resolved. A 2017 stress test required for Fannie and Freddie under the Dodd-Frank

Act found that under a severely adverse scenario, a $100bn capital injection would still be required in 2018, even ten years on from the start of the crisis.[13]

Elsewhere the situation is mixed, with most governments exited or in the process of exiting from their direct equity investments. Thus, the UK government sold its last Lloyds shares in 2017. The Government of Singapore Investment Corporation (GIC) made a loss on its crisis stake in UBS. In the European Union, state aid rules were relaxed during the crisis, but even so capital injections have been insufficient. As shown in Table 4.3, the European share of the total capital injected into banking globally was about 1/3, compared to over 1/2 by the USA even though Europe's banking system is larger. With mortgages and related securities taken out of the picture, the US recapitalisation measures saw American banks quickly get on with supporting recovery. In contrast, European banks have continued to increase their share of non-performing loans at an alarming rate 10 years after the crisis, and the banking system has not played the same role in supporting the economy (discussed in subsequent chapters).

Unconventional Monetary Policy and Interest Rates

Indexes of central bank balance sheets, which reflect their strong buying of assets (quantitative easing), and the 3-month interbank rates are shown in Fig. 5.1. Other than in the USA, where rates have begun to rise and the Fed has announced its intention to start reducing its balance sheet, very little sign of exit from these extreme measures is in evidence anywhere else. In individual economies, these extreme measures tend to weaken exchange rates, but in global terms, this is zero sum with no net effect. So they mainly just have the effect of distorting markets and boosting domestic asset prices without doing anything to improve economic fundamentals—a subject that is taken up in Chapter 9.

[13]See FHFA (2017).

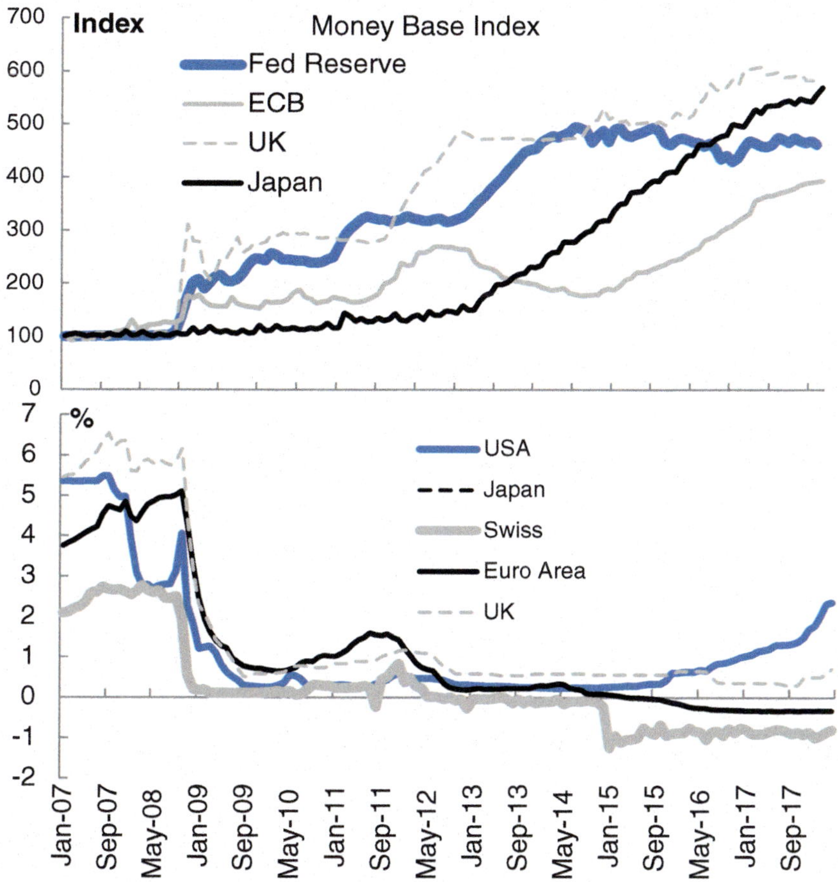

Fig. 5.1 Central bank balance sheets and 3-month interbank rates (*Source* Thomson Reuters, authors)

Requirements for Long-term Reform

If exit from the emergency measures is slow, fundamental reform of the financial system for prudential stability has made even less progress. The earlier chapters of this book suggested that a large number of interactions between globalisation, innovation and poor regulation combined to cause the crisis. To be fair, prudential policy making is extremely

Inconsistent economic policies	Taxation	Regulation	Structure of firms	Board structure	Risk/Fees/Excutive remuneration	Competitive environment	Education/Safety net
Housing ownership incentives & zero equity loans?	Tax advantaged structured products & pass through products	Are instruments treated the same in all jurisdictions?	Too-big-to-fail/implicit guarantee issues?	Independence of directors/Chair & CEO roles	Cash versus equity and links in the share price	Equal treatment of foreign branches & subsidiaries?	Consumer protection laws/codes of conduct
Low interest rate distortion?	Taxing executives' salaries and bonuses	Basel rules/leverage ratio/local rules	Conglomerate structure including an investment banks	Risk sub-committee	Share vesting period	Size/Oligopoly structure/over-banked?	Financial eduction program & firm vs customer responsiblities clear?
Bloated central banks holding of illiquid securities?	Tax treatement of different securities & investors	Regulatory overlaps?	Glass-Steagall-like separation rules in place?	Chair of risk sits on board	Up-front revenue recognition of fee-for-sale	State ownership and subsidied lending?	Rules on prospectuses, disclosure of hidden fees & spreads
Unbalanced large foreign holdings of government securities?	Tax treatment of carried interest in private equity	Deposit insurance/resolution regime in place?	Share of fair value products on balance sheet?	Holistic risk focus including bank long-run strategy and leverage issues	Asymmetry with owners versus executives	Integration of independent operations	Default obligations for unsophisticated pension fund clients?
Capital controls/MFN in Trade/WTO	Local versus federal tax arbitrage opportunity?	Accounting rules applicable	Use of off-balance sheet vehicles?	Voting rule impediments	Asymmetry executive & shareholder versus creditors	Foreign investment barriers to entry?	Caveat emptor versus consumer protection ethos in laws & rules

Fig. 5.2 Incentives, risks and outcomes (*Source* Authors)

difficult, because it has to deal with incentives driven by many factors that lie outside of its purview. Some of the main channels of influence are summarised in Fig. 5.2. A holistic approach would require all of these diverse influences to be working together, in order to swing the arrow at the end of the interaction process towards the positive stable outcome on the right, rather than the crisis outcome on the left. The Basel III process, where authorities have focused their main policy effort, tries to overcome the problems associated with Basel II, which is a very narrow approach.

But it is extremely difficult to get prudential regulations into an alignment with all the elements across the bottom panel of Fig. 5.2. If incentives are not aligned because of policy inconsistencies, then financial market participants will arbitrage opportunities to raise leverage and search out new revenue. Since solving the problem of inconsistent economic policies and global tax reform is a *bridge too far*, it is all the more important to ensure that the other elements of Fig. 5.2 are as consistent as possible. Financial policy makers can affect three very important elements:

- *Regulation*: above all, a leverage ratio for equity capital (less goodwill) to total assets is needed that is at least 5–6%.[14] There are many reasons for this. First, tax laws and regulatory rules are like fixed parameters. If an arbitrage opportunity exists, the parameters don't alter in response to increased trading, quite unlike two identical assets being traded on different exchanges where arbitrage drives prices back towards equality. Tax and regulatory gaps can be exploited endlessly until the trader runs up against a leverage constraint. That constraint needs to be binding at manageable levels. In the crisis, countries showed that it is very easy for the banking system to lose 6% of its assets (Hoenig 2016). Potential losses of this size need to be covered by the leverage ratio which defines the required capital buffer in terms of the entire portfolio and not by adding charges on individual assets without regard to the portfolio's composition and its diversification. The Basel risk-weighting system allows too much scope for banks to game the rules as shown earlier. Banks have always run value at risk models for internal control, but making the weighting process a variable that affects their return on equity puts temptation in the way. In truth, bank managers have no idea about where the next risk shocks will come from—a cyberattack, contagion from other counterparties, fraud, legal penalties for money laundering and so on. The idea that all of this can be modelled and weighted in advance when derivatives can transform cash flows and shift the holding of risk is at best far-fetched and at worst dangerous. Under the simple leverage ratio, management decisions about allocating capital to risky activities would take account of the full market cost of capital, and the

[14]On an IFRS basis. A leverage ratio has always been favoured by the FDIC, as mandated by the FDIC Act. A ratio of at least 5% on an IFRS basis has been recommended by the OECD (2009a) from the outset. The Turner Report (Turner 2009) also supports this approach.

potential risks and rewards of investing in the asset, but would not be influenced by regulatory rules specific to that asset.

- *Corporate governance*: Governments became major shareholders in banks for a time, but did not focus on reforming the process of governance while they had the chance. The equity culture remains, because bank business models have been left intact. Evidence in Chapter 3 suggests that the equity culture is important in IBs and that complex organisations are more difficult to understand and manage risk. This is born out well by Robert Rubin, who was treated as a guru in Citigroup. While always reported as pushing Citi towards more risk-taking prior to the crisis, he later admitted that the business was hard to understand. In an interview reported in the Wall Street Journal, he stated: '*There is no way you would know what was going on with a risk book unless you're directly involved with the trading arena.... We had highly experienced, highly qualified people running the operation*'.[15] This admission lends support to the view that simplifying the structure of the business model of complex banks might be worth considering (the separation issue). Partnership structures might even be envisaged for separated high-risk trading businesses. Other recommendations that might help include: ensuring the independence and competence of directors by strengthening the *fit and proper person test* and extending its coverage, and insisting that the risk officer role benefits from built-in protections.[16]
- *Separation*: Separating high-risk (particularly derivatives-based) business segments potentially achieves a number of goals. First, as just noted, it makes corporate governance more tractable. Second, separating insured deposit banking businesses from investment banking activities reduces the TBTF problem. Where insured deposits are included in the business model, the perception (and reality) of implicit guarantees that give rise to TBTF become inevitable.

[15]See Brown and Enrich (2008).

[16]Their employment contracts should be independent of the CEO, and they should report to the board. See OECD (2009b) for more observations about corporate governance.

Risk-taking needs to be priced without implicit subsidies to ensure that risk does not become underpriced. The underpricing of risk was, at its core, the most fundamental cause of the 2007–2008 crisis. There have been a number of partial attempts at this, including the Volcker rule in the USA and the Vickers approach in the UK. None of these are satisfactory in the view of the present authors, and in Europe, nothing at all has been achieved in this area. Either full separation, like Glass-Steagall, or a non-operating holding company (NOHC) structure may well help to deal with excessive leverage and risk-taking.

The Bank Separation Issue

A complete break-up of banks under a Glass-Steagall approach would create a narrow concept of a deposit bank that could be regulated closely and supported in crises, while allowing *caveat emptor* to apply in the high-risk separated IB business. The idea that consumer banks and IBs make a good countercyclical combination (the consumer bank helps the IB in the crises periods, and the IB helps the bank's earnings in the boom) has been discredited by the events of 2007–2008. The guaranteed deposit bank would create private information, lend on its balance sheet, maintain a strong capital base and have a decent liquidity buffer fully backed up by the lender of last resort. IBs would take on more risk, but would sit outside the well-regulated deposit bank sector.

At the 2008 Reserve Bank of Australia international conference, where these ideas were presented, some participants argued that this structure might still not avoid major systemic problems in the future because banks inside the regulatory fence would still have counterparty relationships with IBs outside the fence—pulling them back through the legal structure into risk exposures. One finance lawyer at a London conference said the following to one of the authors: '*I have a one word response to people who tell me that investment banks need to be separated from the deposit bank.... 'Lehman*''. His point was that Lehman failed and it didn't have a deposit bank subsidising its risk-taking.

Of course, he was a lawyer and not trained in the basics of economic methodology—comparative statics, or getting your counterfactuals right. Lehman had a Basel risk weighting of 20% and was dealing with banks like Citigroup and JPMorgan Chase which did combine deposit banking with their IBs. These banks, themselves subsidised by an implicit guarantee, were trading with Lehman that carried a low capital weight. Now compare this with the counterfactual of a world where a leverage ratio was applied, and where the Citi's and the JP Morgan's had 'separated' IBs. In this world, the separated IB would be trading with Lehman Brothers, and defaults would be allowed to happen. The high-risk IBs would have to pay the true cost of capital, not the cross-subsidised cost of capital, because traders can lose their money in the case of a defaulting counterparty. Leverage and systemic risk would have been commensurately smaller. Regulated deposit banks dealing with IBs too would pay the 'right price' for any trading and would be discouraged from imprudent speculation and derivative-based products.

The Non-operating Holding Company Structure

A second approach is to enforce a NOHC. With this legal vehicle, the parent can raise capital and invest in its subsidiaries, which should be separately listed. There are separate boards and legal firewalls between the subsidiary parts. The objective of the legal structure is to ensure that the creditors of one group can never have recourse to the creditors or capital of another member of the group. The parent invests, but is 'non-operating', and receives a dividend like other shareholders. The advantages are as follows: first, each segment a simplified structure and board members don't have to understand a number of businesses; second, regulatory rules can be tailored to the riskiness of the activities of each of the subsidiaries; third, in the event of a crisis any loss-making subsidiary can be dealt with by supervisors without endangering the whole conglomerate (the problematic segment is easily cut out by resolution authorities); and fourth, shareholders gain through cost synergies (e.g. technology platforms and human resources) and a balanced revenue structure without the risk of contamination effects.

Conclusions

The main cause of systemic failure in the global crisis was seen to be linked to leverage and to contagion risks (which arise from what banks actually do within their business models). Derivatives are powerful tools to transform and shift risks to avoid many regulatory constraints, and to structure products to take advantage of tax loopholes. The scope for innovation under the equity culture, pushing leverage and risk-taking for short-term gains, is virtually unlimited and may again prove too great a temptation for many firms.

Improved corporate governance could in principle bring about safer conglomerates, particularly where partnerships and skin-in-the-game can be introduced. But with the interconnected nature of banking it unlikely that boards can oversee complex mixed businesses. There is therefore an *a priori* case for imposing a simple leverage ratio and for separating risky businesses from deposit-insured consumer banks to reduce contagion risk.

Since the crisis banks have opposed both of these measures on the grounds that they would raise the cost of capital. This of course is the whole point. In the crisis, risk was underpriced. There is a need for risk to be priced by the market in the business segments where it is taken. If this policy shrinks cross-subsidised businesses, then the policy is achieving its goal. With respect to derivatives in particular, it should be recalled that they are essential for consumers and businesses—for example to hedge fuel cost in airlines, to smooth cash flows for pension products in the drawdown phase and so on. There is no reason why these socially useful activities should not be able to be carried out on behalf of clients by depository institutions. But there are also socially non-useful roles for derivatives, such as transforming cash flows and risks to take advantage of regulatory and tax arbitrage opportunities, and speculating with bank capital in hedge funds and proprietary trading. These activities have no business in an insured deposit bank, and conglomerates with such businesses should be forced legally to separate such activities.

The empirical evidence supporting the need for separation and examples of how it would work are considered in the following chapters.

References

Bagehot, W. (1873). *Lombard Street: A Description of the Money Market*. New York: Scribner and Sons.

Blundell-Wignall, A. (2013, March 21). Cyprus: Further Compressing the Coiled Spring. *OECD Insights*.

Brown, K., & Enrich, D. (2008, November 29). Rubin Under Fire Defends His Role at Citi. *Wall Street Journal*.

EBA. (2016). *Recommendation on Harmonisation of Covered Bond Frameworks in the EU*. Brussels.

FHFA. (2017, August 7). *Dodd-Frank Act: Stress Test Results: Severely Adverse Scenario*.

FOMC. (2007). Meeting of the Federal Open Market Committee on August 7.

Gurría, A. (2008, October 11). *Statement by the Secretary-General of the OECD*, before International Monetary and Financial Committee, Washington, DC.

Hoenig, T. (2016, November 9). Strengthening Global Capital: An Opportunity Not to Be Lost—Remarks by FDIC Vice Chairman Thomas M. Hoenig to the 22nd Annual Risk US Conference, New York.

IMF. (2007). *Staff Report on the United States*. Washington, DC.

Lumpkin, S. (2008). Resolutions of Weak Institutions: Lessons Learned from Previous Crises. *OECD Journal Financial Market Trends*, 2008(1), 1–42.

OECD. (2009a). *The Financial Crisis: Reform and Exit Strategies*. Paris: OECD Publishing. Available at: www.oecd.org/dataoecd/55/47/43091457.pdf.

OECD. (2009b, June). *Corporate Governance and the Financial Crisis: Key Findings and Main Messages*. Paris: OECD Publishing.

Shigehara, K., & Atkinson, P. (2011). *Surveillance by International Institutions: Lessons from the Global Financial and Economic Crisis* (Economics Department Working Paper No. 860). Paris: OECD.

Turner, A. (2009, March). *The Turner Review: A Regulatory Response to the Global Banking Crisis* (Vol. 7). London: Financial Services Authority.

6

The Determinants of the Riskiness of Banks

Introduction

The most important cause of the financial crisis was argued in preceding chapters to be the underpricing of risk. This resulted in the failure of some banks and taxpayer support to avoid failures of systemically important banks and other financial intermediaries. Banks in particular faced two broad pressures during the crisis: solvency and liquidity. Banks become insolvent due to falling assets values in relation to liabilities which reduce their net worth to nothing or less. Sensibly calibrated capital rules provide a buffer to absorb losses due to falling asset prices in most circumstances. But where the buffer is too small and asset quality (credit risk) is the problem (typical of a crisis), banks are often able to hide bad assets in a variety of ways for long periods of time: by shifting fair value assets to the banking book (with regulatory forbearance); valuing assets at unrealistic prices; and adjusting the terms of mortgage contracts to avoid defaults (when foreclosure would result in worse outcomes for the bank). This may allow them time to work through their problems.

A. Blundell-Wignall et al., *Globalisation and Finance at the Crossroads*,
https://doi.org/10.1007/978-3-319-72676-2_6

But this requires that liquidity problems do not make it impossible to operate. Such problems can arise through interconnectedness resulting from either dependence on external short-term funding or collateralised agreements. Where derivatives and repos are concerned, events are not within the control of the bank. This is because multiple parties are involved, each depending on the performance of others in chains of payments, making liquidity problems the fastest path to a bank closing its doors. If any link of these chains fails, the result can be to bring down multiple parties. Such failure can arise from either a collapse of counterparty confidence or contractual obligations contained in collateralised agreements. Concerns about the solvency of key players in the chain may be enough to cause liquidity to freeze up—because lending counterparties become unwilling to roll existing funding. Or cash and/or liquid securities to meet margin calls for derivatives transactions and acceptable collateral levels for loans may not be forthcoming.[1] Here, 'immediacy' (with a time and a date) is the issue: the derivative contracts must be settled, either bilaterally or with a clearing house. While the central bank's lender-of-last-resort role should ensure that the system as a whole receives enough liquidity to keep functioning, this cannot be open-ended where solvency concerns are at the root of an individual bank's problems.

Asset price cycles interact with risk-taking in a pro-cyclical way. Thus, risk tends to be underpriced in an asset boom and the supply of products and services (e.g. securitisations, structured products and synthetic bonds) will accommodate excessive increases in client demand. Asset price cycles that lead to concentrated and correlated financial strategies are the breeding pond of systemic risk.

When monetary and liquidity policies become necessary to prevent interconnectedness risk from collapsing the financial system, risk is not destroyed: it simply gets rolled into other areas, putting off needed fundamental policy reforms for another day. If such reform is not forthcoming, then another crisis is likely eventually to emerge. Thus, the post-crisis fixed income bubble has replaced the mortgage securitisation

---

[1]Similarly, fear of insolvency can lead to a 'run' on deposits. This can be the most rapid path to default.

that was in the front seat in the run up to 2007–2008. One decade later, China is discovering how useful off-balance sheet vehicles are for avoiding bank regulations (see Chapter 9).

As Mark Twain is reputed to have said: '*history never repeats itself, but it rhymes*'.

As memories of the crisis fade, it is easy to begin to believe that the regulatory process has gone far enough and may even need to be rolled back—a systematic plan for which has recently been set out in Steven Mnuchin's Treasury in response to a request from President Donald Trump who wants (*inter alia*) to dismantle some key aspects of the Dodd-Frank Act (2010).[2] This, as readers will recall from previous chapters, is the sort of thinking the world went through from the late 1990s.

The Basel III rules have been finalised as of December 2017 after an extended evolution of add-on rulemaking and consultations with the banking industry. This regime does not address concerns about the business models of banks relating to their involvement with 'interconnectedness' as a separate and potentially greater risk than that which can be addressed via capital rules for credit risk. Even still, the Basel '*thought process*' is to try to convert a counterparty risk to a credit equivalent that can be added on as an appendage to the risk-weighted capital rule approach. The Volcker rule of the Dodd-Frank Act, which does address interconnectedness risk (albeit in a partial way), is, at this writing, unfortunately in the gun-sites of the US Administration. Elsewhere, these interconnectedness risks have been ignored in Europe and are only partially addressed in the UK. But before discussing the details of such policy proposals in Chapter 7, it is important to examine the empirical evidence on the relative importance of leverage and capital rules versus interconnectedness risk: is there an empirical case to answer?

[2]See Mnuchin and Phillips (2017), which will be commented on in later chapters.

The Different Aspects of Bank Risk

While bank involvement with fair value securities and collateralised agreements was not unknown in the 1980s and 1990s, the low-return environment associated with globalisation encouraged a housing boom and the increased supply and demand for mortgage products. In a context of large inflows of Chinese financing and sustained low inflation, widely attributed more to monetary authorities' credibility than to the global supply shock, plentiful credit was readily available at low cost. In a 'normal' environment, bank involvement in a range of high-risk activities will 'wash out' to the degree that financial institutions are hedged against market risk. Each exposure has its opposite in collateralised agreements and one bank's loss is another's gain. Losses and gains on individual contracts might be randomly distributed throughout the system and only institutions that have failed to hedge should face net cash obligations or impacts on their balance sheets.

But where exposures remain—collateralised agreements transfer but do not eliminate exposures—counterparty risks also remain. Outside normal conditions, especially when risk is underpriced and asset cycles begin to move in one direction, then leverage begins to rise, and particular sectors like mortgage products can be favoured. Then, these counterparty risks can shift dramatically. Certain types of risk products become over-supplied in relation to strong demand. In this case, the potential for losses is not randomly distributed between banks, and instead, bubble-like trends emerge.[3] Exposures and counterparty risks can be pushed outside of the regulated (and deposit-insured) banking system and into other sectors like insurance companies and other shadow banking institutions.

Typical bank clients are shown in the bottom rung of Fig. 6.1. Low risk-free returns can be enhanced via two basic routes: leverage, which permits a spread return to be magnified,[4] and reusing securities, by

[3]For example, buyers of insurance to enhance the credit quality of CDO tranches (that saw sub-prime mortgage pools rated as senior debt) find ready sellers of underpriced credit default swaps.

[4]A 1% return levered 50 times will yield a 50% return on capital employed.

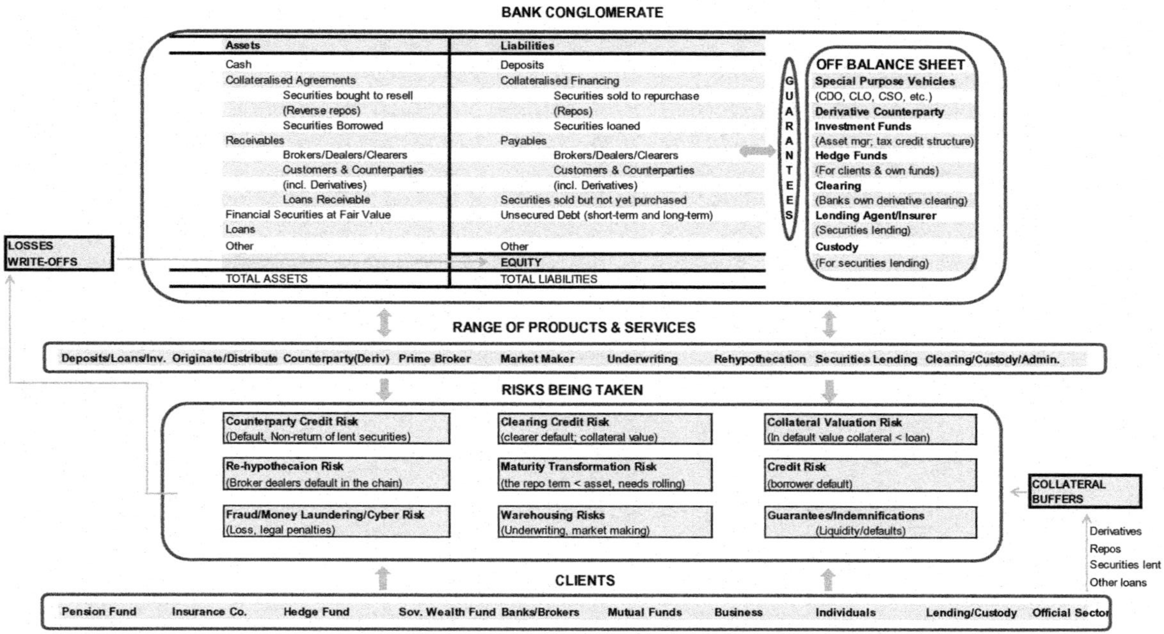

Fig. 6.1 Banking conglomerates and risk (*Source* Authors representation)

borrowing, lending and swapping them via collateralised agreements. Banks increasingly became engaged in both of these paths to achieve higher returns for clients and themselves through the 2000s as discussed in previous chapters.

The range of products and services of banks (*inter alia*) are shown in the middle rung of Fig. 6.1. In the process of undertaking these activities, banks take risks that may lead to losses and insolvency. For collateralised agreements (a repo transaction, for example), the lender bank is buffered by the level and quality of collateral, shown on the right side of the diagram. Where losses are made, banks run down capital shown in the left side of the diagram. If capital is reduced below regulatory limits, alarm bells ring. If equity becomes negative, resolution or rescue of the bank becomes the policy imperative. When uncertainty and fear of insolvencies in the chains of relationships rise between banks, funding via collateralised agreements dries up (on the bottom right of Fig. 6.1), spreading liquidity problems between all of the banks (with similar structures to that shown) that act as counterparties to each other and between banks and other shadow banking counterparties.

The main risks (*inter alia*) are shown in the large section in the bottom half of Fig. 6.1.

- *Credit risk*: borrowers default resulting in non-performing loans. When mortgage concentration builds up in bank portfolios because demand is strong and regulatory rules treat them favourably, then a given default rate will have a bigger impact on bank capital. If there is a move to weaker borrowers as higher quality clients become scarce, this loss impact will be magnified.
- *Guarantees and indemnifications*: to the right of the bank balance sheet in Fig. 6.1 sits its off-balance sheet activities, such as securitisation products (like CDOs), where assets of the bank are transferred, placed in tranches for investors and the bank earns spreads and servicing/administration fees. The bank may provide: liquidity facilities to support SPE obligations; credit enhancement for its securities (such as collateral guarantees); market value guarantees of SPE assets through letters of credit, credit default swaps and total return swaps; entering into derivative counterparty relationships with SPEs

to structure their products for client needs; owning equity and senior tranches of SPE liabilities; and underwriting and making markets in the securities issued by SPEs. The risks associated with all of these activities become correlated when positions become concentrated in sectors (like mortgage securitisation in the crisis) and highly correlated between banks.

- *Warehousing risks*: in the underwriting process of an initial public offering, an off-market book-build process occurs for key client investors. The securities are transferred from the issuer to the bank, and allocations are made after the bids are received. If acquirers don't follow through when the final price is announced, the bank may be stuck with excess inventory that it might have to sell at a loss. Similarly, making markets requires inventory and some speculation on future prices. During the crisis, inventories of mortgages and mortgage bonds built up, particularly as the process began to peak.
- *Counterparty credit risk* (*repos/reverse repos/derivatives*): in Fig. 6.1, collateralised agreements have a prominent place in the hypothetical bank balance sheet, particularly with respect to repos and reverse repos for borrowing and lending cash. A bank might undertake such transactions with other dealer banks in its market-making role; in its prime broker role in lending cash to hedge funds, real estate investment trusts (REITS), etc.; and in lending cash or securities to its own off-balance sheet vehicles. Cash repos may be bilateral or involve re-hypothecation (involving third parties). Securities borrowing and lending operate in the same way as cash repos, but with the added role of lending/custody agents in the process. In either case (repo or reverse repo), the main risk is the default of the counterparty to the transaction in question (e.g. as with Lehman). With re-hypothecation, defaults in any of the players in the chain put the other players at risk. If this occurs (typically when the market concerned turns down), financing repos may not be available. This triggers other outcomes: central bank lending; bank supports for SPVs; lending agents that offered indemnification being put at risk, etc. The same line of argument applies to derivative transactions which were discussed more fully in Chapter 2.

- *Collateral value risk*: securities offered as collateral have a haircut that protects the lender. In a crisis, the value of securities may fall in value and not be sufficient to cover the losses on the lender. This is particularly likely when a trending market bubble swings into reversal: in the boom, thin margins and minimal haircuts are a part of the underpricing of risk. When the reversal comes, collateral is insufficient.
- *Re-hypothecation risk*: the re-pledging of collateral in the re-hypothecation discussion above (see Box 6.1) creates a chain of delivery obligations. The failure of any part of this chain creates liquidity problems for all of the others.
- *Maturity transformation risk*: in repo markets, the maturity of the loan may be shorter than the open position being funded. This requires the repo to be rolled a number of times before the open position matures. However, in a period of stressed market conditions the rolling may not be possible, exposing the bank to liquidity distress and possible defaults.
- *Fraud, money laundering legal penalties, operational risk and cyber risk*: all of which are self-explanatory and may cause the bank to provision for losses. These risks cannot be predicted, and risk-weighting systems that pretend this can be done are, to say the least, disingenuous.

Box 6.1: Repos, Reverse Repos and Securities Lending

A financing repo is the sale of securities and a simultaneous agreement to repurchase them at a pre-specified future price and date. This allows the bank broker-dealer, hedge fund, pension fund, CDO, etc., to borrow cash for a range of purposes: dealers squaring their books, a bank looking to finance its warehousing of mortgage securities; a hedge fund or pension fund short of cash to undertake derivatives transactions, etc. The repo borrower needs cash and deals with a lending counterparty that has surplus cash to invest (another dealer, a money market fund, a corporate treasury, etc., which is doing a reverse repo). The sold general securities act as collateral for the loan typically with a haircut depending on the quality of the collateral ($100 of securities that collateralise a loan of $90 has a 10% haircut). In the event of default by the borrower, the collateral securities held can be on-sold by the buyer/lender to compensate losses.

The seller of the security (the repo borrower) pays interest at the general collateral rate.

A reverse repo transaction is the purchase of a security and a simultaneous agreement to resell them at a specified later date and price. The lender wishes to augment returns on its own portfolio by earning the collateral rate. The collateral (e.g. Treasury securities) may be re-hypothecated, i.e. used as collateral in other repo deals. There may be a velocity of collateral, where the same securities are used a number of times, creating greater liquidity when collateral is scarce, but a pyramid of debt builds up increasing the chain for potential defaults to disrupt the market in a crisis. (NB: collateral scarcity is an issue that has arisen as a result of quantitative easing).

The repo markets may be bilateral or tripartite, where a third party administers and runs all the services associated with the transaction (custody, collateral valuation, etc.). The collateral is delivered to the tripartite agent and managed on behalf of the other two counterparties. This structure is useful when re-hypothecation is involved. The reuse of collateral helps to reduce the cost of repo transactions.

Securities lending and borrowing is an analogous process to a cash repo transaction. A bilateral repo may be undertaken to get hold of specific securities. For example, a bank dealer wants to borrow a security to go short and conducts a reverse repo, i.e. borrows it from another bank or a pension fund and sells it immediately in the belief it will fall in value, so that it can be bought back cheaply in the market to return the security at the due date for a profit. If the broker-dealer view is wrong, and the security borrowed and sold rises in value, the dealer would have to buy it back in the market (to return it to the lender) at a higher price, and a loss is made. When the market is trending up in a boom phase, as with subprime mortgages, the short seller will lose a lot of money. This was one of the themes in '*The Big Short*' film. When the bubble collapses, the short sellers make huge profits and the one-sided previously profitable market in mortgage securitisation makes huge losses.

Once a bank moves from a simple deposits/lending business model based on amortised cost accounting into fair value products and collateralised agreements, the paths to losses and default in a crisis situation become plentiful. Trending markets based on common (groupthink) views, as in the lead up to 2007–2008, brings all of the above risks together in a correlated way. The relative involvement of banks in the above risk activities is the most germane determinant of their risk of default. It may not be enough to have a capital rule (risk-weighted or not) when asset cycles combine with the above risk activities to create macroprudential systemic risk via correlated and concentrated strings of (often illiquid) counterparty transactions.

While it is easy enough to discuss these issues conceptually, the interesting question to assess how important is it? What does the empirical evidence say about capital rules versus business model features of GSIBs?

Determinants of Bank Default Risk

To test the extent to which the nature and size of various bank activities affect its risk of default first requires an observable measure of the latter. The distance-to-default (DTD) of a bank is the market value of its assets minus the book value of its liabilities which, if negative, means that the institution is in a default position. However, it is difficult to measure the default risk of a bank by looking at its reported balance sheet. This is because banks do not like to report the presence of troubled assets, and there is the related issue of the use of complex models to value illiquid (levels 2 and 3) assets.[5] The DTD is measured empirically by using a combination of bank reported data and market information to calculate the number of standard deviations a bank is from the default point, where the (unobservable) market values of assets equal the (observable) book value of debt (expected default risk of the bank). The formula to calculate the DTD is derived from the option pricing model of Black and Scholes (1973) and is shown for the technical reader in the Appendix to this chapter.

The DTD is included as the dependent variable in a panel regression for FSB listed GSIBs from the euro area, Switzerland, the UK and the USA. A number of variables (following the above discussion) were tested for their potential significance including the asset cycle

[5]Under IFRS and FASB accounting rules, assets are divided into 3 levels: level 1, assets traded in liquid markets with readily observable prices; level 2, where mark-to-model can be used (e.g. the value of a swap calculated by a formula with respect to the underlying asset); and level 3, highly illiquid assets where valuations are based on estimated ranges.

that causes pro-cyclical effects; leverage measures; and business model aspects. Different accounting systems apply: US banks and one Swiss bank use GAAP, while all the others are based on IFRS. As collateralised agreement in repos and derivatives is a prime interest for bank risk, the GAAP-based banks are converted to an IFRS basis. The results and main concepts can be found in the Appendix to this Chapter.

Seven important features of the empirical results stand out.

1. The simple leverage ratio is supported by the data, whereas the Basel Tier 1 ratio appears to find no support as a determinant of the DTD.[6] A positive sign: the higher capital relative to the total unweighted assets, the safer the bank.
2. Trading securities are positively related to the DTD for GSIBs, supporting the idea that there is a liquidity benefit for banks with large exposures to collateralised agreements (subject to margin and collateral calls).
3. Wholesale funding has the expected negative sign (more unstable funding makes a bank riskier).
4. The GMV of derivatives is strongly supported by the data with a negative sign. A larger exposure to derivatives makes a bank more risky—independently of the direct effect on leverage. Derivatives exposure is perhaps the best gauge of counterparty risk of a GSIB.
5. CAPM beta has a negative sign and is supported by the data. This is a direct measure of the equity risk premium for the bank relative to the market—the bank's business model interconnectedness makes it more risky than holding the broad stock market (measured by the stock price correlation to the broader mark).[7]
6. The size of a bank in its own market (the TBTF underpricing of risk issue) is also correctly signed (a negative coefficient) and is highly significant. Large leveraged banks that use derivatives are more risky.

[6]Andrew Haldane (2012) also shows that in a single-variable model a leverage ratio is a better predictor of actual default than any of the Basel ratios with data from 45 banks.

[7]GSIBs in the Crisis had CAPM betas that rose well above 1.0 towards 3.0—see Chapter 9 for details.

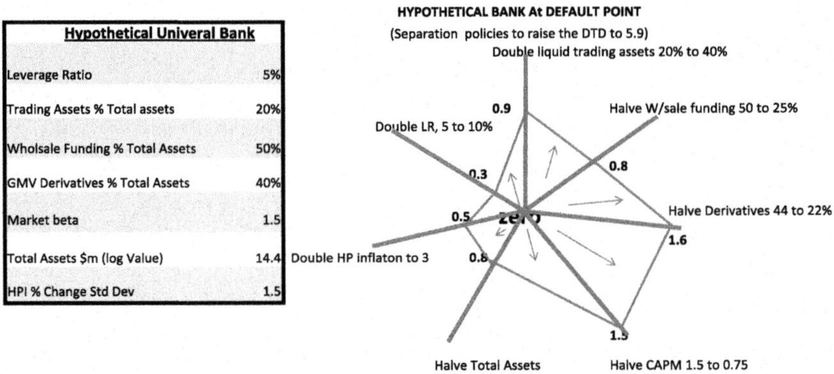

Fig. 6.2 What matters for bank risk (*Source* Authors)

7. The house price cycle is highly significant (positive sign) and illustrates the pro-cyclical effects of the asset cycle.

The business model features consistent with investment banking (collateralised counterparty transactions with repos and derivatives interacting with the asset cycle and correlations between firms) are confirmed by empirical evidence as creating powerful default risk for the GSIBs. It is interesting to note that for GSIBs the leverage ratio has a relatively smaller influence on the riskiness of GSIBs compared to the other terms related to interconnectedness risk.[8]

This is illustrated in Fig. 6.2. Ratios of key business model features of a hypothetical bank conglomerate—similar to some actual GSIBs around the time of the crisis—are shown on the left. The cobweb diagram on the right shows as 'rays' from the centre the impact of changes to the independent variables for each of the elements of the model multiplied by the estimated coefficient for that term (2005–2011 sample). The further away from the zero origin for any term,

[8]This updates Blundell-Wignall and Roulet (2013). The results presented here do not include the causality tests as in the co-integration and error correction tests presented in this earlier study. The point here is to show the original relationships still hold up four years on.

the safer is the bank from changes to that source of risk: where the model sign is positive, the variable is doubled, and where the model sign is negative, the variable is halved (i.e. all 'policy actions' that make it a safer bank). A striking feature of these empirical elasticities is that the business model features are more important than the leverage ratio as sources for policy actions to make GSIBs safer.[9] Notwithstanding the discussion of the crisis in previous chapters and this basic empirical evidence (earlier and more complex versions of which were discussed in international fora), the post-crisis regulatory process has ignored full bank separation and focused instead on capital rules versus risk-weighted assets—itself a flawed concept for which there is no empirical support.

Conclusions

Banks were able to lose 6% of their balance sheets after 2007–2008. Since then, cyber risk and legal penalties (e.g. for money laundering), which certainly cannot be modelled, have become a more important concern for banks. This is clearly being admitted by banks in their response to financial crimes legislation (such as the US Bank Secrecy Act) and the Financial Action Task Force at the OECD—rather than try to understand who is likely to be a criminal or terrorist and treating clients fairly, banks are de-risking. Thus, Americans living abroad are told their accounts are cancelled, indicating that banks have no idea about these things. There is every reason to believe that a simple 6% leverage ratio, requiring no modelling on the part of banks, is the minimum that an ordinary deposit bank should maintain to cover the risk of loss from multiple sources. The Basel capital rules find no support in the empirical evidence—why regulators continue to be fixated on this seemingly flawed approach is something of a mystery. Banks have always monitored their capital at risk internally with value-at-risk modelling. They

[9] These elasticities can't be added up as in a model simulation of policy change with all of the interaction effects—they simply provide semi-elasticities to illustrate what matters based on empirical evidence.

should continue to do so as best they can. But this should never have been the basis for a regulatory capital rule based on risk-weighted assets.

A leverage ratio for a bank at 6% is useful if there are unpredictable asset write-downs to be dealt with (ex post) from time to time. But this does not constitute a pre-emptive approach to promoting financial stability in GSIBs. Other variables play a separately identifiable and important role in GSIB risk, most notably derivatives, the TBTF size of the bank and wholesale funding. This view is quite strongly supported by empirical research. This raises the question of whether beyond some allowable threshold level of derivatives these GSIBs should not be separated into two different entities thereby quarantining these investment banking features from deposit-insured banks. This would reduce bank size, interconnectedness risk and the need for wholesale funding by one simple measure. How this might be done sensibly is an issue taken up in the next chapter.

Appendix to Chapter 6: Modelling the Distance-to-Default

(for the technically interested)

The formula to calculate the DTD is derived from the option pricing model of Black and Scholes (1973) and is set out as follows:

$$\mathrm{DTD}_t = \frac{\log\left(\frac{V_t}{D_t}\right) + \left(r_f - \frac{\sigma_t^2}{2}\right).T}{\sigma_t\sqrt{T}}$$

Where V_t is the market value of bank's assets at time t; r_f is the risk-free interest rate; D_t, is the book value of the debt at time t; σ_t is the volatility of the bank's assets at time t; and T is the maturity of the debt.

However, the market value of assets (V_t) and its volatility (σ_t) have to be estimated. Equity holders have the residual claim on a firm's assets and have limited liability. Equity can be modelled as a call option on the underlying assets of the bank, with a strike price equal to the total book value of the bank's debt. Thus, option-pricing theory can be used to derive the market value and volatility of bank's underlying assets from equity's market value (VE) and volatility (σ_E), by solving:

$$V_t = \frac{\text{VE}_t + D_t e^{-r_f T} N(d2)}{N(d1)}$$

$$\sigma_t = \frac{\text{VE}_t}{V_t} \frac{\sigma_{E,t}}{N(d1)}$$

where

$$d1 = \frac{\log\left(\frac{V_t}{D_t}\right) + \left(r_f + \frac{\sigma_t^2}{2}\right).T}{\sigma_t\sqrt{T}}$$

$$d2 = d1 - \sigma_t\sqrt{T}$$

VE: value of bank's equity; N: the cumulative normal distribution; and σ_E: equity's volatility.

A bank defaults (or is bankrupt) when DD_t equals to 0 (or is negative). All data are extracted from Bloomberg. The total annual debt liabilities (i.e. the difference between annual total assets and annual total equity) are interpolated using a cubic spline to yield daily observations (D_t). The volatility of equity (σ_E) is the standard deviation of daily return multiplied by $\sqrt{252}$ (i.e. 252 trading days by year). The expiry date of the option (T) equals the maturity of the debt. A common assumption is to set it to 1. The risk-free interest rate (r_f) is the 12-month interbank rate.

Model of GSIB Banks' DTD

A panel regression approach is used to explain the differences in DTDs across banks over the period 2005–2011 (to the crisis) and updating to 2016 (see Table 6.1). The sample consists of GSIB commercial and broker-dealer banks. Six banks that failed in the crisis, but which can be considered as systemically important: HBOS, Merrill Lynch, Lehman Brothers, Washington Mutual, Wachovia and Bear Stearns are

Table 6.1 Model estimates: GSIBs

Model variables–35 GSIBs (IFRS accounting)	2005–2011		2005–2016	
	Excluding GSIBs from China and Japan		Excluding GSIBs from China and Japan	
Core Tier 1 capital (% of total assets)	6.137*** (3.67)	–	3.437* (1.75)	–
Tier 1 capital (% of total risk-weighted assets)	–	−1.27 (−0.29)	–	1.306 (0.39)
Trading securities (% of total assets)	4.555* (1.80)	2.857 (0.99)	5.009*** (3.20)	4.680*** (2.86)
Wholesale funding (% of total liabilities)	−3.213* (−1.85)	−2.920* (−1.64)	−3.849*** (−2.96)	−3.137** (−2.10)
Gross market value of derivatives (% of total assets)	−8.110*** (−4.65)	−9.596*** (−4.92)	−6.016*** (−4.25)	−6.507*** (−4.13)
CAPM beta	−2.608*** (−11.97)	−2.594*** (−11.89)	−2.389*** (−10.79)	−2.409*** (−10.48)
Natural logarithm of total assets (harmonised IFRS)	−1.116*** (−3.13)	−1.202*** (−2.98)	−0.826*** (−3.27)	−1.008*** (−4.10)
House price index (year-on-year percentage change over 3 years standard deviation)	0.322*** (6.61)	0.353*** (5.90)	0.230*** (6.00)	0.223*** (5.24)
Constant	22.39*** (4.10)	23.97*** (3.95)	18.54*** (5.38)	20.77*** (6.55)
R-squared	0.474	0.468	0.388	0.371
Fisher statistic (F)	102.5	68.13	67.95	59.22
P-value of F	0.00	0.00	0.00	0.00
Observations	180	154	298	268

Source Authors. OLS panel estimator with cross-sectional fixed effects (variables are not lagged). *Excluding GSIFIs from China and Japan*: this bank sample includes exactly the banks considered in Blundell-Wignall et al. (2013).
*** indicate significance at the 1% level
** indicate significance at the 5% level
* indicate significance at the 10% level

included. Japanese and Chinese banks are excluded as not involved in the 2007–2008 crisis. An OLS panel estimator with cross-sectional fixed effects is used. The DTD model is estimated with two alternatives for leverage: the simple leverage ratio and the Basel RWA concept (positive sign expected). Trading securities are the sum of the trading book and available-for-sale securities and are expected to have a positive sign (a liquidity buffer). Wholesale funding (liabilities other than deposits and long-term debt) is expected to have a negative sign. The gross market value of derivatives as a share of the banks' total assets, but converting all US banks and one Swiss bank to the IFRS concept for consistency (a negative sign). Total assets of the bank are harmonised to IFRS concepts for all banks (a negative sign). Beta is the covariance of the firm's stock price with the national stock market, using daily data to calculate annual observations, divided by the variance of the national stock index (a negative sign). The house price index refers to the annual percentage change in the national house price index (a positive sign as loan-to-value ratios fall with higher house prices).

References

Black, F., & Scholes, M. (1973). The Pricing of Options and Corporate Liabilities. *Journal of Political Economy, 81*(3), 637.

Blundell-Wignall, A., Atkinson, P. E., & Roulet, C. (2013). Bank Business Models and the Separation Issue. *OECD Journal, Financial Market Trends, 2012*(2), 1–23.

Dodd-Frank. (2010). Wall Street Reform and Consumer Protection Act (see US Congress).

Haldane, A. (2012). The Dog and the Frisbee. Speech Given at the Federal Reserve Bank of Kansas City's 36th Economic Policy Symposium, The Changing Policy Landscape, Jackson Hole, WY.

Mnuchin, S. T., & Phillips, C. S. (2017). *A Financial System That Creates Economic Opportunities: Banks and Credit Unions.* US Department of the Treasury.

7

Why Bank Separation Must Complement the Leverage Ratio

Introduction

In 2017, Secretary Mnuchin's Treasury has suggested some rollback of the Volcker Rule that went some way towards prohibiting risky activities of banking conglomerates. However, in the preceding chapter, empirical evidence was presented to show that Global Systemically Important Banks (GSIBs) are very different from national deposit-taking banks due to large portfolios of derivatives which give rise to interconnectedness risk is a more significant and separate source of risk for GSIBs.[1] It is critical to have business model policies for GSIBs such as the Volcker Rule. This chapter discusses what sorts of bank separation policies make the most sense.

While Basel III has propelled reform of capital rules, there has been no consensus between countries on what to do about business model risk. Approaches to the latter include the Vickers recommendations for the UK; the Dodd-Frank Act Volcker rule for the USA; the (stillborn)

[1]With the elasticities shown in Fig. 6.2, it seems likely that no reasonable cut in leverage would have sufficient impact to offset that of a large rise in derivatives as a share of assets.

A. Blundell-Wignall et al., *Globalisation and Finance at the Crossroads*,
https://doi.org/10.1007/978-3-319-72676-2_7

Liikanen proposal for Europe; and a resolution regime approach in Switzerland.[2] Most international organisations have focused on replacing Basel II with Basel III, improved supervision, better disclosure and cross-border cooperation. Better resolution regimes are proposed to deal with TBTF.[3] Academics have stressed the difficulties of interpreting rules based on separation proposals, and some have been strongly against it.[4]

Business Model Risk for GSIBs Cannot Be Dealt with by Capital Rules

The problems with derivatives and repos that lead to margin and collateral calls cannot be handled by the Basel III reforms aimed at establishing more capital for banks with add-ons such as the CVA charge to deal with counterparty risk—the amounts that could be required to avoid default in a crisis are likely to be too large.

This can be illustrated with the distance-to-default (DTD) calculation of the previous chapter. A DTD of 3 standard deviations implies a less than 1% chance of bank failure over the period of the maturity of the debt (e.g. 1 year). An illustrative calculation in an earlier paper concerning the crisis (when banks did reach the default point) asked what additional capital levels would have been required to keep the DTD at 3.0 in each year, thereby reducing the chance that the bank would default.[5]

---

[2]See UK Government (2011b); See section 619 of Dodd-Frank in US Congress (2010); Liikanen, E. (2012); and FINMA (2013).

[3]For example, see Ötker-Robe et al. (2011), p. 2.

[4]See Duffie (2012) for the former, and Goodhart (2013) for the latter.

[5]See Blundell-Wignall et al. (2013a). The DTD model of equation is first solved as in the appendix to Chapter 6. The DTD is then set to 3.0, and (for maturity of $T=1$) target bank capital K^* is calculated by solving for the V/D ratio that satisfies that condition for any bank below the critical 3.0 standard deviation threshold: i.e. $3.0\,\sigma_t - \left(r_f - \frac{\sigma_t^2}{2}\right) = \log\left(\frac{V_t}{D_t}\right) = \propto_t$. Given that $D = \mathrm{TA} - K$, where TA is total assets, it is then possible to calculate K^* holding σ and V at their original solved values, given the historical observations of TA: $K_t^* = \mathrm{TA}_t - \frac{V_t}{e^{\alpha_t}}$. The gap $K^* - K$

This gap was calculated for 21 of the GSIBs in the USA and in Europe (as defined by the FSB) and for 48 other large banks.

From 2002 to 2007, the size of extra capital injections is not material for all of the banks in the study, underlining the point that most banks don't need capital until they need it in a crisis. However, in 2008, an additional \$2.2tn was needed to keep all bank DTD levels at a minimum of 3.0 standard deviations, a tripling compared to actual T1 capital of \$1.1tn these banks had at the time. Of the total, \$1.6tn was required by the GSIBs and \$600bn was required by the other banks. In 2009, \$4.5tn more capital was required (quadrupling actual capital of \$1.6tn), of which \$3.6tn was due to the GSIBs.

This analysis suggests that GSIBs are very different to the traditional bank group because of counterparty risk. Many of these banks would have failed without massive support because of the nature of their business models. GSIBs needed much more equity than any reasonable capital rule would allow.

GSIBs are typically very large and combine elements of traditional banking—deposit taking and lending—but also carry out investment bank (IB) functions such as: prime broking, market making, broking, dealing, underwriting, derivatives and structured products, securities lending, rehypothecation, and often ancillary businesses such as clearing, custody and administration. These activities give rise to interconnectedness risk, which is cross-subsidised by the implicit guarantee from governments and central banks, particularly when insured deposits are included in the business mix. If risk is underpriced in this way, the size of the activities becomes larger than otherwise and, as the crisis showed, these institutions become too big to fail (TBTF). If such activities were separated from the core deposit banking function, and the separated securities firms were fully (and credibly) resolvable, then risk would be priced according to where it is taken without the implicit guarantee. This idea is explored in the next section.

---

is then computed for each bank and summed over the system. The idea is to see what *ex ante* amount of extra capital would be needed, without taking into account any subsequent impact on σ and V that an actual injection of $K^* - K$ might have on σ, and other variables.

The Structural Separation Proposal

Following the 2008 crisis, the OECD was amongst the first to propose separation as necessary for the future stability of the financial system.[6] A non-operating holding company (NOHC) structure for banks based on a separation threshold related to the extent of counterparty risk is the legal structure most consistent with the empirical evidence on determinants of the DTD. Once a bank moves beyond that threshold, the derivatives and related counterparty businesses should be separated into an independent legal entity (essentially ring-fencing it from the deposit-insured bank). The general policy aim of separation is to ensure that deposit banking is safe, so that the central bank and/or the taxpayer do not need periodically to support the bank each time uncertainty about interconnectedness risk rises in a crisis situation. This would help remove the implicit guarantee for the investment banking activities while the deposit-taking institution remains well protected.

The threshold would be set at a level that allows the deposit bank to carry out passive hedging functions for itself and on behalf of clients (with appropriate use of exchanges and clearing), but not OTC derivatives and related securities functions associated with IB functions. These IB activities would be conducted in the legally separate investment bank—by definition smaller than the conglomerate—that would be resolved in the event of default. Of course, the cost of investment banking transactions would rise, but only to the extent that the implicit guarantee tied up with TBTF and depositor protection is removed. This is the entire point. These activities are underpriced and periodically lead to crises.

The recommended threshold would be the share of derivatives on an IFRS basis (no netting) in the area of no more than 10% of total assets. Examples of banks that went through the crisis without requiring public support, such as Wells Fargo, Santander, Westpac and others, all had derivatives on an IFRS basis meeting this limit.[7]

---

[6]See, for example, OECD (2009).

[7]See Blundell-Wignall et al. (2013b).

At the legal structure level, the aim is to write the law to ensure that the creditors of the securities subsidiary must not be able to pursue the assets and capital of other subsidiaries (and notably the core deposit bank) or the non-operating parent. This smaller investment bank would be easier to resolve, but the structure proposed would greatly reduce the probability of default because risk would be priced according to the nature of the activities undertaken there. The subsidiaries would not be able to trade on the reputation and credit rating of the parent (i.e. they would have their own credit rating for debt issuance). The legal structure would ensure that capital, assets and liabilities would not be able to be shifted between subsidiaries directly or via the parent. Assets would not be able to be pledged or otherwise encumbered between the subsidiaries. In Fig. 7.1, the areas circled with the broken line would be subject to the threshold, and the broken vertical line would block-off guarantees for off-balance-sheet structures that may be associated with the deposit bank. The functions of the deposit bank are circled on the bottom left, and for the IB on the bottom right.

Counterparties dealing with the separated investment bank would do so in the knowledge that their obligations would not be guaranteed by the official sector in the event of default. This would raise the cost of counterparty transactions since higher margins and collateral haircuts would have to replace the implicit guarantee and more care would be taken with respect to co-mingling cash and rehypothecation permission. The size of the business would decline to levels that would be less disruptive in the event of default. In the event of the latter, closeout netting would come into effect without intervention and support from the authorities.

Derivatives are chosen for the threshold as they permeate most of the IB functions and carry with them liability structures that take wholesale funding well beyond the deposit base. There are socially useful derivatives needed for hedging purposes. But there are uses which are not socially useful, and these include structuring products for tax avoidance and arbitraging bank capital rules (e.g. with synthetic securitisation discussed earlier). These latter activities are prone to take derivatives activity beyond the 10% threshold. There is no reason why normal hedging

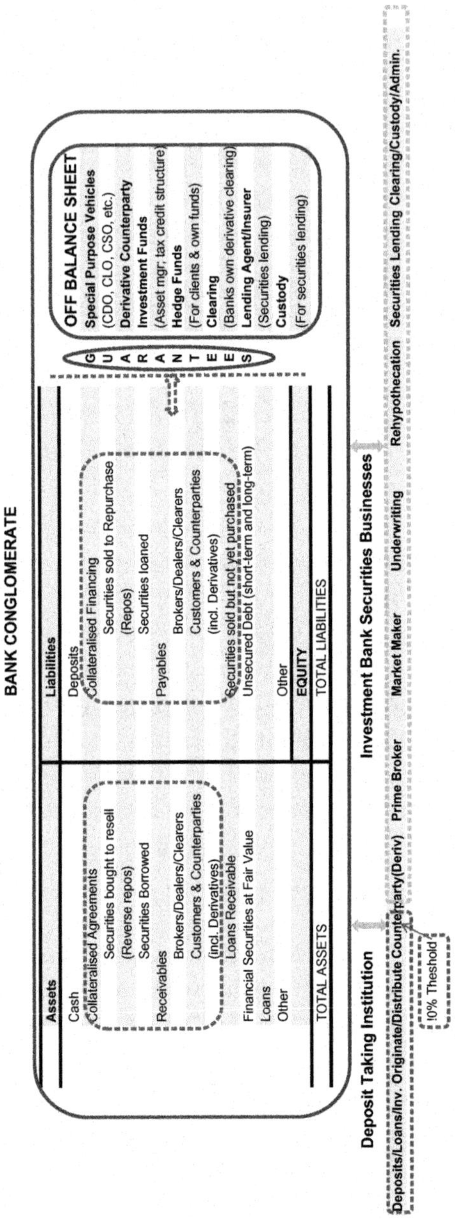

Fig. 7.1 Separation (threshold) proposal for bank conglomerate (*Source* Authors)

activity cannot continue (using jointly owned exchanges and clearers) within the 10% threshold.

This proposal is about getting risk priced appropriately by removing the implicit guarantee for IB functions. That the regulator can shut down the IB without affecting deposit banks removes the need for so-called living wills. Resolution mechanisms for smaller, legally separate IBs would be more credible than those needed for large mixed conglomerates—helping to deal with the TBTF issue. Deposit insurance and other guarantees would apply to the deposit bank without being extended to the legally separate IB.

Illustrating the Separate Effects of Leverage Ratios and Investment Bank Separation

Figure 7.2 provides a simple hypothetical example of the separate effects of leverage and separation rules on bank business models. It illustrates why both are necessary for the safety of banking.

Case A shows the conglomerate combined deposit-taking and investment bank untouched by either rule. The parent raises $100 on the equity market and invests it evenly in both businesses.[8] The deposit bank leverages its equity into debt (deposits) by say by 20 times, and its total balance sheet of assets (debt plus equity) is $1050. If it earns a net 1% on assets, it makes $10.5 profit and has a return on equity (ROE) of 21%, which it returns to shareholders. An upper range to its maximum potential loss is (say) 2.5%, or $26, well inside its capital. The IB takes on more risk activities and levers its equity 50 times, for a total balance sheet of $2550. If it earns the same 1%, it makes $25.5 in profit and an ROE of 51%, more than double the deposit bank purely because of the higher leverage of its activities. If its maximum potential loss is the

[8]The parent may try to use double gearing if permitted: instead of raising $100 in equity, it borrows half as debt. Debt and equity would be invested as 'equity' into the subsidiaries, then the rate of return on equity and the leverage ratio could be doubled versus true equity. It is imperative that the concept of capital to which leverage ratio rules apply should be for equity only.

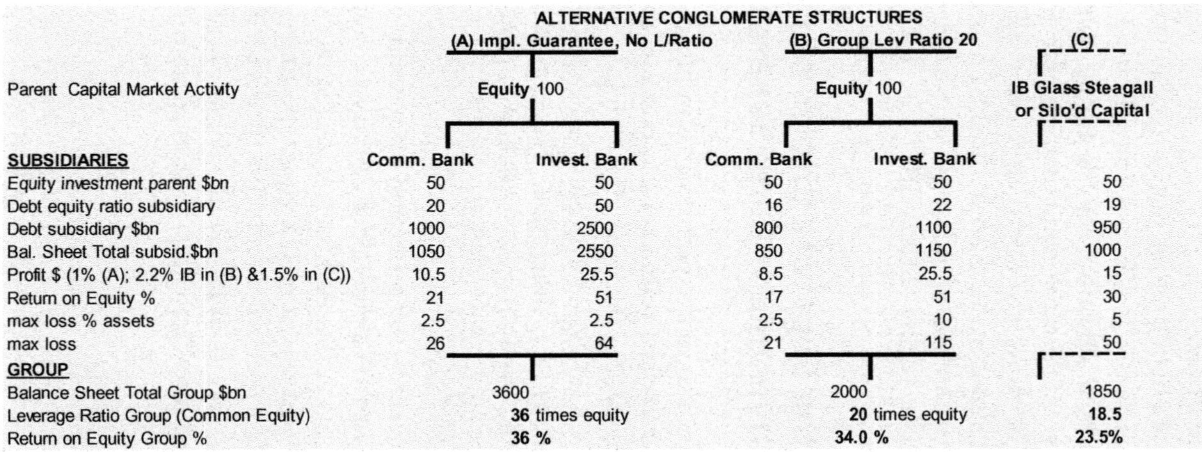

ALTERNATIVE CONGLOMERATE STRUCTURES

	(A) Impl. Guarantee, No L/Ratio		(B) Group Lev Ratio 20		(C)
Parent Capital Market Activity	Equity 100		Equity 100		IB Glass Steagall or Silo'd Capital
SUBSIDIARIES	**Comm. Bank**	**Invest. Bank**	**Comm. Bank**	**Invest. Bank**	
Equity investment parent $bn	50	50	50	50	50
Debt equity ratio subsidiary	20	50	16	22	19
Debt subsidiary $bn	1000	2500	800	1100	950
Bal. Sheet Total subsid.$bn	1050	2550	850	1150	1000
Profit $ (1% (A); 2.2% IB in (B) &1.5% in (C))	10.5	25.5	8.5	25.5	15
Return on Equity %	21	51	17	51	30
max loss % assets	2.5	2.5	2.5	10	5
max loss	26	64	21	115	50
GROUP					
Balance Sheet Total Group $bn	3600		2000		1850
Leverage Ratio Group (Common Equity)	**36** times equity		**20** times equity		**18.5**
Return on Equity Group %	**36 %**		**34.0 %**		**23.5%**

Fig. 7.2 Alternative bank structures (*Source* Authors)

same as the deposit bank at 2.5%, then a potential loss of $64 would be greater than its capital. The conglomerate would have to run down capital allocating from the deposit bank to the IB (weakening the deposit bank).

In Case B, a group leverage ratio of 20 times is imposed—so with $100 equity, the total balance sheet can only be $2000, as opposed to $3600 in Case A. While there are a large number of ways to meet the rule, they all involve the IB having to cut its leverage. In the example shown the cuts are shared, with the deposit bank moving to a debt/equity ratio of 16 and the IB to 22. But this poses a problem for the IB as its leverage route to profits is reduced. Consequently, it has an incentive to take on higher spread risk activities to maintain its ROE at the 51% level expected by investors in Case A—it needs to earn not 1% but 2.22% to maintain its ROE of 51%. This extra risk-taking raises the maximum potential loss to, say, 10% in a crisis event. But in this case, the loss could be as high as $115, more than double its equity. Still worse (and very consistent with events in the crisis), the maximum potential loss for the whole group is $115 for the IB plus $21 for deposit bank. This would be a total potential loss of $136, or 36% more than the capital of the whole group. The taxpayer is still on the hook. Without official support in a risk event, the whole group would fail, and deposit insurance would have to be paid out for the $800 of deposits in the deposit bank.

In Case C, the deposit bank is left as it is in Case B, but it is separated as a NOHC from the IB with a new legal structure. The IB must also meet the leverage rule of 20 times equity. In this case, the IB is not cross-subsidised by the implicit guarantee—it can and will be resolved if the potential risk event is realised. Market discipline would come into play (higher margins, deeper haircuts and less permission for the reuse of assets) to ensure that the maximum loss is less than or equal to the capital of the IB. Its total balance sheet is $1000, and it must control risk to ensure a maximum loss of 5% of its assets; i.e. its maximum loss of $50 is no more than its equity capital (in the example, it cuts the risk spread to 1.5% from the 2.2% in Case B).

Comparisons with Other Separation Proposals

The NOHC proposal is compared to the Volcker rule in the USA, the Vickers rule in the UK and the (defunct) Liikanen proposal for Europe in Table 7.1. The US and UK approaches are the only ones that made it into regulatory laws. In Europe, nothing was done with the Liikanen proposal due to banks lobbying their governments to block the legislation,[9] while in Switzerland, a resolution approach was adopted (wrongly asserting its equivalence with legal separation). In very broad terms, the NOHC proposal and the UK Vickers rule are similar in that they separate the bank conglomerate into the deposit-taking institution and the IB, ring-fencing them by law.[10] The Volcker Rule and the defunct Liikanen proposal attempt to do something quite complex—to separate out some speculative functions that can't be done in a bank holding company while leaving many similar IB functions in place.

The Attempt to Separate Speculative Functions (Volcker & Swaps Push-Out Rule)

The Dodd-Frank Act section 619 'Volcker Rule' prohibits depository institutions from engaging in proprietary trading and from investing in covered funds (like hedge funds and private equity) beyond small limits (see Table 7.1). The trading restriction is complex, and there are three tests: *the market risk capital rule test*—instruments covered by that rule can't be traded for proprietary gain; *a status test*—if the transaction would normally require the entity to be registered with the CFTC or SEC as a dealer then it can't be done; and *a purpose test*—that the trade cannot be made for the purpose of short-term resale, benefiting from short-term price movements, realising arbitrage profits, and hedging any of the foregoing. This latter blanket ban has come under fire from the Mnuchin et al. (2017) review which recommends removing

---

[9]See Brunsden (2017).

[10]The OECD views were solicited by the secretariat of the Commission, see UK Government (2011a).

Table 7.1 The NOHC structure compared to the US and UK proposals

	Regulatory Approaches to Bank Separation			
	Non-operating Holding Company (NOHC) (Business model separation)	**Vickers** (Business model separation)	**Volcker Rule** (Partial functions separation)	**Liikanen/Barnier/France/ Germany** (Partial functions separation)
AIM	Better allocation of risk and improved resolvability. Continuous provision of services by bank affiliate in the event of a crisis.	Insulate retail banking & SME lending from international shocks. Improve resolvability within groups. ↓ taxpayer risk.	Reduce speculative losses to banks & focus on intermediary functions serving customers.	Safe, stable & efficient banking. Remove TBTFas main risk. Facilitate recovery & resolution.
Features	Non-operating parent invests in ring-fenced affiliates with their own governance. Legal structure stops creditors of distressed affiliates seeking redress against the others in the group. Allocates risk more efficiently between the regulated bank & less regulated IB.	Ring-fence retail from w/sale & IB divisions within a holding Co. Tougher capital standards for ring-fenced bank Promote competition in retail banks & IBs separately. Foreign banks welcome.	*Prohibits:* (a) prop. trading by any insured depository instit. in commodities, financial securities & derivatives that do not benefit customers. (b) Investment in Priv. Equity & hedge funds by deposit. Insists. (3% rule: of capital of any fund & of total capital of bank)	*Prohibits:* (a) prop. trading of securities & derivatives; (b) lending to hedge funds & private equity. Separates: market making, hedging activities & underwriting from depository institution beyond a threshold into separate legal entity (10% of assets). NB: All domestic & foreign banks (branches & subs)

(continued)

Table 7.1 (continued)

	Regulatory Approaches to Bank Separation			
	Non-operating Holding Company (NOHC) (Business model separation)	**Vickers** (Business model separation)	**Volcker Rule** (Partial functions separation)	**Liikanen/Barnier/France/ Germany** (Partial functions separation)
Functions	Maintains all business units in the group. Bank mandated to take deposits & provide overdrafts/ loans. Bank prohibited from IBs: prime broking; structuring OTC derivatives market making; underwriting; securities lending; rehypothecation; guarantees to SPEs.	Maintains all business units in the group. Bank mandated to take deposits & provide over-drafts/loans. Bank prohibited from: structuring OTC derivatives; equity & ETFs; security market making; & underwriting. Trade finance & aspects of w/sale are OK.	*Permitted activities:* traditional banking, trading in US government debt; underwriting; market making exemption (inventory limit); risk-mitigating hedging; trading for customers; liquidity management; investments in 'Small Business Inv. Companies'; limited investments in covered funds & advisory businesses; advisory businesses; foreign trading by non-US banks.	*Permitted activities:* deposit taking and lending, & full participation in the payments system for depository institution. Market making hedging & underwriting in the seoarate legal entity.

(continued)

Table 7.1 (continued)

	Regulatory Approaches to Bank Separation			
	Non-operating Holding Company (NOHC) (Business model separation)	**Vickers** (Business model separation)	**Volcker Rule** (Partial functions separation)	**Liikanen/Barnier/France/ Germany** (Partial functions separation)
Administrative & industry concerns	That it is difficult to separate functions into entities. But this lobbying view is refuted by events in Australia (Macquarie). Entities & functions were 1st defined by regulator (Bank & IB). Restructure instruments grant relief to regulatory impediments to separation arising from corp. & income tax laws to the entities as specified. 'Transfer certificates' issued by regulator to transfer of assets & liabilities between the entities. Was carried out in a few months of 2007 (legislation & implementation) to avoid bank default risk.	UK banks and lobbyists claim that it is difficult to implement & have convinced the authorities to give them until 2019 to sort it out. They would do well to examine the NOHC legislation in Australia. Applies to foreign subsidiaries operating in the UK.	Global competition disadvantage to deposit institutions in the USA. Extra-territoriality: foreign bank affiliates in USA that control funds deemed banking entity for the V-R even if funds only offered abroad. Prop. trading definition too complex based on intent (for S/Term gain or serving client demand. Market making inventory limits too tight & reduce liquidity. Covered fund restriction goes beyond hedge fund & priv. equity; restricitive (e.g. venture capital). Costly to small firms which should be exempt.	Related German & French Separation Proposals: were consistent on the prohibitions but not permitting market making, hedging and & underwriting within the depository institution.
Effective date	2007 (July) in Australia for Macquarie. Was voluntary. Not proposed elsewhere.	2019–linked to Basel III timetable.	2015 (July)	Was to be 2017, but bank lobbying succeeded in killing all of it. EU withdraws legislation in Oct 2017.

Source OECD, & various Treasury, regulatory agency, legislative documents, and inquiry reports

this element because it is subjective and leads to conservatism and costly documentation.

In the lobbying process, banks successfully argued that the Volcker rule should continue to allow underwriting and market making for depository institutions, in spite of the blanket ban on speculating on short-term price movements. The exemption for market making asks that banks don't build inventory beyond reasonable forecasts for serving expected client demand which otherwise would cause excess inventory. Once again, the Mnuchin review attacks this because it asks traders to forecast the impossible—particularly for illiquid OTC derivatives—and documentation is costly to firms. The review suggests that such forecasts shouldn't be required if the firm stands ready to buy and sell the instruments, the activity is fully hedged, and compensation arrangements for gains (fair value claims) are in place.[11]

With respect to the ban on investing and sponsoring covered funds (such as the right-hand side of Fig. 7.1), the Mnuchin review suggests that it is too extensive and may not limit itself to hedge funds and private equity which are not defined clearly enough. It argues that this might exclude the seeding of venture capital and other useful things to support economic growth. It suggests longer seeding periods (from the current 1 year to 3 years).

Because of these and other concerns, the Treasury review goes further than the above specific recommendations to a more general set of suggestions:

- That all depository institutions with less than \$10bn in assets should be exempt from the Volcker rule—they are too small for systemic risk concerns and record keeping is too costly for them. This will help community banks.
- Larger firms should also be exempt if they have less than \$1bn in trading assets or the latter constitutes no more than 10% of their balance sheet (which is in any case consistent with the existing market risk rule thresholds).

[11]Consistent with the Duffie (2012) views.

- Banks with a large enough leverage ratio should also be exempt. Mnuchin suggests that the Financial Choice Act 2017 proposal that a 10% (unweighted) leverage ratio should place a bank '*off-ramp*' for the Dodd-Frank Act—totally exempting it from the Volcker Rule.

The Dodd-Frank Act did contain a partial separation proposal in section 716. This prohibits the granting of US federal assistance (including Fed discount window access and FDIC deposit insurance) to entities that are registered with the CFTC or SEC as swap dealers or major swap participants. This would limit a US insured depository institution's ability to engage in such derivatives activities. Such activities were to be '*pushed out*' into separate execution facilities. This provision was amended making the push-out rule to be marginal and largely immaterial to risk. The amendment (apparently involving Citigroup) was tacked onto a spending bill to ensure it passed both houses.[12] Banks can now hold virtually all swaps on their balance sheet, including the credit default swaps discussed in reference to the crisis in earlier chapters.[13]

Thoughts on the Mnuchin Review

There is a lot of sensible thought in the Treasury review and also a very big BUT…On the side of agreement, the Volcker rule does have too much complexity and inconsistency. For example, GSIBs are allowed to carry out market-making activities, which requires banks to maintain an inventory of assets because the activity is about immediacy for clients (see Duffie 2012). Speculation on short-term price movements for a profit is inherent in this business—the profit incentive is the driving mechanism for efficiency in the market. It is unreasonable to restrict quantities of inventories to levels forecast by some past *rule of thumb*—a sure-fire way of introducing inefficiency. It is clear too that compliance

[12]See https://dealbook.nytimes.com/2014/12/12/citigroup-becomes-the-fall-guy-in-the-spending-bill-battle/.

[13]An exception is structured finance swaps (ABS swaps). See Warren (2015).

cost are high, demonstrating 'intent of a trade' is difficult and that small uninvolved financial institutions (such as community banks) should be exempt.

However, the big '*BUT*'... should be staring the reader in the face. It is very strange for a country that prides itself on the benefits of the market to be prescriptive about functions and the intent of traders. Under the NOHC rule, there is no need for any of this. Investment banking is ring-fenced, and the entity is resolvable. IBs have to manage their own risks in a free manner. The reality seems to be that the big banks don't want this, because they like inefficiency which makes for profits via implicit and explicit subsidies from the government. Having avoided separation, these banks (supported by the US Treasury) are now in a strong position to argue for the rollback of cumbersome and inefficient rules. These banks are not arguing to replace Volcker with IB separation. Rather they want to move closer to what they had prior to the crisis—the support of an implicit government guarantee.

Furthermore, and contrary to the Mnuchin Treasury view, the earlier empirical evidence and analysis in this chapter show that the leverage ratio is not an efficient tool for dealing with interconnectedness risk. Leverage risk and interconnectedness risk are separate, and during the crisis (particularly without taxpayer support), there would have been no reasonable leverage ratio that would have prevented defaults (not even the 10% proposed in the Financial Choice Act).

European Liikanen Proposal

The Liikanen proposal is now formally defunct. Its aim was to limit the TBTF implicit guarantees, enhance resolvability, and strengthen governance (see Table 7.1). To do this, a bank with above 15–25% trading securities should be considered for separation in a second-stage review by supervisors. If the supervisor deemed it necessary a subsidiary for the activity would have been be formed, still within the conglomerate but subject to tougher Basel rules. Market making was to be within the trading entity, but underwriting could have stayed with the deposit-taking institution. Bail-in bonds were also recommended for the trading group. The Basel risk-weighting approach for the trading group would have been a very poor risk-mitigating mechanism, as shown by the earlier research on the distance-to-default. Objections from constituent countries (notably France and Germany), under the advice of their national champion banks, were the prime reason the whole adventure failed.[14]

The UK Vickers Rule

The Vickers rule ring-fences UK retail operations of large banks (see Table 7.1). The separated securities-focused subsidiaries can also have banking licenses, setting up as wholesale/investment banks anywhere around the world. The aim of Vickers is to ring-fence the domestic retail business from international financial shocks and to limit taxpayer costs for losses given default. This proposal of ring-fencing, which passed into law, is closest to the NOHC proposal.

Switzerland Resolution Approach Is a Non-starter

The Swiss authorities have opted against separation and/or ring-fencing for their two giant universal banks (Credit Suisse and UBS) and instead chose to rely on 'single point of entry bail-ins': i.e. the creditors of the top holding company or parent bank (which owns all the companies in the group) are bailed into the extent necessary to recapitalise the whole group of companies in the event of default. This is argued to buy time to resolve some non-viable part of the group, presumably if management feels like it.[15] It is difficult to see how this reduces proprietary risk-taking behaviour of a bank in the same way that actual separation does. The cross-subsidisation of high-risk businesses (notably derivatives) is not eliminated prior to the universal bank itself moving to full

[14]For example, banks could not accept that market making was to be moved to a subsidiary.
[15]See FINMA (2013).

default, which the authorities can't possibly allow to happen. It is not a pre-emptive approach, and risk-taking will continue to be subsidised.

Indeed, creditor counterparties to derivatives trades will be very pleased to do business with both Swiss banks: they can reasonably assume defaults will not be allowed for any business segments and that the holders of contingent convertible bonds (CoCos) for the whole group will be bailed in at the first loss and the taxpayer will be there for anything beyond that. The creditors of one group do not even have to pursue the assets or capital of others in the group—which the NOHC proposal is designed specifically to avoid—the 'bail in' builds this pursuit into the very process. This is not the way to align the pricing of risk with the extent of risk being taken in the various business segments and to enhance credible resolvability.

Criticisms of the Full Bank Separation Proposal

Banks of course resist separation proposals because they would remove the implicit government subsidy and cut rent-seeking profits. Supporters of banks in this respect offer five broad sets of criticisms of the NOHC and full separation proposals. These are:

1. That Lehman Brothers and AIG were not universal banks that could be considered for separation, and yet they caused systemic events.
2. That it was not the GSIBs that failed during the crisis; it was the specialised mortgage banks involved in the real estate boom and busts in the USA, the UK, Ireland and Spain that mainly failed.
3. That separating core deposit banking will force investment banks into more unstable wholesale funding, making their business more costly and unstable.
4. That it is legally too complex to separate assets and liabilities while meeting all of the tax and corporate laws of the country concerned.
5. That separation with full ring-fencing of all subsidiaries is essentially Glass-Steagall, so why bother with NOHC ring-fencing?

That Lehman and AIG Were Not Bank Conglomerates

The Lehman Brothers point was already dealt with in Chapter 5. The most basic methodology of economics is to get the counterfactuals straight. One needs to ask how big would Lehman have been if its counterparties were not TBTF unseparated universal banks like Citigroup, JP Morgan, UBS, Credit Suisse, Barclays, Bank of America, Deutsche Bank, BNP Paribas and Societé Génerale, but ring-fenced boutique subsidiaries of those banks with no official guarantees? And what if Lehman, as a consequence, had a 100% Basel risk weight instead of the 20% at the time? With respect to AIG, the exposures that took the company down were sold CDS contracts written for banks for the explicit purposes of them reducing the capital they were required to hold under the Basel risk-weighting system. The banks were essentially bailed out by the US taxpayer. The history of the past decade would have been very different with NOHC separation combined with a leverage ratio.

That It Was Mainly Mortgage Banks That Failed

This second criticism does not stand up to scrutiny. First, the GSIBs were explicitly supported by direct capital injections, official liquidity support by their central banks on an unprecedented scale and the US Government paying out the AIG counterparty claims. Second, the specialist mortgage banks had adapted their own business models to take advantage of the fee-for-sale securitisation boom. Countrywide Financial is a good example. Table 7.2 shows its net income evolution from 2001 to the year just before its demise.

Line 9 shows net income, and the very bottom memo line shows what net income would be without its fee-for-sale securitisation business income. In 2001, Countrywide was already heavily reliant on fee-for sale, but as the subprime boom gained momentum net interest income began to fall after 2004 (due to the pushing for more subprime borrowers), and fee-for-sale (in line 3) boomed. In 2006, this

Table 7.2 Countrywide financial business model evolution

$ Thousands	2001	2002	2003	2004	2005	2006
(1) Interest income	3,178,670	3,926,572	6,116,218	6,774,939	8,593,626	12,751,703
(2) Interest expenses	1,726,358	1,442,806	1,935,023	2,608,338	5,615,941	9,133,682
Memo: Net interest income	1,452,312	2,483,766	4,181,195	4,166,601	2,977,685	3,618,021
(3) Non-Interest income (fee for sale)	1,502,737	1,665,770	3,843,810	4,226,652	7,985,658	9,257,050
(4) Gains on securities	108,301	369,929	1841	493,677	(6496)	(284,849)
(5) Non-interest costs (staff etc)	2,063,224	3,111,811	4,108,815	5,155,952	6,670,755	7,981,570
(6) Provisions	50,058	63,149	64,685	120,329	115,685	233,847
(7) Taxes	361,295	501,244	1,472,821	1,398,299	1,619,677	1,659,289
(8) Other (minority int, extraordinary)	299	1,482	7,575	14,776	22,640	40,670
(9) Net income (=1−2+3+4−5−6−7−8)	588,474	841,779	2,372,950	2,197,574	2,528,090	2,674,846
Memo: Net income without fee-for-sale	(914,263)	(823,991)	(1,470,860)	(2,029,078)	(5,457,568)	(6,582,204)

Source Annual reports, authors

non-interest income was $9.26bn. Without that, its net income would have been a loss of $6.58bn (bottom right). In the following year, securitisation stopped, and so did Countrywide. Pointing to institutions like Countrywide in this debate is flawed thinking—they were very much a product of the holistic picture of the mess of financial regulation and innovation of the 2000s.

That Investment Banks Will Shift to 100% Wholesale Funding

That of course is the whole point. Under separation, IBs will fund themselves with equity, like an insurance company, and wholesale borrowing. That is what investment banks are supposed to do—they are not supposed to be the recipients of implicit subsidies from government guarantees. Smaller resolvable IBs will be forced to price risk at levels commensurate with their business activities once separated from deposit-insured banks. A competitive level playing field would apply to all IBs. Goldman Sachs is perhaps a model of an IB that is well run with appropriate hedging strategies. They should be competing with equally hungry and well-run institutions separated from the inefficient subsidised structures of bank conglomerates and preferably with skin-in-the-game 'partnership' governance structures.

That Banks Are Too Complex to Separate

This criticism has been very typical of lawyers and consultants employed by bank conglomerates. It was argued strongly in the UK when Vickers was first announced—although Vickers has now died down as an issue. But there is a better example of the weakness of this argument, which can be seen when banks really want to do it for survival reasons—as opposed to defending their rent-seeking business models. The Wallis (1997) Review of the Australian financial system recommended the NOHC as a sound legal structure, without trying to impose it as a regulation. It was seen as a sound method to quarantine entities in a group containing a depository institution (to protect against creditors of one entity seeking to pursue the assets and capital of other entities of a group). However, while the 1998 Financial Sector (Shareholdings) Act amended the 1959 Banking Act to permit NOHC legal structures, there was no actual adoption due to corporate and tax law complications (impediments under the Corporations Act, 2001, and the taxation laws).

However, in 2007, Macquarie Bank had highly levered securities businesses mixed into the holding company, and after the volatility, at the start of the year, the bank saw the NOHC structure as being in its own interest. Importantly, it was also encouraged this way by the Australian Prudential Regulatory Authority (APRA). To deal with the complexity issue, a new restructures bill was quickly passed (see Australian Government 2007). This created two simplifying instruments:

- *Restructure instruments*: to grant relief to the specific statutory impediments to NOHC affiliates complying with the requirements of corporate law.
- *Internal Transfer Certificates*: issued by APRA, to facilitate the rearrangement of assets and liabilities of the different activities into their separate business lines.

To complete the process, a number of amendments to the Income Tax Assessment Act 1997 were passed: i.e. amendments to the consolidation rules and capital gains tax aspects that were impediments to restructuring. Macquarie Bank adopted the NOHC structure in 2007, the very same year as the changes in law, and this structure served it very well as the global crisis unfolded. If banks want to do it, then it's not so complicated after all.

Isn't Ring-Fenced NOHC Really Just Glass-Steagall via Another Name?

Finally, this fifth comment may be right—that one might as well move to full separation. Nevertheless, there are still advantages of legally ring-fenced entities belonging to a NOHC structure. These include synergies in the technology platform, and back office and human resources sharing. Cross-selling would also be permitted, though with arms-length pricing. Finally, the business model has great advantages for the equity investor, who will receive dividends from properly diversified sources. If traditional banking falls on hard times dividends may still be paid from the IB, and vice versa, without contamination effects.

Concluding Remarks

The above analysis shows that business models of GSIBs have evolved to such a complex and interconnected state that there is no reasonable capital rule that can be put in place in normal times to protect the financial system in the event of a major crisis. Leverage and interconnectedness risks are separate concerns—two issues that need two policy instruments. This point is not reflected in the 2017 Mnuchin Review in the USA.

The necessity of structural separation has been recognised in a number of jurisdictions, and new regulatory approaches have been proposed. These, however, are inconsistent across borders, particularly as to where the lines of separation should be drawn.

The bank regulator's paradox is that large complex and interconnected banks need very little capital in the good times, but they can never have enough in an extreme crisis. Separation is required to deal with this problem. The study suggests banks should be considered for separation into a NOHC structure with ring-fencing when they pass the key allowable threshold of 10% for the share of derivatives in total assets on an IFRS basis (no netting). Both the separated deposit bank and the IB should also have a binding and meaningful leverage ratio on an IFRS basis, with no deductions from the denominator. The pricing of interconnectedness risk would be appropriate in this structure. Finally, and importantly, separation with a NOHC gets rid of the need to have complex rules about the intent of traders and the need to exempt some institutions on the grounds of the costs versus benefits of compliance costs. Other than maintaining a leverage ratio, IBs in this structure would be lightly regulated.

References

Australian Government. (2007). Financial Sector Legislation Ammendment (Restructures) Bill 2007, Federal Register of Legislation, Available at: https://www.legislation.gov.au/Details/C2007B00112.

Blundell-Wignall, A. Atkinson, P. E., & Roulet, C. (2013a). "Bank Business Models and the Separation Issue". *OECD Journal, Financial Market Trends, 2012*(2), 1–23.

Blundell-Wignall, A., Atkinson, P. E., & Roulet, C. (2013b). Integration Versus Interdependence and Complexity in Global Trade and Finance in the Post-war Period. In Morten & Gnan (Eds.), *50 Years of Money and Finance: Lessons and Challenges, SUERF 50th Anniversary Volume*. Brussels: Larcier.

Brunsden, J. (2017, October 24). European Commission Withdraws Bank Separation Proposal. *Financial Times*. Available at: https://www.ft.com/content/ddbedcd9-2dea-3b68-b8e2-2e1bc1eda13f.

Duffie, D. (2012). *Market Making Under the Proposed Volcker Rule* (Working Paper). Stanford University Graduate School of Business. Available at: www.darrellduffie.com/uploads/policy/DuffieVolckerRule.pdf.

FINMA. (2013, July). *FINMA Position Paper on the Resolution of Systemically Important Banks, Swiss Financial Market Supervisory Authority* (FINMA), Switzerland. Available at: www.finma.ch/e/aktuell/Pages/mm-pos-sanierung-abwicklung-20130807.aspx.

Goodhart, C. A. E. (2013). "The Optimal Financial Structure", *LSE Financial Markets Group Paper Series*, Special Paper 220. Available at: http://www.lse.ac.uk/fmg/assets/documents/papers/special-papers/SP220.pdf.

Liikanen, E. (2012, October). *High-Level Expert Group on Reforming the Structure of the EU Banking Sector: Final Report*. Brussels. Available at: http://ec.europa.eu/internal_market/bank/docs/high-level_expert_group/report_en.pdf.

Mnuchin, S. T., & Phillips, C. S. (2017). *A Financial System That Creates Economic Opportunities: Banks and Credit Unions*. Report to President Donald J. Trump. Executive Order 13772 on Core Principles for Regulating the United States Financial System. US Department of the Treasury, Washington.

OECD. (2009). *The Financial Crisis: Reform and Exit Strategies*. Paris: OECD. Available at: www.oecd.org/dataoecd/55/47/43091457.pdf.

Ötker-Robe, I. J. Fiechter, J. Surti, M. Hsu, A. O. Santos, A. Ilyina. (2011). "Subsidiaries and Branches: Does One Size Fit All?." *SSRN Electronic Journal*. Available at: https://papers.ssrn.com/sol3/papers.cfm?abstract_id=1805316.

UK Government. (2011a, April). *Interim Report: Consultation on Reform Options*. Independent Commission on Banking. London. Available at: https://s3-eu-west-1.amazonaws.com/htcdn/Interim-Report-110411.pdf.

UK Government. (2011b, September). *Independent Commission on Banking: Final Report Recommendations* (Vickers Report). London. Available at: http://webarchive.nationalarchives.gov.uk/20131003105424/https:/hmt-sanctions.s3.amazonaws.com/icb%20final%20report/icb%2520final%2520report%5B1%5D.pdf.

US Congress. (2010). Dodd-Frank Wall Street Reform and Consumer Protection Act (2009). H.R. 4173—111th Congress. Available at: www.govtrack.us/congress/bill.xpd?bill=h111-4173.

Wallis, S. (1997). *Financial System Inquiry Final Report*. Canberra: Treasury. Available at: http://fsi.treasury.gov.au/content/FinalReport.asp.

Warren, D. R. (2015). Developments in Banking Law. *Review of Banking and Financial Law, 34* (pp. 439–450, Section V, on 'Congress's Rollback of the Dodd-Frank Swaps Push-Out Rule').

8

Assessing the Finalised Basel III Banking Regulation Regime

Introduction

The Basel reform saga through phases I, II, II.5 and III has been a very unsatisfactory process. There is a need to keep an open mind on this, because 'groupthink' has become increasingly embedded in the process. Nevertheless, the spectacular and continuing increase in size, complexity and scope for arbitrage of a substantially unchanging regulatory framework is striking.

Basel I consisted of 13 pages of simple text, free of jargon, plus some short appendices. Basel II was based on hundreds of pages of text, quantitative impact studies and many years of work. It was introduced with a confidence that brushed off critics and critiques. Yet its anticipation by banks actually contributed causally to the crisis by lowering the capital weights that would apply following its implementation. One might imagine that this would have caused the Basel Committee for Bank Supervision (BCBS) to tear up the flawed framework and start from scratch (see Appendix to Chapter 2 for methodology flaws). But that wasn't to be. Instead, Basel III has proceeded as a piecemeal string of adjustments and announcements running into many thousands of pages. Each step was

A. Blundell-Wignall et al., *Globalisation and Finance at the Crossroads*,
https://doi.org/10.1007/978-3-319-72676-2_8

subject to consultation and negotiation with banks, with seemingly endless technical add-ons and changes of mind. The BCBS members are confident that the more granular Basel III will be different this time.

Key Elements of the First Phases of Basel III Reforms

Prior to the final phase of the reforms, the BCBS locked in a number of changes to the Basel II framework, while leaving the basic method for risk-weighted assets (RWA) and the use of models in the internal ratings-based (IRB) approach largely untouched. These changes include *inter alia*:

- *A better quality of capital*: focused on the Common Equity Tier 1 (CET-1) ratio to move gradually to 4.5% of RWA (with various deductions) to be phased in by 2019.[1]
- *A Capital Conservation Buffer* (*CCB*): of 2.5% of RWA above the CET-1 minimum, to be built up in good times and run down in bad—within the range 4.5–7% capital distribution restraints apply in order to build it up again to the full amount (2019 for full compliance).
- *A GSIB Higher Loss Absorbency Requirement* (*HLAR*): thought necessary due to the externalities created by GSIBs (due to size, interconnectedness, etc.). This will result in an extra CET-1 capital charge as a percent of RWA according to (annual) rankings of these banks into 5 'buckets' of risk (from bucket five for the highest risk down to bucket one, respectively: +3.5%, +2.5%, +2%, +1.5%, +1.0%).
- *A minimum Tier 1 ratio*: to be phased into 6% of RWA by 2019, and 8% for total capital including Tier 2. Tier 1 capital is made up on CET-1 capital plus other allowable instruments such as most preferred shares and contingent convertible bonds (CoCos).

[1]Deductions such as goodwill, deferred tax assets and a number of intangibles are to be phased in by 2019.

- *A minimum Leverage Ratio* (*LR*): of Tier 1 (T1) capital to an exposure measure (not risk-weighted) to be phased into 3% by 2019. Importantly, the denominator of total assets allows derivatives to be accounted according to (legally binding) netting sets, i.e. the single-netted dollar replacement cost amount.[2] The same netting applies to some securities financing transactions (SFTs, like repos), provided that it is mark-to-market, legally enforceable, net gain and losses allowing for collateral can give a single figure, and the non-defaulting counterparty can terminate the contract. Off-balance sheet items are included by applying their credit conversion factor (CCF).
- *A Total Loss Absorbing Capacity (TLAC) minimum for GSIBs (FSB initiated)*: of 16% of RWA by January 2019 and 18% by 2022 (and to be 6 and 6.75% of the LR denominator by those dates).[3] Total regulatory capital may be applied to TLAC (but not the regulatory buffers), and other instruments issued by the resolution entity (or group, such as a bank holding company) are then added to this and must be 'paid in'; unsecured; non-callable; not redeemable; not subject to netting; at least one year to maturity; and exclude exposures to other entities in the GSIB group. Excluded are deposits, derivative liabilities, debt with derivative links (like structured notes), tax liabilities, encumbered securities and securities where bail-in can be legally challenged.
- *An improved securitisation framework*: allowing a choice between using the IRB approach, external ratings or the standard approach (SA). The latter is based on inputs that start with the 8% capital charge that would apply had the exposure not been securitised (the underlying pool). It then makes adjustments for delinquencies, etc. See the Appendix to this Chapter for details.
- *A revised market risk (MR) framework:* which first deals with the boundary issue between banking and trading books and introduces a more risk-sensitive approach to MR. It is expected to significantly

[2]The replacement cost of the netting set is the fair value of the netted amounts minus the variation margin received plus the variation margin provided by the non-defaulting bank.

[3]For details see FSB (2015).

raise capital charges for MR. With regard to the boundary, there is now a clear list of presumptive inclusions for each book, based more clearly on intent-to-trade versus hold-to-maturity. The standardised and internal models approaches MR were revised in the final version. While more complexity is involved in calculating default exposure, these are still based around the basic idea that an exposure at default (EAD) calculation can be multiplied by 12.5 and added to RWA where the 8% capital rule will apply. See the Appendix to this Chapter for details.

- *Counterparty credit risk* (*CCR*): is incorporated into Basel III to have a capital charge for the risk of losses due to counterparties in derivative transactions defaulting before meeting all their contractual obligations on bilateral transactions. CCR exposures are calculated as a multiple of the replacement cost of the exposure (for an immediate close out) plus the potential future exposure. CCR for derivatives is calculated either by using the standardised approach (SA-CCR) or by using internal models.[4] Some of the calculations for CCR are used in the formulas for the credit valuation adjustment (CVA) discussed below. See the Appendix to this Chapter for some details on CCR.
- *A 'large exposure framework'*: is to be phased in by 2019, since the capital charge as a percentage of RWA is not designed for exposure to a single counterparty.[5] Large exposures have to be reported (above 10% of eligible capital), and there is a limit of 25% of capital to a single counterparty (or connected group), and 15% for one GSIB to another GSIB.
- *A Liquidity Coverage Ratio* (*LCR*): that requires high-quality liquid assets (HQLA) like cash and government bonds to be equal to 100% of the amount of liquidity that would be needed to cover a stressed environment for 30 days.[6]
- *A Net Stable Funding Ratio* (*NSFR*): whereby '*available*' stable funding (e.g. customer deposits) must be 100% of '*required*' stable

[4]See BCBS (2014).

[5]For derivatives and for SFT.

[6]See BCBS (2013).

funding (which is a function of the liquidity and maturity characteristics of the bank's assets).
- *Margin and Collateral Rules*: related to the Basel III process and following a G20 request, BSBS/IOSCO rules for margins and collateral (clearing requirements and the quality of assets) have been introduced. [7]

The Final Phase Basel III Reforms

The finalisation of Basel III involves six main elements:

- Enhancing the standardised approach to credit risk;
- Constraining the inputs to internal models;
- A revision to the CVA capital charge for derivatives;
- A revised method for operational risk (OR);
- A LR buffer for GSIBs; and
- Output floors when using internal models.[8]

These are considered in turn.

Changes to the Standardised Approach to Credit Risk

The changes to the standardised approach are summarised in Table 8.1. The main change to the risk weights is to make them more granular—just more of them are added on. This approach is possible due to the linearity of the portfolio invariance assumption of Basel maths set out in Chapter 2.

[7]Clearing and margin rule improvements under Dodd-Frank and European Market Infrastructure Regulation (EMIR) have helped to reduce systemic risk for broker dealers. These tend to vary between jurisdictions and have evolved: use of swap execution facilities; pre-determined minimums for initial and variation margins on un-cleared derivative transactions; the quality of collateral; trade reporting to repositories, etc.

[8]See BCBS (2017b).

Table 8.1 The finalisation of Basel III treatment of credit risk in December 2017

Risk Weights Under Basel III (Pillar 1), %

(NB: GOVERNMENT & INTERNATIONAL ORGANISATION BONDS AS BEFORE)

	BANKS					COMPANIES			PROJECT/OBJECT FINANCE (a)		
External Rating	S/Term	L/Term	Standardised	S/Term	L/Term	External	Standardised	R/W	External	Standardised	R/W
AAA to AA-	20	20	Grade A	20	40	20	Invest. Grade	75	20	Pre-operational	130
A+ to A-	20	30	Grade B	50	75	50	Non I/grade	100	50	Operational	100
BBB+ to BBB- &unrated	20	50	Grade C	150	150	75	SME	120	75	Op-High Quality	80
BB+ to B-	50	100				100			100		
Below B-	150	150				150			150		

RESIDENTIAL REAL ESTATE (b)			
LTV Band	Loan	Income Prod.	
< 50%	20	30	
50-60	25	35	
60-70	30	45	
70-80	30	45	
80-90	40	60	
90-100	50	75	
>100%	70	100	
RETAIL R/W (c)	Transactor	Revolving	Other
Non-revolving	75		
Revolving	45	75	100

COMMERCIAL REAL ESTATE		
LTV Band	R/W	R/W: Income Producing
≤ 60%	Min(60%, RW C-party)	70
> 60%	RW C-party	na
60-80	na	90
> 80		110
When NA	R/W Counterparty	150
Land Acquisition/Dev/Construct. Loan		R/W
To Company. or SPV		150
Residential only development		100

COVERED BONDS			
External Rated		Standardised	
	R/W	R/W Issuing Bank	R/W Bond
AAA to A-	10	20	10
A+ to BBB-	20	30	15
BB+ to B-	50	40	20
Below B-	100	50	25
		75	35
		100	50
		150	100

CREDIT CONVERSION FACTOR OFF-BALANCE-SHEET	CCF
Unconditional Cancellable Commitment (UCC)	10
Commitments (not UCC)	40
Note Issuance & Revolving Underwriting Facilities	50
Self Liquidating Letters of Credit	20
Direct Credit Substitutes	100

SUBORDINATED DEBT & EQUITY EXPOSURES	R/W
Subordinated Debt	150
Equity legislated prog. (d)	100
Speculat. unlisted equity	400
Equity	250

SUMMARY OF CREDIT RISK BASEL III
Make all the elements more 'granular'.
Change the treatment of mortgage risk using LTV
Add covered bonds.
Add project and object finance

Source BCBS (2017a, b). *Notes* (a) Project finance is where bank consortiums fund an infrastructure project in stages. Object finance is for a ship, a plane, satellite, etc.; (b) there are some hybrid cases—see BCBS—where loan value below 55% of the value has a 20% R/W and the rest has the R/W of the counterparty. Similarly for commercial, there is a category of the minimum of 60% or the R/W of the counterparty for loan value below 55%; (c) non-revolving is essentially instalments; and revolving is where there is discretion for the borrower to draw down as a source of credit, like a credit card, overdraft and charge cards. The low 45% R/W applies if the card has been fully paid at each date for at least a year; (d) legislated sector for loans with government support to a sector of the economy

- For exposure to other banks where external rating is allowed, there is little change to Basel II, but more granularity is introduced for the stand-alone approach circled. For the standardised approach, categories A, B and C are based on due diligence by the lender. Category A means the bank borrower has adequate capacity to meet its commitments; B means its capacity is reasonable if things go well; and C refers to material default risk in an adverse scenario. Rated and stand-alone risk weights are introduced for bank covered bond holdings (see middle right of Table 8.1).
- For exposures to companies, shown in the top panel, similar comments apply, and rated and stand-alone categories are introduced for project and object finance. Investment grade can be supported by enhancement from credit default swaps (CDS) and total return swaps.
- A major change concerns exposure to real estate, which now (sensibly) are based on loan-to-value percentage bands. This applies to both residential and commercial real estate, and a distinction is made for borrowing for income-producing (investment) properties which have a higher risk weight.
- Retail lending exposures make a distinction between whether the credit is to cover a specific transaction or to act as a source of credit (and repayment history becomes a factor for the lowest risk weight).
- Off-balance sheet exposure CCFs for risk-sensitive categories are specified, shown in the bottom panel (left).
- Subordinated debt and equity exposures of banks are specified in a more granular way (also shown in the bottom panel).

While a lot of work has gone into all of this, the criticisms of Basel II set out in earlier chapters still apply. With the portfolio invariance assumption, there is an endless possibility for best-guess risk weights to be added to ever more granular categories. But it is impossible to fix timeless risk weights on asset classes. The very act of doing this becomes an input into the dynamic process of financial innovation to shift exposures and alter the riskiness of securities with derivatives and other instruments.

It must be recalled that the BCBS had confidence in their methods to announce Basel II, which turned out to be a fiasco. Banks will continue to optimise any risk weights up to the true limits provided by a simple

LR in order to minimise their capital costs and maximise their ROEs. With a LR, provided it is strict enough, there is no need for the costly pretence that risks can be assigned values by civil servants. Banks have an internal capital allocation process, and they have always looked at risk models to assess the risks to the use of their own capital. Banks use models to determine these allocations according to risk and return estimates, and they are probably best at doing this—provided that process is not corrupted by making these outputs the basis of regulatory capital minimums. Risk assessment in this way is an internal process and that is where it should stay. Civil servant attempts to fix risk weights should have been stopped after 2008.

Restrictions on the Use of Bank Models

Earlier chapters of this book have summarised the severe criticisms levelled at the BCBS for allowing banks to use their models for regulatory capital charges. So it is to be welcomed ten years on that the BCBS has accepted that banks' use of their models will result in very uneven capital weights between similar banks. But instead of getting rid of this methodology, the BCBS has become more prescriptive.

Banks use models to estimate the probability of default (PD) for an exposure, the loss given default (LGD), EAD and sometimes the effective maturity of exposures. These plug into the Basel formulas for capital rules (typically based on 12.5 times a default exposure that then is added to RWA). Under the final Basel III, the advanced IRB approach will not be used for banks' exposures to (other) banks and financial institutions, nor will it be used for large and mid-size companies. Exposures to these entities are now regarded as too difficult for banks to model, and LGD and EAD outputs were seen as important sources of variation among bank outputs. Instead, the foundation IRB approach (F-IRB) will be used for these exposures. This allows banks to continue to estimate the PD (with a floor and based on improved referencing to past default experiences), but BCBS-determined parameters will be used for LGD and EAD in determining risk weights. For equities, the SA is to be used. For specialised lending, the advanced IRB is allowed to be used alongside the F-IRB and the SA.

The advanced IRB will still be able to be used where robust estimation is regarded as more likely (mortgages, retail, etc.). In all cases, input floors to parameters for the PD (in basis points), the LGD ranges and EAD (on- and off-balance sheet weightings) will apply. This is intended to encourage more conservative outputs. There is also more prescriptiveness in the parameter estimates including LGD parameters for the advanced approach.[9] Given these changes, banks negotiated the removal of the 1.06 scaling factor for RWA intended to make up for variability in outcomes for credit risk discussed in Chapter 2 (see Eq. 2.1).

In short, the banks have defended the use of models in the capital rules quite well. The PD is still a key variable even for the F-IRB, since the risk weight depends upon it, the IRB approaches still apply for many exposure calculations, and the 1.06 scale factor is gone.[10] Nevertheless, to the extent that new constraints do reduce variability between banks for risk weightings, it is to be welcomed. Banks that are not to use the IRB methods will use the weights in Table 8.1.

This final determination on the use of models, in the opinion of the present authors, does not remove the bulk of earlier criticisms, and the onus still remains for the LR to shoulder the main burden of making banks safer.

The Credit Valuation Adjustment for Derivative Counterparty Exposures

Credit Valuation Adjustment (CVA) risk refers to potential mark-to-market losses that arise due to the deterioration in the creditworthiness of a counterparty in response to credit spreads and MR factors that drive prices of derivative transactions (not conducted with a central counterparty) and SFT (like repos) that are reported at fair value for accounting purposes. The BCBS estimated that 2/3 of the counterparty-related losses in the crisis were due to CVAs and only 1/3 to actual defaults.

[9]And new metrics for haircuts apply where collateral is involved.

[10]The RWA is equal to 12.5*[EAD*Estimated Capital Required]. But the estimated capital requirement depends on a complex formula that includes the estimated PD.

In the final version, the BCBS now believes that CVA risk is too complex, and: '*Accordingly, the Committee is of the view that such a risk cannot be modelled by banks in a robust and prudent manner*' (BCBS 2017a, p. 7). While one might say '*hallelujah*' to that, it is not clear that the final version provides a lot of comforts. Two approaches are proposed for banks above a certain threshold: (i) a standard CVA approach (SA-CVA) and (ii) a basic approach (BA-CVA). Banks need to be approved by supervisors to use the SA-CVA, and otherwise must use BA-CVA. Any banks whose notional aggregate exposure to derivatives is less than €100bn can count CVA risk as a simple multiple of their CCR. For consistency with the approach to MR, the CVA risk is based on fair value sensitivities to MR factors. Sensibly, any eligible hedges used to offset CVA risk must be excluded from benefit in the MR capital charge calculation.

There is a simple option for less sophisticated banks (that don't hedge CVA risk via a CVA desk) known as the 'reduced' or 'stand-alone' version. This approach doesn't recognise hedging and is based on netting sets for each of the bank's counterparties. Prescribed risk weights are based on the credit quality of the counterparty. The capital requirement for a counterparty exposure is a simple calculation of the risk weight for the counterparty multiplied by the sum across all netting sets with that counterparty of exposure amounts.[11] These capital requirements are then added up across the counterparties according to a BCBS formula.

The full basic approach gives a 25% weight to the above 'reduced version' calculation and a 75% weight to capital requirements that are for hedged CVA risk. The latter is calculated like the reduced or stand-alone approach, but gives recognition to the use of single-name hedges and index hedges with correlation factors.[12] However, hedging can't take the

[11]Exposure amounts are by netting set: the effective maturity, times the EAD, times a Supervisory Discount Factor.

[12]For example, a bank like Goldman Sachs might hedge its exposure to AIG CDS insurance of its structured mortgage products by buying a calibrated CDS on AIG itself, as a single-name hedge, or (with less precision) it could buy a put on the insurance sector index. Single-name hedge offsets to CVA have their own supervisory-determined correlation between the credit spread of the counterparty versus that of the hedge name; their own risk weight; their notional amount; and a supervisor discount factor. Similar thinking goes into index hedges.

capital charge to zero, as a misalignment factor for the uncorrelated or idiosyncratic part is included to avoid this.

To be able to use SA-CVA, the bank must have an independent risk unit, a CVA desk, a modelling capacity to calculate CVA exposure, and it must do so at least once a month. A CVA desk is responsible for implementing hedges for CVA risk. Bank trading desks take positions, and these can be hedged with internal or external counterparties. Internal hedges are exactly offsetting positions (opposite between CVA and trading desks). There are six types of risks covered: interest rate; foreign exchange; counterparty credit spread; credit spread of the reference security (that drives the derivative exposure); equity; and commodity. SA-CVA is then the sum of all the capital charges for sensitivity risks ('*delta*' and '*vega*') calculated for the entire CVA portfolio and including all of the eligible hedges. These are essentially simulations based on inputs from the sensitivity calculations. Like the other parts of the Basel framework, these are based on PD, expected LGD and simulated future exposures to counterparties. Included are the effects of collateral and illiquid counterparties that are accounted at fair value. Audit processes and databases are mandated and are intended to improve robustness. Banks have the right to choose to '*carve out*' any number of netting sets from the SA-CVA approach and treat these via the basic approach (presumably if it is to their advantage to do so).

The calculations use a methodology consistent with that for MR. First, *delta* and *vega* sensitivities are calculated for each risk type (for the position and hedges). These are essentially marginal change coefficients. Weighted sensitivities are then obtained by multiplying the calculated sensitivities by its prescribed risk weight. Net sensitivity is obtained by adding that for the CVA and the hedges. Then for each bucket of risk-weighted sensitivities are aggregated using prescribed correlations. Thus, for the interest rate risk factor *delta* and *vega* sensitivities are calculated for the buckets consisting of the bank's domestic currency and seven major currencies which tag the securities concerned. The risk factors are the absolute change in inflation and remaining periods to maturity for the instruments (referred to as 'tenors' in the BCBS publications). For equities, the buckets might be size, region and sector tags, and so on. The sensitivities are the CVA response to a tiny change in the risk factor. Bucket-level risk charges for this and the other risk factors are then aggregated using prescribed correlation factors.

Operational Risk

Operational Risk (OR) was also a source of loss in the crisis, and the BCBS has included a streamlined approach to deal with this. It works like this: OR is a function of (i) a business income components (BICs) (net interest, dividends and lease income; fee income; trading book income; and banking book income from fair value through profit or loss accounting) and (ii) a loss component (LC). Bigger income is assumed to imply a more complex business. Three buckets of risk are set: for €1bn; greater than €1bn but less than or equal to €30bn; and greater than €30bn. Marginal coefficients for these groups are set at 0.12, 0.15 and 0.18, respectively. The BIC is the sum of the business income segments multiplied by their respective coefficients depending on size. The LC is 15 times the average loss over the past 10 years. An Internal Loss Multiplier (ILM) is then an increasing function of LC/BIC. OR is then set equal to ILM*BIC.

This is not worth much time criticising. Suffice it to say OR is idiosyncratic. It depends on boards, bank culture and due diligence. Big losses also stimulate improvements in these latter items. The Basel concept of OR cannot be thought of as a useful measure of risk.

The Leverage Ratio

The LR is one of the centrepieces of what makes a banking system safer—as prior chapters of this book have tried to make clear. For Basel III, the LR is Tier 1 Capital divided by an exposure measure (not total assets as it is often defined in this book). The final version of Basel III leaves the permitted ratio at 3% for non-GSIB banks and introduces a LR buffer for GSIBs set at 50% of their risk-weighted Higher Loss Absorbing Requirement (HLAR). The final capital rules for the RWA concept and the LR are summarised in Fig. 8.1.

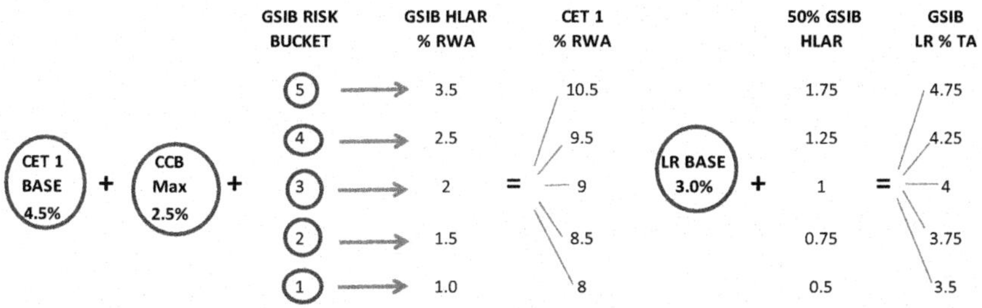

Fig. 8.1 GSIB capital requirements at full implementation (*Source* Authors' representation, BCBS)

When these capital requirements are not met, either for CET-1 or for the LR, they are to be subject to distribution restrictions as a percentage of bank earnings.

The exposure measure is modified in the final version. One can only imagine the amount of lobbying involved in deciding on this. After the usual deductions (e.g. deductions from the Tier 1 numerator are also deducted from the exposure denominator), it is left up to supervisors as to whether something needs to be done if they notice derivative transactions that move assets off-balance sheet, use of agencies to transact in derivatives and repos in ways that mitigate or remove them from inclusion in the exposure measure, and so on. Clearly, a less-inclusive denominator makes the LR look better, i.e. higher. Some of the things supervisors can 'do' in these cases seem derisory in the light of the discussion in previous chapters: that is, that the solution is that there could be more supervisor oversight and (at worst) a second pillar capital charge for the transaction might be imposed by said supervisors (see BCBS 2017b, p. 144). Supervisor worries about de-leveraging can also make adjustments the other way (to be less strict). Similarly, central bank reserves can be excluded from the exposure measure in periods of macroeconomic need.

Derivatives are included at replacement cost at the netting set level (netting out offsetting trades subject to 'novation' and which are legally enforceable) less any cash variation margins received plus those that are paid. An allowance is made for potential future exposure (calculated as for CCR). Securities financing are not subject to netting. Off-balance sheet exposures are included (where control is present) multiplied by the CCFs (see Table 8.1). The netting set issue is discussed in the assessment of Basel III below.

Output Floors

The present authors pointed out that a LR and a risk-based capital rule would not sit well together—that the LR minimum would essentially become a maximum to the capital that banks would hold, since risk weights could be managed to ensure that no more capital than necessary was held: '*This process will likely be very distortionary, as it has been in the past, pushing banks towards lower-weighted assets and shifting promises outside the banking system – with the risks of creating new bubbles and/or unintended shadow banking developments* via *the regulatory arbitrage process*'.[13]

The BCBS finally agreed to place a limit on regulatory capital benefits arising from the use of internal models versus that which would apply from the standardised approach of Table 8.1. This was perhaps one of the most hard-fought battles in the process with EU GSIB banks and policy makers holding out to make sure it was not too onerous. In 2016, the Vice President of the European Commission in charge of financial stability stated in relation to this proposal: '*As things stand, the proposals Basel has issued for consultation ……. (latest data) …. shows it undermines risk sensitivity and could lead to significant capital requirement increases. We want a solution that works for Europe and does not put our banks at a disadvantage compared to our global competitors*'.[14] As good a '*coming clean*' as one might ever hope to hear from a policy maker in Europe.

The final revision is as follows: in meeting all of the above capital requirements, the RWA must be calculated as the higher of: (i) the

[13]Blundell-Wignall et al. (2010, p. 17).

[14]See Dombrovskis (2016). The European Banking Federation republished the speech under its own banner.

approach banks are approved to use, and (ii) 72.5% of the RWA calculated by standardised approaches as set out above (e.g. for credit risk, as set out in Table 8.1). Credit risk, CCR, the CVA charge, MR and OR are all included in this rule.

To put this into perspective, the reader is asked to go all the way back to Table 2.1, which set out the Basel II regulatory benefit for risk weights achieved by using models (the IRB approach) based on the quantitative impact study at the time. Under the final revisions of 2017, banks (notably GSIBs) can achieve a 27.5% cut in RWA by using their models compared to the SA for all categories. The average percent cuts for RWA in Table 2.1 for Basel II were: 21.9% for banks and financial firms; 61% for residential mortgages; 6.5 to 74.3% for retail (depending on component); and 21.9 to 41.4% for corporates and commercial real estate (depending on component). These unrestricted model benefits of Basel II have been impinged upon: for example, models can't be used for exposures to other banks, and the 61% relief for mortgages is reduced. But then again, the SA in Table 8.1 for banks is similar to Basel II, and for mortgages LTV ratios have to get up near 90% before the old 35% weight is surpassed. In other asset classes, the new floor seems to sit within the ranges that could be achieved with Basel II. In short, this is no revolution, and the banks should be reasonably well pleased (despite all the private sector outcries about a 'Basel IV' during the process).

Assessment of the Revised Basel III

The fundamental problems with the Basel methodology were set out in the Appendix to Chapter 2. The current version of Basel as it stands in early 2018 does not address these:

- *Portfolio invariance*: that idiosyncratic risk can be identified, separated out, modelled and risk weighted to calculate capital charges that can simply be added up to derive sensible capital requirements without regard to a portfolio's composition.

- *Single global risk driver*: that Basel is applied across all jurisdictions for all banks and has nothing to do with clustering of risk in given jurisdictions.
- *Treatment of financial promises in the same way*: so that banks can at their discretion shift risk between institutions within and outside of banking to mitigate capital requirements.
- *Subjective inputs*: notwithstanding the Basel III attempts to impose floors on parameters and to restrict model use, much discretion remains and the constraints on model output are not very tight.

Repeated efforts to deal with past failures of the Basel methodology by introducing more granularity and imposing model restrictions reflect, in a sense, an implicit recognition of big methodological problems. But not once, since 1988 has the BCBS questioned that methodology; where problems have emerged, they have been attributed to insufficient granularity in the framework's coverage, formulas and models.

A fundamental philosophy of this book is that pricing risk without implicit subsidies is the best way to encourage prudent bank behaviour. At the same time, owners of deposit-taking institutions must be made to face the negative consequences of their own mistakes so that they fully factor the risks into their decision-making. Trying to work out how much 'rainy day' capital banks need to cover possible losses by a formula on the basis of model-based stress scenarios is bound to fail—particularly when large banks and their creditors know they will always be saved in a crisis. As soon as models of any kind are used to determine capital requirements in the standard or IRB approaches, they are contaminated and subject to dynamic influences as banks manipulate them to maximise the return on equity. Banks know their businesses better than regulators, and they are incentivised to mismanage risks when management and shareholders enjoy unlimited exposure to the upside while they are insulated from the downside. Banks achieve this by maximising leverage so that they are working as much as possible with someone else's money while keeping TBTF structures in place to reassure the markets that a safety net is in place for lenders to the bank.

The most prudent approach is to separate investment banking from deposit banking in excessively complex banks, especially those with large derivative operations. Deposits should be insured, to encourage stability if confidence is threatened, and deposit banks should hold enough equity to provide significant loss-absorptive capacity to insulate counterparties without necessitating government financial support. The authors of this book suggest that a LR of CET-1 capital to total consolidated assets (based on IFRS standards) of at least 6% should be maintained to cover loan losses.

The separated smaller investment banks should have no explicit state guarantee. Withdrawing the implicit guarantee remains a challenge, but for banks with no deposit liabilities the threat to allow such failure should be credible. Still, such institutions should also adhere to leverage limits both to ensure some exposure of their own capital to the MRs they incur and to cover risks that cannot be modelled (including fraud, cyber risk, legal penalties, ORs and the like). This will expose investment banks to effective market discipline. Since counterparties will bear the full brunt of inappropriate collateral and variation margin transfers (i.e. because it would be credible that state bailouts will be absent), pricing will fully reflect risk. Like deposit banks, the investment banks will of course run their own risk models—as they always have—but this process will not be contaminated by making internal capital allocation assessments the focal point of capital regulations.

This type of fundamental reform has been left out of consideration during the Basel III process and avoided because banks don't want it. Subsidies are good for profits—and policy makers in Europe have been easier to convince than those in the USA (see Box 8.1) due to issues about the economy; in particular, structural differences with the USA; and the relative weakness of the European economy.

Structural Differences Across Economies That Lead to Regulatory Competition

Bank finance has been dominant throughout the post-war period in financing the economy in continental Europe and Japan, while capital markets have played a greater role in Anglo-Saxon countries. This means that a one-size-fits-all approach to regulation like Basel III will not be able to satisfy policy makers in any jurisdiction and will always be pushed towards the lowest common denominator. The same rule might be perceived to penalise banks and the economy too much in a bank-dominated region like Europe, compared to the USA where capital markets play a larger role in funding companies. Regional competitiveness begins to creep into decision-making. The parallel writing of the Basel rules and additional regulatory measures in individual jurisdictions make for significant differences.[15] Thus, for example, the USA has moved much more strongly on capital rules than has Europe, see Box 8.1.[16] Bank business model separation of risky activities has been implemented in some form in the USA and the UK, but this has been resisted in continental Europe.

Box 8.1: US Regulatory Features That Are Tougher Than Basel

In parallel with the Basel III reform process, and perhaps reflecting different interpretations of the gravity of the events of 2007–2008 and frustration with the delays and bickering over Basel III proposals, the USA pushed ahead with its own stricter reform process with the Dodd-Frank Act. Importantly, this eliminated trust-preferred securities from Tier I capital and included the Volcker rule relating to separation. Its Collins Amendment ensures that capital rules are tougher than those agreed at Basel. The Dodd-Frank Act has many more features which diverge from the less-strict Basel rules. This chapter does not attempt to go through the details of Dodd-Frank, but some of key features which go beyond things contained in Basel III (and in addition to the Volcker rule) include *inter alia*:

- The creation of the Financial Stability Oversight Council (FSOC) to coordinate between the US regulators (the Federal Reserve, FDIC, Comptroller of the Currency) and with a special focus on large interconnected financial institutions.

[15]These include leverage reforms in the USA, rule writing under the Dodd-Frank Act and the continuing amendments to the European Union's CRD IV (Capital Requirements Directive for Prudential Supervision) and capital requirements regulation (CRR).

[16]A buffer of 2% versus the Basel leverage ratio of only 3%—for bank holding companies (BHCs) with $700bn of assets or $10tn under custody. This must be a 6% LR for insured depository institutions (IDIs) within the group. These rules will be effective from 1 January 2018. Smaller foreign IHCs will have to undergo stress testing if consolidated assets are $10bn.

- The creation of an independent Consumer Financial Protection Bureau (CFPB) which provides education and deals with complaints and investigates illegal practices.
- Banks with consolidated assets above \$50bn are to be subject to enhanced prudential standards (much of these Basel-related as regards capital and liquidity). Foreign bank organisations (FBOs) in the USA with US assets above the \$50bn threshold must form an intermediate holding company (IHC)[17] which must adhere to the tougher US regulations.[18] IHCs had to be established by 1 July 2016. BHCs and FBOs with consolidated assets greater than \$10bn have to form risk committees.[19]
- BHCs, IHCs and financial institutions designated for supervision by the Federal Reserve with consolidated assets of \$50bn (or more) must submit a 'living will'. These are to set out clear resolution plans in the event of default.
- The Collins Amendment (section 171) establishes minimum risk-based capital and LRs for BHCs, insured depository institutions (DIs) and non-bank financial holding companies designated by FSOC for supervision by the Federal Reserve. These ratios cannot be less than those in effect for DIs at the July 2010 enactment of Dodd-Frank. The upshot of Basel III with rulemaking consistent with Dodd-Frank was the introduction of an Enhanced Supplementary Leverage Ratio (ESLR)—a buffer of 2% versus the Basel leverage ratio of only 3% (which was judged by the US agencies to be insufficient for an event such as that in 2007–2008) for BHCs with \$700bn of assets or \$10tn under custody. This must be a 6% ratio for insured DIs within the group (including off-balance sheet exposures). These rules became effective as of 1 January 2018.
- Annual stress testing by the Federal Reserve is required for BHCs and IHCs with consolidated assets of \$250bn under the Comprehensive Capital Analysis and Review (CCAR) rules.[20] The BHC/IHC must show not only that it meets minimum standards but that it has a capital plan to deal with its own unique risks in a stressed environment scenario: thereby adding a qualitative element to the review.
- Dodd-Frank Act Stress Tests (DFASTs) apply to state non-member banks and savings and loans. These have to submit a bank-run stress test (separate from CCAR) if they have assets above \$10bn, with the FDIC providing the scenarios for the test.[21]

---

[17]Smaller foreign IHCs will have to undergo stress testing if consolidated assets are \$10bn. The European Union established a similar rule at €30bn.

[18]For any two or more institutions owned by a non-EU parent with assets of branches and/or subsidiaries greater than EUR30bn.

[19]See also Federal Reserve (2012).

[20]See Federal Reserve (2013).

[21]There is a slightly faster cycle for publishing the result if banks have over \$50bn in consolidated assets.

These US rules are tougher than the Basel minima. Europe, more prone to the influence of its 'national champion universal banks', has stuck closer to the Basel script and (as noted in Chapter 6) has quietly dropped any effort to separate investment banks from deposit banks.

However, the Dodd-Frank Act has been reviewed by the US Treasury (see Mnuchin et al. 2017), and a number of reforms are proposed: more coordination amongst regulators; a greater role for Treasury (particularly with respect to the assumptions for CCAR scenarios); a 2-year cycle for CCAR; increasing the threshold for DFASTs from $10 to $50bn; to exempt any bank with a 10% LR from the need to comply with the Act at all; a LCR for internationally active banks only; the Basel single counterparty credit limit to apply only to banks selected for enhanced prudential standards; the Basel NSFR to be delayed for further research; greater budget control over the CFPB and reduced independence for its director; living wills needed only for those banks above the threshold for enhanced supervision (and only every two years); and to enhance liquidity in the financial system by excluding cash on deposit with the Fed, Treasury securities and initial margins for centrally cleared derivatives from the exposure measure for the ESLR. These reforms are aimed at better coordination of regulation, reduced costs for smaller banks and improved liquidity. Many of these make sense (in contrast to Treasury's views of the Volcker rule discussed in Chapter 7).

Sequencing of Policies in Europe

Another problem pushing regulation outcomes to the lowest common denominator is the sequencing of policy since the crisis. As pointed out in earlier chapters, in response to a crisis policy makers need to deal with non-performing loans (NPLs) early. The USA more or less followed this sequence while Europe did not.[22] NPLs are shown in Fig. 8.2.[23] US NPLs peaked in 2010 at 4% and subsequently have

[22]This is sometimes put down to Brussels State Aid laws (the use of public funds) relating to competition policy in Europe, which is a complicating factor for a Bad Bank of any meaningful size.

[23]All charts are based on a global sample of publicly traded and non-listed commercial banks over the 2008–2016 period. If no data were available for 2016, then 2015 data are used. The sample consists of 1845 commercial banks (302 in Europe, 116 in Japan, 15 in Australia, 91 in Latin America, 281 in Asia and 1040 in the USA). This analysis is based on annual consolidated financial statements extracted from SNL Financials and Bloomberg.

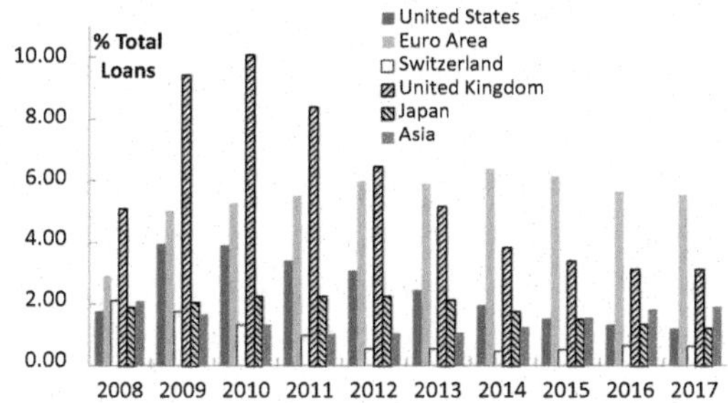

Fig. 8.2 Non-performing loans by region (*Source* Bloomberg)

fallen in every year to around 1.5% in 2016 (about the same level as for Japan). In contrast, European NPLs were around 5% in 2010 and have risen on average to 6.5% in 2016, with considerable country diversity (well into the double digits in the south of Europe). While it is true that a lot of bad mortgage securities sit within the Fannie and Freddie '*conservatorship*' and are guaranteed and dealt with by the government, this is a policy choice. They are separated from the rest of the system. It is the ultimate form of a '*Bad Bank*' that Europe desperately needs.

The failure of Europe to deal with its NPL problem means that this bank-dominated economic region (without the capital markets depth of the USA) contributes to economic weakness which in turn reinforces the NPL build-up and increases resistance to proper regulatory reform. Because Basel is a global process, European resistance to reform pushes that process to the lowest common denominator—and helps explain why the USA has gone further than Basel III.

Leverage Ratios: The Equity and Netting Issues

Two issues relating to LR measures are critical: the numerator of the ratio, designed to measure loss-absorptive capital capacity, and the denominator, designed to measure exposure to loss. With respect to absorptive capacity, only equity net of certain deductions such as goodwill, deferred tax asset, etc., is available to absorb losses. Accordingly, the main Basel regulatory ratios use CET-1 capital and add extra buffers for GSIBs to measure absorptive capacity. But for the LR, the Basel rules use the broader Tier 1 capital in the numerator. This includes preferred equities and CoCos which make it easier to respect the leverage limit. But contingent capital does not add *'going-concern'* loss-absorption capacity in a useful way as it requires trigger points (e.g. a capital ratio, a credit spread or regulatory discretion on these). This adds to undesirable dynamics. The interests of management and shareholders are not aligned with those of hybrid security holders. The holders of equity don't want to be diluted and may undertake fire-sale selling of assets to avoid conversion of debt into equity.

With regard to exposure, the netting of gross derivative positions vis-à-vis each counterparty bilaterally understates true exposures, in important cases by large amounts. Netting simplifies procedures in the event of an actual default: where a bank is \$50 million down on a CDS and \$60 million up on an interest rate swap vis-à-vis the same counterparty and the seniority of these claims is the same, then the most the bank could lose in a close out is \$10 million. This compares to the \$60 potential loss in the absence of netting. These procedures make sense for *ex post* close outs and, provided they are permitted under the contractual arrangements, reduce exposures to counterparty risk. But they do nothing for MR since the GMV of each contract can change if the state of the world changes, as it always will. An *ex ante* preventive philosophy which acknowledges these risks makes more sense for regulation purposes. Use of such netting to measure exposure for the LR (also for CRR and CVA risks charges) understates exposures and does not sit well with an *ex ante* approach to regulation.[24]

Consider the simplified picture in Fig. 8.3.[25] Netting exposures for set of assets and liabilities by counterparty reduce exposure and reward a movement away from diversification benefits. On the left side of Fig. 8.3, Bank A has multiple counterparties (two here for simplicity) and the gain/loss exposures are shown. The CVA is additive and in the diverse counterparties case results in a positive capital charge related to

[24]See Blundell-Wignall, Atkinson, in collaboration with Eddins (2011).

[25]This example is drawn from Blundell-Wignall and Atkinson (2015).

A. Diverse Counterparties	
P1: Netting Set 1	
IRS up	100
CDS down	-90
Net	**10**
P2: Netting Set 2	
IRS up	90
CDS down	-100
Net	**-10**

B. Concentration Case	
One netting Set	
IRS up	100
CDS down	-90
IRS up	90
CDS down	-100
Net	**0**

Fig. 8.3 Netting set example (*Source* Authors)

the \$10m positive exposure. On the right side is the case of only one large netting set, where the previous positions together now net out to zero. Bank B has no exposure to derivatives necessitating a CVA charge at all.[26]

The larger the netting set the more scope there is for offsets and relief to capital, so the incentive is to reinforce concentration in GSIBs: to use only other very large TBTF banks that deal in derivatives to make the netting set as large as possible. That is, it will reinforce the trends towards the (already) highly oligopolistic derivative markets. Risk is increased, because diversification is reduced while capital to absorb unexpected large losses in a crisis is minimised. TBTF is incentivised to get worse.

Some examples illustrate the potential enormity of netting. In 2010, Bank of America had \$1519bn in gross derivative assets, but with counterparty netting of \$1406bn, and allowance for cash collateral, this reduces to only \$73bn. JP Morgan Chase had \$1529bn that nets to \$80bn. Citigroup had \$654bn that nets to \$50bn. In 2008, EUR1224.5bn in gross derivatives at Deutsche Bank netted to EUR104.1bn. Banks did not try to lose money in the crisis, but a huge amount of the losses were related to counterparty CVA risk despite netting and a belief that they were not exposed to the extent they were.

[26]Presumably, if there were only 2 counterparties for the large universe of all derivatives, the banks could expand gross derivative assets towards infinity with no risk charge at all.

Netting makes an enormous difference to *ex ante* LRs and consequent capital requirements if they are to suffice to prevent crises.

The impact of the differing concepts on the various leverage constructs can be seen in the following illustrations. The LR here is defined using IFRS accounting rules, which only allow netting on a very restricted basis, in the denominator, and CET-1 is used to measure loss absorbing capital in the numerator. Comparisons by region are shown first, and then the case for GSIBs in 2017 is presented.

Leverage by Region

Weighted averages of the two ratios are shown by region in Fig. 8.4. All series use CET-1 to measure loss-absorptive capital. Ratios using RWA to measure exposure (according to the phase of Basel I, II and III reform prevailing at the time) are shown with solid lines towards the top of the graph. The LR, calculated with no netting of derivative positions in the exposure measure, is shown towards the bottom (with matching broken lines). Banks on average have managed to keep regulatory ratios

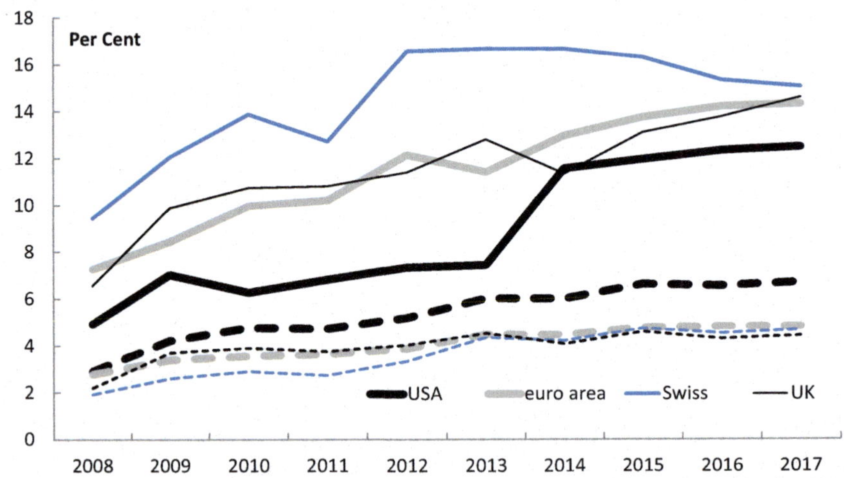

Fig. 8.4 Basel CET-1/RWA (solid line) v simple leverage ratio (based on bank total assets shown in matching dotted line) (*Source* SNL, authors)

based on risk-weighting well above even the current Basel III minima in recent years. The upward trend is remarkable. However, this has not translated into a matching trend for the simple LR, though the USA looks better than Europe.

To put this in some perspective, the average level of NPLs for Europe was 6.5% (and much higher in southern countries), yet European banks on average have LRs that barely exceed 4%. This comes back to one of the themes in this book: if banks are able to manipulate risk weights that determine the denominator of the ratio, there is no effective leverage constraint. Leverage is a key mechanism for bank profits, and banks have worked hard to keep regulators as far away from this variable as possible. The output floors in the final Basel III rules recognise this problem, but as noted earlier they are not that challenging. Banks have done well in defending their patch in the final Basel III.

Leverage by GSIBs

All GSIBs already meet all of the Basel III requirements versus RWA, without exception. In contrast to this, Fig. 8.5 shows the simple LR of CET-1 capital to total assets based on IFRS (with no netting of derivatives). The left column for each numbered bank refers to the 2008–2010 average and the right column to the 2017 level. All GSIBs have improved compared to the earlier period. However, most of the GSIBs do not meet this book's recommendation of a 6% minimum LR based on the IFRS no netting definition.[27] Four US banks are close to the recommendation. No GSIB from the euro area, the UK, Switzerland, Sweden or Japan are above 6%. Three of the four GSIBs in China are above the 6%.

This capital shortage in risky institutions remains a significant concern from a financial stability perspective. As Thomas Hoenig (2016) points out, US bank losses and the Troubled Assets Relief Program together summed to be 6% of total assets of the US banks concerned

[27]This definition would require higher minima to meet official minimums where netting is allowed.

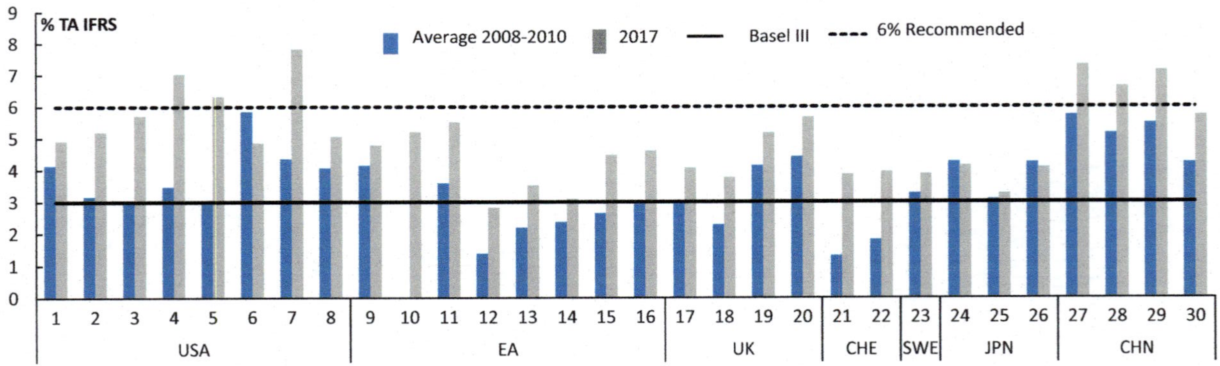

Fig. 8.5 The leverage ratio core Tier 1/(Total IFRS Assets) GSIBs 2008–2010, and 2017 (*Source* Bloomberg. *Note* USA: United States; EA: euro area; UK: United Kingdom; CHE: Switzerland; SWE: Sweden; JPN: Japan; CHN: China)

(Hoenig 2016). Since such an outcome actually happened in the recent past, the suggested 6% rule should be a minimum.

The Derivatives Threshold and the Need to Separate Excessively Complex Banks

Derivatives (gross market value) beyond a certain threshold are the best gauge of the sort of business model a bank has—i.e. on which side of Fig. 7.1 it sits with the threshold of around 10% recommended in this book. Not all GSIBs would need to be separated by this criterion (e.g. Wells Fargo, a profitable and very large bank, sits well below 10% on a gross basis before netting).

Figure 8.6 shows the gross market value (GMV) of derivatives by region, as a weighted average of the banks included. Switzerland, dominated by two large banks, has seen its banks' derivatives share reduced from an average of over 40% to a still very high 20%. Currently, the USA has the largest average derivative intensity (even with national banks with little derivative businesses included). The UK (with the city of London) is very large, and other Europe also plays a significant role (appearing lower than the other investment banking countries on an average basis due to the large role of traditional banking in funding

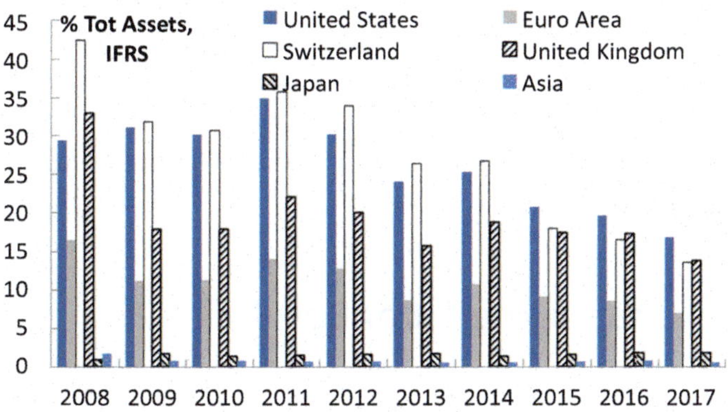

Fig. 8.6 Banking derivatives by regions (weighted averages) (*Source* Thomson Reuters, SNL, authors)

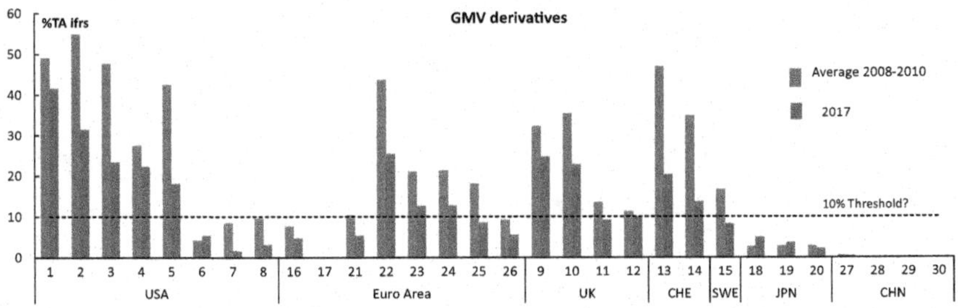

Fig. 8.7 Derivatives as a share of total assets by GSIBs (*Source* Bank reports, authors)

the economy). The banks of Asian countries do not play a large role on average in investment banking—Australia being relatively high amongst them. There is nothing wrong with high derivative intensity in investment banks, provided they are separated from deposit banking and implicit subsidies; the problem is that this is not the case.

Derivative Intensity by GSIBs

The break between above and below the 10% threshold in the US GSIBs is very clear. Three GSIBs are well below 10% threshold, and this was true even looking at the 2008–2010 average (Fig. 8.7). Five US GSIBs are well over the 10% threshold. These banks need investment and deposit banking to be separated. In the euro area, four of the GSIBs should be separated. In the UK, two GSIBs are well above 10% and the other two are on the borderline for separation. The two Swiss GSIBs should be separated based on the 10% threshold and one in Sweden is on the borderline.

Conclusions on the Final Basel III

A lot has been done since the global crisis to make the banking system safer. The greater focus on CET-1 (quality) capital is to be welcomed. However, the central place given to RWA has always been the weakest aspect of the regulatory toolbox. It gives scope for banks to minimise the impact of regulation on actual leverage. Bank lobbying and the economic aftermath of the crisis (particularly in Europe) have combined to keep regulatory intrusion under the Basel framework as a one-size-fits-all lowest common denominator. The USA chose to take a tougher line.

Leverage and the related size of derivative exposures (on which fees are based) are an important influence on GSIB revenue. Derivatives are also an important part of shifting exposures and transforming risk to minimise risk weights.

Losses can come from many sources: credit defaults; counterparty defaults, fair value asset valuation shifts as credit quality moves; mismatches between assets and their funding; illiquidity; fraud; cyber-attacks or failures; operational failure; disruptive innovations; legal penalties for money laundering; warehousing of unsold securities; and more. These cannot be modelled and predicted. The reality is that in trending '*goldilocks*' market banks don't need much capital, and losses seem far away. But when something happens and a crisis emerges, models, correlations and normal distribution-based risk metrics are useless.

Regulation of banking needs to encourage *ex ante* incentives that work to reduce risk. For this purpose, pricing risk is more effective than quantities linked to some sort of modelled loss possibility prediction based on crudely calibrated metrics. It is important to separate banks that are heavily involved in investment banking and to impose an adequate simple LR on all banks. Risks need to be priced without the distortion of subsidies from deposit insurance and other guarantees, and capital needs to be held to cover losses that can't be predicted. Derivative exposures need to be taken fully into account.

Banks have always allocated their capital with an internal assessment of risk and used quantitative tools to do so. Banks don't need regulators to tell them to do this. A fundamental mistake in the approach to regulation has been to contaminate risk management tools by linking them to capital charges. Banks know their businesses better than regulators, but they will always mismanage risks when prices are distorted. The greatest business model possible is to leverage up the reward for risk-taking supported subsidies and guarantees.

Appendix to Chapter 8: Technical Details of Revisions to Securitisation, Market Risk and Counterparty Credit Risk Capital Charge Frameworks

Revision to the Securitisation Framework

Securitisation (discussed in Chapter 2) was perhaps one of the most important drivers of the crisis. Securitisation involves many players that ultimately generate investable instruments based on underlying pools of assets (that can be held on balance sheet or structured as liabilities of SPVs in senior, mezzanine and equity tranches with external credit ratings). The role of credit rating agencies in this process was very problematic (see Chapter 4). Banks can be originators of securitisations and/or investors in the liabilities. Regulatory treatment of off-balance sheet vehicles depends on the degree of control over the SPV. Where there is some control relationship, the revised rules try to reduce the role of external ratings—which is only partially achieved.

The new framework introduces a hierarchy of three choices: (i) if approved for the IRB modelling approach in the capital framework, then use it (and internal assessments can be used for asset-backed commercial paper); (ii) if not IRB approved but approved for external ratings, then use those; and (iii) where neither of these is possible, use the SA. The last of these becomes necessary in many cases as the new framework has more granular tranches (and also distinguishes the so-called thickness of tranches) that need to be rated. The SA applies typical Basel formulas to calculate the securitisation capital charge, based on inputs that start with the 8% capital charge that would apply had the exposure not been securitised (the underlying pool). It then makes adjustments for delinquencies and the attachment and detachment points of the tranches (see Chapter 4). If none of the above three approaches can be used, then a risk weight of 1250% is applied to the exposure.

There are likely to be mixed pools in this process—for example, where the IRB approach applies and but where the standardised approach is needed for parts that can't be modelled. Further complicating the picture is the use of maximum risk weight caps for senior tranches based on good quality underlying pools (which might have risk weights as low as 15%). Furthermore, when all the capital charges are added up, the bank can apply a maximum capital charge of no more than what it would have been for the underlying (not securitised) pool of assets. The reason for these caps is that policy makers want to encourage the rejuvenation of the securitisation markets to help the economy.

The amount of discretion available to banks in this framework still allows plenty of scope for bank optimising their capital requirements.

Market Risk Reform

MR relates to risk of losses on- and off-balance sheet arising from changes in market prices of the so-called trading book assets. Recall from Chapter 2 that the capital to be required to cover for MR is included in the RWA formula scaled up by 12.5[28]:

$$\text{RWA} = 12.5(\text{OR} + \text{MR}) + \text{SUM}[w(i)A(i)]$$

Prior to the fundamental review of the trading book and the resulting final reforms, MR was based on default risk and an incremental charge related to rating migration risk (rating changes that trigger mark-to-market losses) and an additional value-at-risk (VaR) capital charge based on a stressed scenario. Securitisation was excluded (treated separately from MR in the banking book). Otherwise, the boundary between what should be in the trading book and in the banking book was left unchanged.

The fundamental review is expected to significantly raise capital charges for MR.[29] It first clarifies the boundary between banking and trading books: there is now a clear list of presumptive inclusions in each based on intent-to-trade versus hold-to-maturity. Second, a more risk-sensitive approach is adopted for the standardised and internal models approaches to MR in the final version.

[28]Note that the 1.06 scalar for credit weightings in Eq. (2.1) has been dropped as part of the Basel III finalisation—see below.

[29]This brief summary follows a reading of BCBS (2016a).

Standard Approach to MR

The SA to MR is the sum of three elements: (i) a sensitivity-based method (SBM) risk charge; (ii) a default risk charge (DRC); and (iii) a residual risk add-on (RRAO).

- *For the SBM*: there are seven risk classes: general interest rate risk (GIRR); credit spread risk (CSR) for non-securitisation; CSR for securitisations not correlated to the trading portfolio; CSR for securitisations that are correlated; equity risk; commodity risk; and foreign exchange risk. Risk factors are mapped into these risk classes: that is, variables in the pricing function used by the bank trading desk for given instruments for reporting profit and loss positions to management.[30] These risk factors are shocked for a stress scenario, and sensitivity risk positions are calculated. These are then multiplied by prescribed risk weights and risk positions with common characteristics ('*buckets*') are aggregated. Diversification benefits are allowed within each risk class but not between them.
- *The DRC*: is to capture stress events in the tail of the default distribution not captured by credit spread shocks in mark-to-market risk. A jump-to-default (JTD) is calculated, which is a function of the notional value of each position (separately), its market value and the prescribed LGD. Some offsetting diversification benefits are allowed so that net JTD can be calculated. These are allocated to risk buckets, and the appropriate risk weight is applied. Total DRC adds up these elements.
- *The RRAO*: is for instruments where model sensitivities cannot be calculated.[31]

The three risk positions are then added to obtain trading book MR (which multiplied by 12.5 gives the RWA).

---

[30]For example, for GIRR this might be corporate bond curves affected by market implied inflation risk and other correlated variables.

[31]It is '*the simple sum of gross notional amounts of the instruments bearing residual risks, multiplied by a risk weight of 1.0% for instruments with an exotic underlying and a risk weight of 0.1% for instruments bearing other residual risks*' (BCBS 2016a, p. 19).

Internal Models Approach to MR

For the internal models approach (for approved sophisticated banks), the main innovation compared to previous Basel attempts is to move away from VaR method towards the concept of '*expected shortfall*' (ES) under a stress scenario, which is somewhat tougher. VaR asked what the maximum 1-day loss in dollar terms would not be exceeded at the 99% confidence level over a given trading period. ES asks, conditional on a tail event actually occurring (i.e. being in the tail beyond the 97.5 confidence level), what could be the potential loss? This change requires risk factors for modelling losses to use more complex metrics from back-testing over a stressed period, using the finance concepts of *delta*, *vega* and *curvature* risk (see Glossary).

All banks must calculate the SA charge (even if they use the internal model approach). Much stricter conditions apply for banks being able to use internal models for nominated trading book portfolios. In particular, they have to be based on a database of verifiable market prices. Both the SBA and the DRC are treated as being able to be modelled for trading book exposures, but the RRAO is not.

Counterparty Credit Risk

CCR for derivatives (risk of bilateral counterparty default) is calculated either by using the standardised approach (SA-CCR) or by using internal models.[32] CCR exposures are calculated as a multiple of the replacement cost of the exposure (for an immediate close out) plus the potential future exposure. The replacement cost of un-margined derivatives is the maximum of: (i) zero or (ii) the sum of mark-to-market exposures within a netting set, minus any related collateral held. For margined derivatives, it is the maximum within a netting set of: (i) zero; (ii) the sum of values in the netting set less associated collateral; or (iii) the largest exposure that would not trigger a margin call net of any

[32]See BCBS (2014).

independent collateral held.[33] Potential future exposure is a multiplier (to allow for over-collateralisation) times an aggregate add-on for each netting set within an asset class (interest rate, foreign exchange, credit equity and commodity derivatives) based on the notional amount, its maturity and its delta-adjustment to the underlying price.

References

Basel Committee on Banking Supervision. (2013, January). *Basel III: The Liquidity Coverage Ratio and Liquidity Risk Monitoring Tools.*

Basel Committee on Banking Supervision. (2014, January). *The Standardised Approach for Measuring Counterparty Credit Risk Exposures.* Available at: https://www.bis.org/publ/bcbs279.pdf.

Basel Committee on Banking Supervision. (2016a, January). *Minimum Capital Requirements for Market Risk.* Available at: https://www.bis.org/bcbs/publ/d352.pdf.

Basel Committee on Banking Supervision. (2017a, December). *High-Level Summary of Basel III Reforms.* Basel. Available at: https://www.bis.org/bcbs/publ/d424_hlsummary.pdf.

Basel Committee on Banking Supervision. (2017b, December). *Finalising Basel III Reforms.* Basel. Available at: https://www.bis.org/bcbs/publ/d424.pdf.

Blundell-Wignall, A. & Atkinson, P. (2010). Thinking beyond Basel III: Necessary Solutions for Capital and Liquidity. *OECD Journal, Financial Market Trends, 2010* (1), 9–33.

Blundell-Wignall, A., & Atkinson, P. E. (in collaboration with Samuel Eddins). (2011). Global SIFIs, Derivatives and Financial Stability. *OECD Journal, Financial Market Trends, 2011*(1).

Blundell-Wignall, A., & Atkinson, P. E. (2015). Basel Regulation Needs to Be Rethought in an Age of Derivatives. In J. Danielsson (Ed.), *Post-crisis Banking Regulation: Evolution of Economic Thinking as It Happened on Vox.* London: CEPR Press.

---

[33]A bank is exposed to the default of the counterparty of a derivatives trade when it is in the money (has a positive mark-to-market value of the position). Within each netting set, negative (out of the money) mark-to-market positions can be offset against the bank's exposures for the purposes of the capital charge.

Dombrovskis, V. P. (2016, September 29). Embracing Disruption. *Speech to the European Banking Federation.*

Federal Reserve. (2012, December 14). Proposed Rules to Strengthen the Oversight of US Operations of Foreign Banks.

Federal Reserve. (2013, March 14). Comprehensive Capital Analysis and Review 2013: Assessment Framework and Results.

FSB. (2015, November). *Principles on Loss-Absorbing and Recapitalisation Capacity of G-SIBs in Resolution.* Basel. Available at: http://www.fsb.org/2015/11/total-loss-absorbing-capacity-tlac-principles-and-term-sheet/.

Hoenig, T. (2016, November 9). *Strengthening Global Capital: An Opportunity Not to Be Lost*—Remarks by FDIC Vice Chairman Thomas M. Hoenig to the 22nd Annual Risk US Conference, New York.

Mnuchin, S. T. & Phillips, C. S. (2017). *A Financial System that Creates Economic Opportunities: Banks and Credit Unions.* US Department of the Treasury.

9
Globalisation and Finance at the Crossroads

Introduction

Globalisation and finance are at the crossroads. The crisis was an opportunity to take a courageous path for full banking reform in the advanced countries and for a greater rapprochement with an emerging China in open trade and investment. Instead, the opposite is happening. Monetary policy is aimed at cushioning the effects of the crisis on large banks to nurture the rebirth of the interbank market in advanced countries; these are the same banks which have fended off serious reform. China is creating its own brand of risk for themselves and the world economy through a financial repression approach to monetary policy while trying to finance a strong and more high-tech domestic economy. Assisted by the cheap and seemingly endless supplies of loanable funds from its financial system, China is striking out to build an alternative to the OECD/Washington Consensus open-economy model of economic development. This risks segmenting world trade and investment.

Growth in a world of rapidly changing technology requires open trade and investment conducted on a level playing field for all—this

A. Blundell-Wignall et al., *Globalisation and Finance at the Crossroads*,
https://doi.org/10.1007/978-3-319-72676-2_9

enables scale economies by the most innovative competitors that, in turn, create income via derived demand for work from other companies in the supply chain. This was discussed with evidence in Chapter 1. Open trade and investment must be supported by the financial sector, based on sensible business models that do not raise the cost of capital and lead to periodic crises.

This is not the approach that policy makers seem to be taking. The globalisation process appears to be well on its way to heading in the wrong direction. This chapter discusses four important issues that will influence how globalisation plays out:

- Monetary policies in advanced countries directed at cushioning the impact of the crisis on large banks by absorbing their assets until the 'bad asset' digestion process is complete and the interbank market (as a consequence) is nursed back to health. Monetary policy has subsidised banks, distorted prices for investors and encouraged excess demand for alternative products.
- This monetary policy, when combined with the approach to regulation discussed in Chapter 8, sustains TBTF banks and their associated high interconnectedness risk.
- China is building a separate large trade and investment bloc based on subsidised finance and principles inconsistent with multilateral trade and market openness.
- China's approach to development at home and abroad has put vast demands on its banking system as it attempts to diversify and move up the value-added chain. This is proving to be very difficult with China's financial repression approach to monetary policy, which has resulted in Chinese banks becoming involved in vast off-balance-sheet activities perhaps on a scale larger as a share of the economy than those of US and European banks prior to the crisis.

These developments suggest globalisation and finance have reached a difficult point: a crossroad. Each of these topics is explored in the following four sections and possible implications are then drawn in conclusion.

Advanced Country Monetary Policy Supporting Banks and Distorting Returns

Financial reform, as discussed in Chapter 8, did not fundamentally restructure the business models of banks that played the key role in the crisis. These banks are still perfectly recognisable, though with larger shares of counterparty business following some significant mergers during the crisis. Instead, regulation has evolved along lines that banks can live with, and monetary policy has been directed towards seeing them through to a state where borrowing and lending in the interbank market can return to normal. Only when this happens, can policy rates be returned to reasonable levels and the vast quantities of private debt acquired by central banks in the quantitative easing process gradually be reduced.

In the lead up to the crisis, globalisation in conglomerate banking (in London, New York, Paris, Zurich and Frankfurt) took the form of increased interdependence as counterparties to each other. This allowed them to achieve scale economies in underwriting, prime broking, funds management and cross-selling opportunities for structured products. Banking grew explosively and this ultimately resulted in the crisis. As the underlying asset quality of securities plummeted, uncertainty rose about which entities would survive and which products would incur large losses and/or defaults; so the interbank market stopped functioning. Global interest rates, already low, fell further as policy rates were cut to zero (or below), and quantitative easing resulted in massive central bank buying of illiquid assets from banks.

It has always been an objective of the central banks of advanced countries to return to normal operations in the interbank market, allowing central banks to operate in a more conventional way. This has not been possible in most countries that host the GSIBs, because too many banks were suspected of holding too many bad assets related to the crisis. Many securities simply could not be used as collateral for the normal functioning of repo and derivatives markets and in the reuse of assets between non-banks. And banks did not want to deal with each other since these assets, with honest accounting, could have taken the counterparties they were using into insolvency. This indigestion did not sit well with increased demands for new and cheaper financial products brought about by low interest rates. Pushing central bank cash into the system served as a substitute for an interbank market—albeit in an unconventional way—while providing GSIBs with a path for building revenue again (i.e. as intermediaries in the reuse of securities as pension funds, insurance companies and other private investors struggled to cut cost and improve returns).

This approach to policy cannot be reversed overnight. That would mean pouring assets back into the banking system without the same credit quality as central bank cash. Only high-quality assets (such as government bonds, highly rated corporate securities and central bank cash) can play the role of collateral in repo and derivatives transactions.

Central banks in countries that host GSIBs do not like to discuss openly the real reasons for unconventional monetary policy. Instead, in public, the subject is most often still discussed in terms of inflation targeting. Inflation is '*below the comfort*' zone, and policy must stay unconventionally easy until it picks up. Convenient as this might be in the circumstances, it is wearing thin after a decade of no inflation. In Chapters 1 and 5, the case was made that the Phillips curve has likely become more global through global supply chain mechanisms, digitalisation and other technology. Other than for price-level changes induced by exchange rates and volatile price elements like food, taxes and energy, local monetary policy will be less connected to inflation while this goes on.

As a simple illustration, Fig. 9.1 shows the trade-off between inflation and unemployment in the USA since 1995, when the high inflation of the 1970s had long been eradicated. Very little trade-off has been evident, as for more than 20 years unemployment has ranged between 4 and 10%, while inflation has remained within a 1 and 2-1/2% zone. There is no sign of a pickup in core inflation, yet interest rates are beginning to rise and the gradual reversal in QE has at least begun. In the UK, where GSIB banking structures are similarly important, inflation has accelerated, but monetary policy has not moved. This does not mean that inflation is no longer a monetary phenomenon—it simply means its transmission will be slower depending on excess capacity in global as opposed to domestic supply chains.

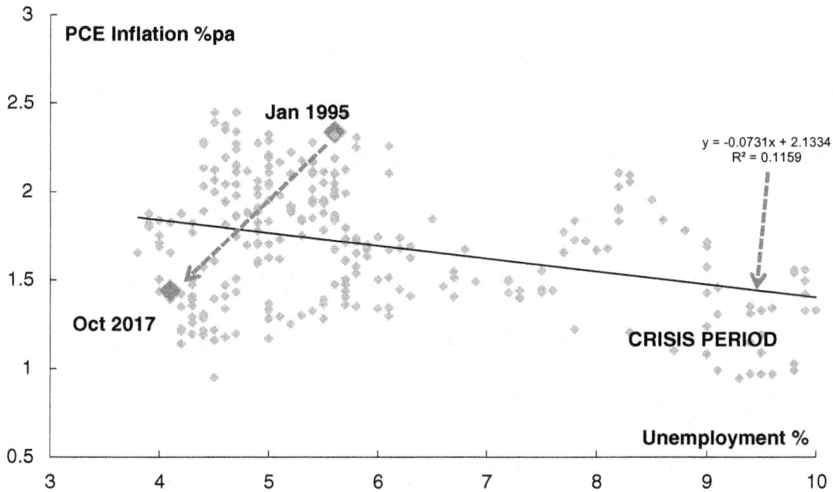

Fig. 9.1 US inflation and unemployment trade-off, 1995–2017, monthly (*Source* Thomson Reuters, authors)

In the near-term, the best gauge for returning to normal (as opposed to restrictive) interest rates, and for reversing QE policies, will be when the GSIB banks get through their medium-term asset-cleansing process and move towards dealing with each other with acceptable liquid private securities again.

Which country has GSIBs whose state of health might warrant a return to normalcy? It should be no surprise that this happens to be the country that is now moving rates up and is tapering the central bank balance sheet despite no inflation. Figure 9.2 shows the ROEs on the GSIBs broken into four global regions. The US GSIBs have recovered nicely, as shown in the top left. The key factors contributing to this are: (i) the recovery of asset prices; (ii) the concentration of bad assets in the Fannie and Freddie conservatorship; (iii) the huge balance sheet of the Federal Reserve; and (iv) the keeping of regulations to acceptable levels (with the Trump Administration promising more relief to come). The euro area and non-euro Europe have not yet delivered the same success as the USA. While the euro area has fought hardest of all to keep regulation at bay, there are some important differences with the USA:

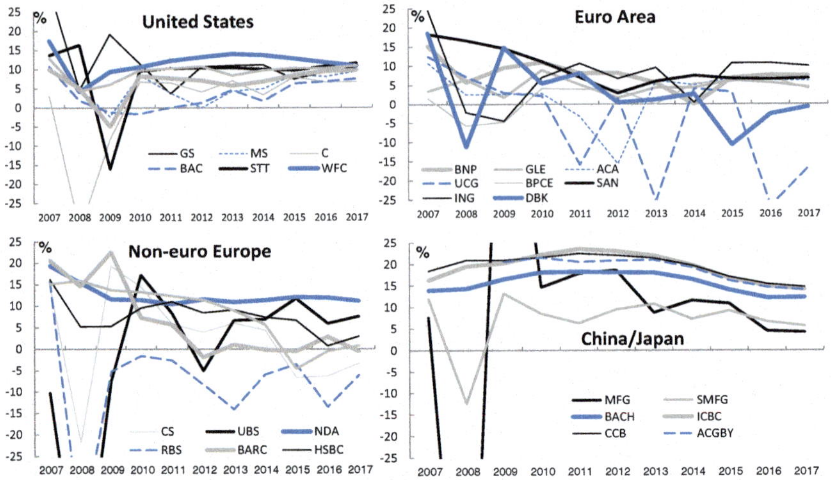

Fig. 9.2 GSIB ROE recoveries since the crisis (*Source* Bank balance sheets. Tickers: GS: Goldman Sachs; MS: Morgan Stanley; C: Citigroup; BAC: Bank of America; STT: State Street; WFC: Wells Fargo; JPM: JP Morgan; BK: Bank of NY Mellon; BNP: BNP Parisbas; GLE: Societe Generale; ACA: Credit Agricole; UCG: UniCredit; BPCE: Groupe PBCE; SAN: Santander; ING: ING; DBK: Deutsche Bank; CS: Credit Suisse; UBS: UBS; NDA: Nordea; RBS: Royal Bank of Scotland; BARC: Barclays; HSBC: HSBC; STAN: Standard Chartered; MFG: Mizuho Fin. Group; SMFG: Sumitomo Mitzui Fin. Group; BACH: Bank of China; ICBC: Industrial & Commercial Bank of China; CCB: China Construction Bank; ACGBY: Agricultural Bank of China)

- In the Europe, there is no Fannie or Freddie to hold bad mortgage assets.
- The European Central Bank was late in moving to buy up private assets from the banks and to provide cash liquidity—indeed, like 'fighting the last war' (inflation), it raised interest rates before being forced to reverse the error.
- The one-size-fits-all monetary policy in the euro area and the absence of exchange rates to adjust have meant weaker growth—particularly in the case of Italian banking (and EU further-southern countries) where NPLs have been high.
- Europe depends more on banking for finance than the USA, and many of the banks are not complex investment banks—they are hurt by the low interest rate strategy while not benefiting from investment banking fees.

In the non-euro European area, banks in the UK and Switzerland are further away from returning to normal compared to the (one) high-performing Swedish bank shown. UK and Swiss corporate governance in certain banks was particularly poor in the lead up to the crisis (as was discussed in Chapter 3). In the UK, having let the situation get out of hand, authorities were slow to understand and to accept there was a problem. More recently, Brexit issues have created uncertainty for large global banks and the future of the city.[1] These countries too will return to normal when portfolios slowly improve (bad assets mature and are written off), and banks can increasingly use their own assets to operate in the interbank market.

Globalisation and the Monetary Response to the Crisis Distorting Markets

An historical perspective on asset prices shows just how much distortion has been involved in saving the GSIBs. Table 9.1 reports historical data summarising US financial market performance, for which long and consistent series are readily available for inflation, equities and bonds from: 1920 to 2017; since China joined the WTO in 2001; and the period since the crisis.

Inflation over almost 100 years averaged 2.6% (at a compound annual rate), but since 2001 has fallen to 2.1%. Over the decade of the easiest monetary policy in history, it averages 1.8% per annum. The real 10-year yield has fallen over each of the three periods: 2.3, 1.3 and 0.7%, per annum, respectively. In contrast, real equity returns paint a different picture. Over nearly 100 years, real equity returns came in at

[1]In Mervyn King's 2012 BBC lecture, he famously said that: '*With the benefit of hindsight, we should have shouted from the rooftops that a system had been built in which banks were too important to fail, that banks had grown too quickly and borrowed too much, and that so-called "light-touch" regulation hadn't prevented any of this*'. Of course, you can only shout from the rooftops if you understand what was happening with the benefit of foresight. The Bank of England, as recent minutes make clear, at first thought it was a liquidity crisis—and presumably a narrow one, given covert lending to a few banks in the beginning. They had no idea about the '*Run on the Rock*' and other problems. This all came later, when it was clear to the man in the street.

Table 9.1 Long-term returns compared to recent years

	1920–2017	2001–2017	2009–2017
			(% per annum)
CPI	2.60	2.05	1.77
S&P 500	5.83	3.25	13.05
Real S&P	3.23	1.20	11.28
Div Yield	3.98	1.95	2.02
Real S&P Tot. Ret.	7.21	3.15	13.31
10 yr	4.87	3.38	2.44
Real 10 yr	2.27	1.32	0.67
Asset allocation return real 60% equity 40% bonds	5.24	2.42	8.25

Source Authors' long-term database and Thomson Reuters

7.2% per annum. Since 2001 (enveloping the crisis) real equity returns fell to a 3.2%. However, since the crisis, US real equity returns have averaged 13.3% per annum. Low-inflation and massive-liquidity injections have been very supportive for equity markets.

Overvaluation of equities is also likely at the end of 2017. Warren Buffett (2001) has been credited with the view that a reliable measure of equity value is simply the market capitalisation versus GDP. But when company earnings come increasingly from global markets and supply chains, this indicator should decline in its usefulness on a national basis. However, this criticism cannot be true of the world economy. Figure 9.3 shows world equity market capitalisation divided by world nominal GDP. At the end of 2017, this indicator is at the highest point over the period shown. This is not sustainable, and how it unwinds will not be comfortable for investors. This distortion of 0.7% real bond returns versus 11.3% real equities since the crisis is due in large part to the need to save GSIB banks.

Banks Versus Pensions and Insurance

Figure 9.4 shows an adding up of global bank balance-sheet assets (with and without China) and survey data on pension and insurance company funds under management. The trend lines over the period are also shown. The effect of easy money and the fending off of regulation on banking is in evidence. Over this period, global banking assets have

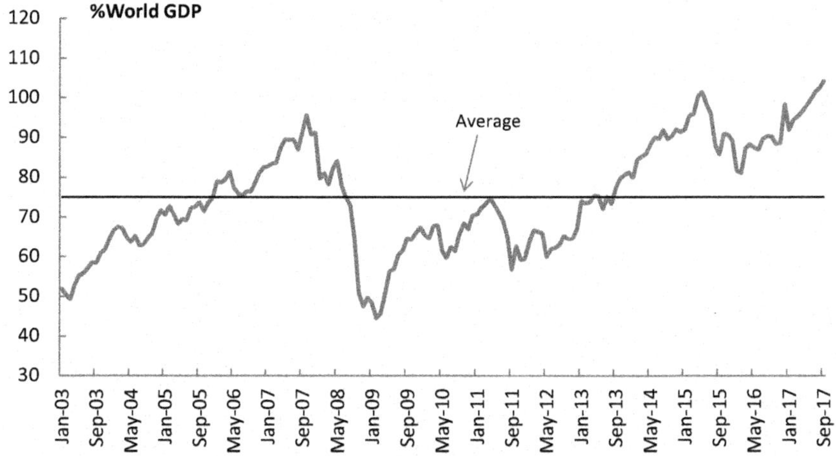

Fig. 9.3 World market cap versus world GDP (*Source* World Federation of Stock Exchanges and IMF)

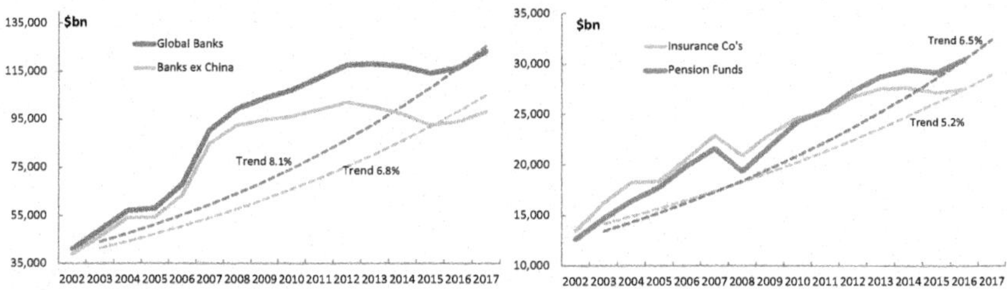

Fig. 9.4 Global banking versus pensions and insurance (*Source* OECD, Thomson Reuters. Banks excludes central banks. OECD countries and China)

grown on average at 8.1%. If China is excluded, banks assets grew at a 6.8% pace globally. The large contribution of China reflects the effect of the (perhaps ill-considered) state-driven credit creation boost in 2009. With unconventional policy buying up bank assets (such as commercial paper and mortgage securities) and low rates driving up asset prices GSIBs, not unsurprisingly, did not collapse and have instead achieved a soft landing. This compares to 5.2% growth for insurance companies and 6.5% for pension funds: in both cases, their financial assets were hit by falling assets prices during the crisis. Since 2009, pension funds, with

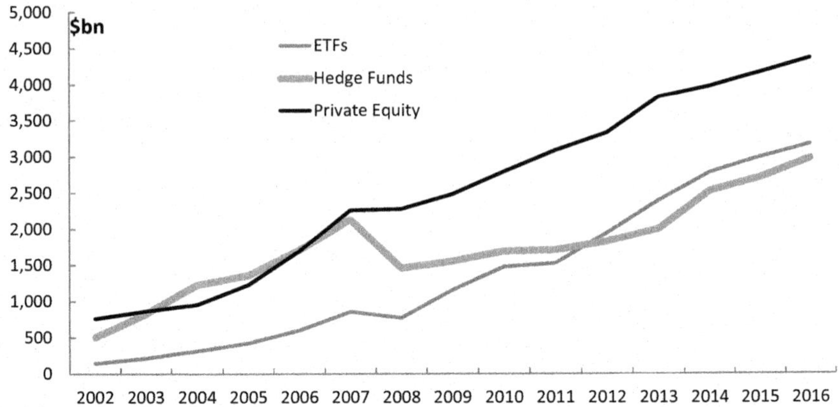

Fig. 9.5 Hedge funds, ETFs and private equity (*Source* OECD, FSB)

a bigger allocation to equities, have outperformed insurance companies, benefiting from the equity boom. Over this period, the only poor-return year was 2015 during the China and emerging market growth scare.

Pension funds are also investors in hedge funds, private equity and exchange-traded funds (ETFs) shown in Fig. 9.5. These products are also owned by sovereign wealth funds, wealthy clients and retail investors. They have benefitted from fund inflows in response to the low-interest-rate environment, as investors seek to enhance returns. Policies to support GSIBs via low interest rates following the crisis have resulted in both strong equity markets and increased demand for alternative assets. Private equity funds and ETFs have been the star performers: private equity because there is a belief that managers in this assets class focus on long-term risk premiums that cannot be obtained in equity markets; and ETFs because they are cheap which is attractive when risk-free interest rates are so low.

Other funds benefiting investment banking and broker-dealers include:

- *Absolute return funds*: These promise-positive returns in both rising and falling markets. They use: a wide number of assets; are not tied to traditional benchmarks; and short securities via derivatives and other methods.

- *Total return funds*: These promise low-risk ways to maximise gains from income (interest and dividends) and capital gains (securities that appreciate over time). Downside risk is hedged with derivatives.
- *Risk parity funds*: These focus on the allocation of risk (volatility as opposed to dollar capital). Using volatility metrics, the product leverages low-risk assets while deleveraging high-risk ones. Derivatives and repos are used in the process.

GSIBs have been akin to subsidised and supported public monopolies: they have benefitted not only from QE directly targeted at the recovery of the crippled interbank markets, but also from new ways to generate fee income in a low-inflation environment. Bank broker-dealer activity, origination and investment banking are at the very centre of all of these activities which generate fee and spread income. While traditional deposit banking is squeezed by low interest rates, GSIBs find new ways to benefit from the situation that they played such a major part in creating. As their past bad assets mature and disappear, GSIBs look forward to a return to more profitable days.

The Cost of GSIB Interconnectedness

The cost of equity is the return expected by investors to compensate them for the extra risk they are taking compared to investing in a risk-free asset. For investing in a bank versus the stock market, this is calculated using the capital asset-pricing model: the firm-specific equity risk premium is derived from that for the general equity market; and this is added to the risk-free government bond rate.[2] Thus, the dividend yield plus expected trend growth in earnings for the equity market should, in equilibrium, be greater than the risk-free government bond rate. The relationship between the individual stock and the overall equity market is measured by its beta. Beta is the covariance of the firm's stock price with the national stock market. Beta greater than 1.0 for a bank tells

[2]See Campbell et al. (1997).

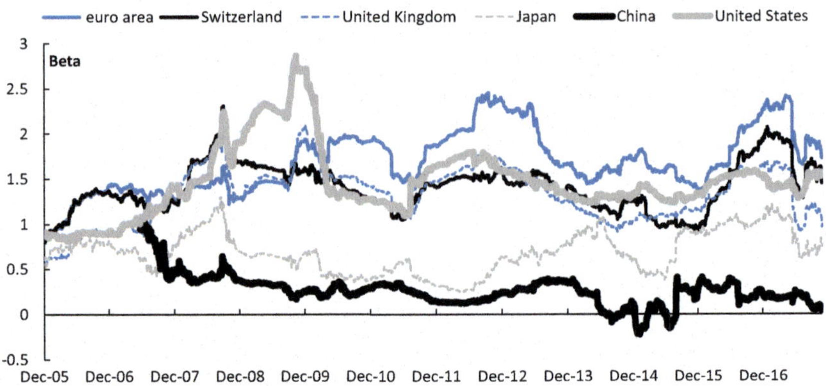

Fig. 9.6 GSIB beta outcomes (*Source* Authors' calculations. BETA is the covariance of the firm's stock price with the national stock market, using daily data regressions to calculate annual observations, divided by the variance of the national stock indexes)

the analyst that risk factors driving markets will have a larger effect on banks than on other sectors and vice versa. Any tendency for beta to rise suggests that compared to the overall equity risk premium, investors would need higher returns to invest in a bank given the equilibrium relationship with a risk-free investment.

Figure 9.6 shows the betas for the GSIBs, averaged according to the country where they are headquartered. The countries with the most important investment banking centres—the USA, the euro area, the UK and Switzerland—all have betas greater than 1.0 on average. During crisis periods, or periods where risk is perceived to be rising, these betas can move into the range of 1.5–2.5 which is indicative of higher systemic risk.

- The 2008 crisis, led by the USA, saw beta move to around 2.5 in the 24 months to December 2009. There was contagion to European banks, but at that point most EU policy makers and analysts had not understood the full global interconnectedness of GSIBs.
- The European bank crisis occurred two years later in 2011–2012, when beta for the euro area moved up well above 2.0.
- In 2016, the euro area led the rise in bank betas again. General problems in European banking had been made worse by the

zero- and negative-interest-rate environment and the rise in non-performing loans discussed earlier. More specifically, Deutsche Bank was threatened with a €14bn potential fine due to the alleged breaking of US laws while its business model is still struggling to deal with past investments and a return to sustained profitability. Deutsche Bank's CoCos fell sharply at one point as investors feared a 'bail-in' of bond holders could occur.

The fine for Deutsche Bank has apparently been forgiven by the Trump administration as of early 2018, but this does not detract from the more general problem of the need for fundamental reform of GSIB banks. Deutsche Bank has been an on-the-record opponent of separating investment banking from deposit banks: '*Diversified income streams enhance the stability in an integrated bank, and this has systemic importance. It is noteworthy that in 2008, the investment banking or "broker-dealer" model virtually disappeared in the US: Bear Stearns and Lehman Brothers gone, Merrill Lynch taken over, and both Goldman Sachs and Morgan Stanley converted into Bank Holding Companies (in other words, able to take deposits). In good parts of the cycle, investment banking profits can be used to invest in services which benefit retail or private customers*' (see UK Parliament 2009). The subsequent 8 years of history speaks for itself. GSIBs in the USA and Europe need to be reformed appropriately.

This systemic risk comes at a cost to the economy in apparent contrast with Asia. Figure 9.6 shows that the bank betas for Japan and China are lower than in the countries that host the large interconnected investment banks—in China's case significantly so.

Bank betas multiplied by the market equity risk premium and added back to the risk-free government bond rate provide a measure of the cost of equity for banks. Bank cost of equity measures is shown in Fig. 9.7. When Tidjane Thiam the CEO for Credit Suisse said European banks are not investable,[3] it is because their ROEs are lower

[3]See Financial Times 28 September 2016, *Europe's Banks Not Really Investable*, https://www.ft.com/content/00606dc2-7739-30c9-b13c-1f56de2ccb66.

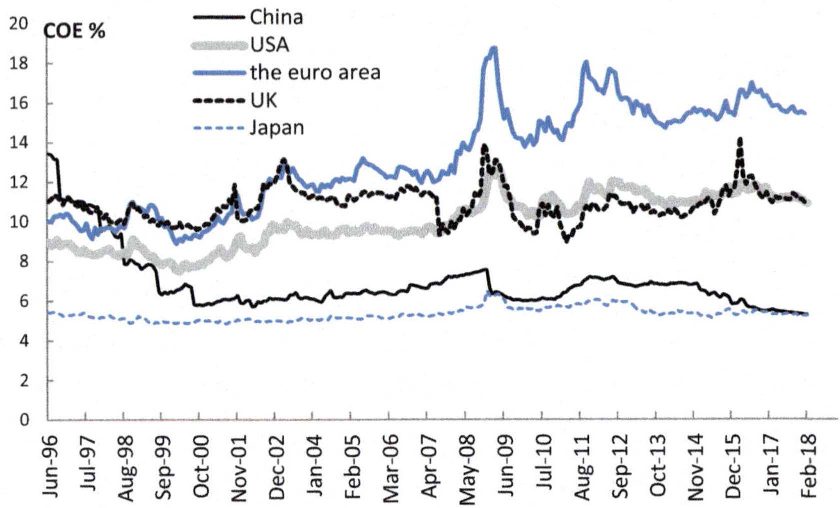

Fig. 9.7 Bank cost of equity by country (*Source* Authors' calculations, Thomson Reuters)

than the cost of equity—this means that it isn't possible to create value for shareholders that compensates for the risk they are taking. When banks are un-investable, they cannot raise needed equity and can't function as appropriate allocators of risk. This is true for all of the countries that host the GSIBs that embody investment banks. Japan and China have very large banks, but they do not play to the same extent on the global investment banking stage. These two high saving countries have a low cost of equity for banks because they are less interconnected and have low betas. In the case of China, the main equity investor is directly or indirectly the state which is always ready to recapitalise them or to guarantee client money when problems arise (see below).

A low cost or equity is important for long-term investing. If a longer-term project fails, equity prices fall and the investor carries the risk. If the investment is funded by debt, the burden remains and the company is put at risk with debt service and no offsetting revenue streams. Taking long-term investment risk requires equity. Paradoxically, the TBTF implicit subsidy for GSIBs in advanced countries feeds through into underpricing of risk for trading, which raises the risk premium that is a cost for the real economy in terms of infrastructure and other forms of long-term investment. This is another example, argued throughout this book, that regulation in advanced countries has not struck the right balance. The contrasting low cost of equity in China is also very important for thinking about the subsequent section concerned with the direction globalisation is taking and which part of the world will enjoy greater economic success in the future.

Figure 9.8 shows the return on equity of selected GSIBs in 2016 and 2017 and the gross market value of their derivatives as a share of total assets over the same period (converting US banks' and Credit Suisse' accounts to a comparable IFRS basis). The overall relationship is negative. Three US banks (top right) that are primarily investment banks have ROEs at around 10% despite high levels of derivatives—though still below the cost of equity. The culture in these banks is not mixed with that for retail deposit banking. Other mixed culture universal banks appear to do less well. This raises a question as to how they

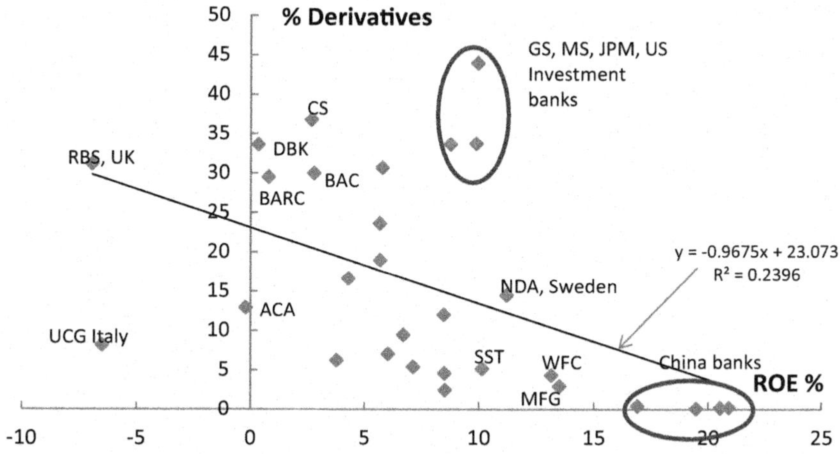

Fig. 9.8 ROEs 2016–2017 average versus derivatives share of balance sheet (*Source* Bank balance sheets, authors. GS: Goldman Sachs; MS: Morgan Stanley; JPM: JP Morgan; RBS: Royal Bank of Scotland; UCG: UniCredit; DBK: Deutsche Bank; ACA: Credit Agricole; NDA: Nordea; SST: State Street; WFC: Well Fargo; MFG: Mizuho Fin. Group)

convinced policy makers not to separate them. Very large banks that do not play a great role in the complex interconnected derivatives counterparty businesses (bottom right) have made higher returns than both: (i) universal banks with a mixed culture; and (ii) those that are more purely investment banks.

China's Belt and Road Initiative: An Alternative Globalisation Strategy

In Chapter 1, the '*China Shock*' issues were discussed: that Chinese SOEs, supported by state-owned banks, have built up huge capacity in many industries and, since their entry into WTO in 2001, have penetrated world markets to a meaningful degree. The China price and the challenge this has posed to other countries have led to a more intensive approach to technology in advanced countries, and both of these have combined to keep downward pressure on wages earned by less-than-college-educated workers. This has led to resentment and resistance to Chinese direct investment and to anti-dumping duties. These pressures from advanced countries are likely to grow as China moves towards becoming the largest economy in the world.

Looking to the future, these risks have contributed to China's implementation from 2015 of a very ambitious globalisation strategy—the Belt and Road Initiative (BRI)—that does not include advanced industrial countries. Instead of rapprochement with advanced countries in trade and investment, by early 2018 it has signed 72 countries into the BRI. The BRI countries in the main are run by governments that play a large role in the economy through state ownership and, in a large majority of them, democratic processes are not present.[4] The BRI countries are rich in minerals and energy, but have been held back from fully exploiting and exporting them by lack of infrastructure. China is making itself the centre of providing this infrastructure on an unprecedented scale, funded by China's Policy Banks (see below), while at the same

[4]New Zealand, near neither the so-called belt nor the road, is an odd (to say the least) exception.

time acquiring technology from advanced countries, both via acquisitions and by documented cases of alleged illegal means.[5] Moving up in the value-added chain within a large BRI trade bloc, based around Chinese technical standards and leadership, is the essence of the strategy.

Supported by banks with a low cost of equity, as set out in the previous section, this strategy is to develop infrastructure that rejuvenates the old Silk Road routes through central Asia all the way to Russia and Poland (the 'Belt'), while also creating a shipping route joining up ports that also broadly moving from east to west (the 'Road': from the South China Sea, through south-east Asia, Indonesia, Myanmar, India, Pakistan, Kenya, Djibouti, Saudi Arabia, Turkey and Europe).

The Belt and Road Strategy Versus the Washington Consensus

The Washington Consensus, as summarised by Williamson (2004),[6] emphasised ten key features for economic development: (1) fiscal discipline to avoid balance of payments crises; (2) reordering public expenditure priorities to promote growth and inclusiveness; (3) tax reform to

[5]The OECD and EUIPO (2016) estimate that in 2015 pirated goods imported into the USA amounted to between $58 and $118bn. $85bn of US goods were also sold elsewhere in the world. 87% of goods seized by US border protection originate from China. US companies such as Tiffany are in litigation with Chinese companies and banks that pass money back to China. Other countries are in the same boat (e.g. Gucci of Italy has been in strong litigation against China). Pirated software and stolen trade secrets are even larger problems than goods. With respect to the latter, the cases of Harvest Funds versus Krane and Tang Energy versus AVIC are instructive examples. Commission on the Theft of American Intellectual Property in Washington, DC, estimates that counterfeiting, stealing trade secrets and software theft cost the USA between $225bn and $600bn per annum. See http://ipcommission.org/report/IP_Commission_Report_Update_2017.pdf. Litigation in the courts is frustrating due to complex corporate structures that make it difficult to establish '*alter ego*' relationships with the parent companies in China and, since SOEs are prevalent in these cases, sovereign immunity claims become a major barrier.

[6]Preceded by Fukuyama (1989) on pondering the end of Communism, asserting that a consensus emerged that competition and markets are the best way to organise society, as Communism collapsed in the Soviet Union. Fukuyama wrongly, as it turns out, postulates that: '*Chinese competitiveness and expansionism on the world scene have virtually disappeared*'. The BRI shows us that rumours about the end of history were indeed premature.

promote incentives while funding government; (4) liberalising interest rates combined with stronger prudential supervision; (5) competitive exchange rates; (6) trade liberalisation; (7) liberalisation of inward foreign direct investment, but not for hot money which might cause volatility; (8) privatisation with anti-corruption measures and appropriate regulation; (9) product deregulation focused on barriers to entry and exit, but with work safety or environmental controls; and (10) property rights.

The IMF, the World Bank and the WTO became the institutional side of promoting these principles. Borrowing in developing countries became conditional on adherence to World Bank Structural Adjustment Programs (SAPs). The conditionality implicit in this framework (i.e. for financial support from these institutions and their advanced country membership) has meant little meaningful development has been generated from these sources and certainly when compared to that provided by China over a short period of time. Apart from anything else, countries where corruption runs at high levels avoid Washington Consensus principles. Bearing such concerns in mind, China's approach is to respect non-interference in domestic issues and to provide infrastructure funded from China and built by Chinese construction companies, often with concessions to run the infrastructure on agreed terms over the repayment period.

This investment is now well underway. The east–west land and sea bridges of the BRI are joined in north–south directions with six main economic corridors:

1. *New Eurasia Land Bridge*: involving rail to Europe via Kazakhstan, Russia, Belarus and Poland. Within China, Jiangsu and Xinjiang are the most affected and linked (reflecting regional aspirations).
2. *China, Mongolia Russia Economic Corridor*: including rail links and the steppe road—this will link with the land bridge.
3. *China, Central Asia, West Asia Economic Corridor*: linking to Kazakhstan, Kyrgyzstan, Tajikistan, Uzbekistan, Turkmenistan, Iran and Turkey.
4. *China Indochina Peninsula Economic Corridor*: Vietnam, Thailand, Laos, Cambodia, Myanmar and Malaysia. Within China, Yunnan and Guangxi are the most affected provinces.
5. *China, Pakistan Economic Corridor*: Xinjiang Province will be most affected. This important project links Kashgar city (free economic

zone) in landlocked Xinjiang with the Pakistan port of Gwadar a deep-water port used for commercial and military purposes.
6. *China, Bangladesh, India, Myanmar Economic Corridor*: This is likely to move more slowly due to mistrust over security issues between India and China.[7]

There are six broad objectives for the BRI strategy that have important implications for advanced countries and the open trade and investment regime promoted by the WTO, the OECD and other organisations:

1. To move excess capacity in low-technology industries which cause air pollution, such as steel and energy, away from Beijing and towards the Western Provinces, Mongolia and other parts of the Asian region. The western regions of China and Mongolia are lagging in prosperity, and shifting production to where there is demand created by the BRI construction projects makes more economic sense.
2. To move China up in the areas of digitalisation and higher-value-added production, with BRI countries taking over more of the lower value-added industries—but with China as the central hub.
3. To transfer technology from advanced countries to China as quickly as possible via mergers and acquisitions and by joint ventures in Western countries where patents can be understood and absorbed. Once China has mastered these technologies, Western companies find they become less welcome in China.[8]
4. To have Chinese technology used as the default technology in BRI partner countries, to cement economic interdependence with China—which is best achieved by China winning contracts with cheap funding and China-led building projects.[9]

[7]See, for example, Patil (2015). India lies between 2 countries with which it has fought wars in the last 60 years and mistrusts the strategic objectives of BRI. It has repeatedly asked that the BRI project is designed with India's participation as an equal partner.

[8]The automobile industry is a good example within China, and the AVIC turbine business is an example of this within the USA.

[9]A recent example of this was the hard-fought battle with Japan for the Bandung to Jakarta high-speed rail.

5. To create a trading and investment zone with countries which broadly adhere to the Bandung Principles of non-alignment and non-interference in domestic economic and political affairs.
6. To deepen cultural exchanges and cement the strategy though: scholarship programmes for BRI students to study in China; the hosting of business fairs; and investing in the spread of Confucius Institute networks.

Table 9.2 shows China's cumulative investments in construction projects abroad and its acquisition investment of advanced country companies.

BRI construction investment sums cumulatively to $444bn from 2005 to 2017, with the next largest beneficiary being sub-Saharan Africa at $164bn. The typical model for China is a complete package—to win the contract, fund it via a state-owned bank consortium and build it with Chinese technology and labour. The funding repays itself for many projects, as the deal is often structured as an agreement for China to run the completed infrastructure as a concession for a fixed period (like 30 years) at agreed tariffs and related protections. The funding comes from state-owned Policy Banks, but also from large state commercial banks and (to a smaller extent) the '*Silk Road Fund*'. BRI investment in

Table 9.2 Chinese construction investment & corporate acquisitions outside China, cumulative 2005–2017

Region	Corporate investment $m	Construction investment $m
Belt and Road Initiative	273,910	443,670
North America	220,460	1,930
Sub-Saharan Africa (ex BRI)	65,070	164,460
Latin America	108,560	66,700
Europe (ex BRI)	275,720	8,210
Middle East and North Africa (ex BRI)	260	33,880
Australia	90,950	12,710
Japan	6,620	0
Other	9,180	2,560
Total	1,050,730	734,300

Source Company Announcements. American Enterprise Institute

the latest Five-Year Plan is slated to move well above the amounts in the table. While many of the BRI countries have junk credit-rating status, the above structuring of the deals reduces financial risk.

The low cost of equity for Chinese Policy Banks is a great advantage in funding BRI projects. In project finance, equity needs to be at a sufficiently high level in order that debt can be held at levels low enough to be supported by project cash flows, while also meeting the equity risk premium for shareholders. Infrastructure projects have zero of very little cash flow in the investment phase. A low bank equity risk premium makes the hurdle rate needed over the life of the project more achievable in higher-risk countries where variability of cash flows might be high. With state-owned banks and a low cost of equity, there is less risk that the debt capacity of projects will be too high.

In Table 9.2, it can be seen that even greater sums have been spent on acquiring technology from advanced countries through the acquisition of foreign companies. Increasingly, these acquisitions have been switched away from resources and energy towards higher-technology firms (e.g. medical, pharmaceutical, telecommunications, robotics, agricultural processing, automobiles, aviation, shipping, entertainment and tourism). Since 2005, foreign company acquisitions have cumulated to more than $1tn.

As these projects are completed in the longer run, there will be trade benefits for China at the centre of an alternative trading platform. The spreading of Chinese technology and control over infrastructure products will give China pre-eminence in a region currently equal to around 43% of world GDP. This may not be good for the global collective interest—though that may be the point since geopolitics is also in play. China plays a long game not based on the next election cycle. The local name for China means the '*middle kingdom*', and this fits very well with the BRI. China sees itself as a global civilisation that was a pre-eminent global power for perhaps 2000 years, only losing this status by missing the industrial revolution. They are now enjoying that revolution, and the aim is to take a huge part of the world with them. If segmentation in world trade does occur, the benefits of multilateral trade will be reduced. Resuscitating the Trans-Pacific Partnership and taking strong Western leadership in the Asian Infrastructure Investment Bank (AIIB) via a large capital stake to match the China Policy Banks would be a prudent strategy to balance things. But this seems increasingly out of reach with current Western policy.

China's GSIBs and Off-Balance-Sheet Risk

The large SOE banks (policy and commercial) are the prime source of funding for economic activity within China, and the Policy Banks provide the bulk of the funding for the BRI. A brief guide to the Chinese financial system is set out in the Appendix to this chapter and is helpful in understanding issues in this section.

China controls banking more directly than in advanced countries via changes in reserve requirements, caps on deposit and lending rates and other quantitative methods (see the appendix). The picture of a financial repression approach is completed by its use of strong capital controls that limits foreign funding of the banking system. While there is an attempt to move more towards an 'interest rate corridor' approach (see the appendix) it is very far from having a market-based system and this dichotomy is very much at the heart of current financial stability issues in China.

In 2009, China expanded credit and fixed asset investment via the SOE sector to stave off the risk of being drawn into the crisis-driven recession underway in the West. The money supply accelerated from around 15% in the 12 months to November 2008 to a peak of 30% in the 12 months to November 2009. The economy responded quickly, and from 2010, China attempted to rein back what had become excessive credit growth.

As noted in the BRI discussion, China is developing a strategy to become a more diversified higher-value-added economy with diverse financial needs that does not sit well with financial repression. Urbanisation, housing, small business needs in a rapidly changing technological environment, local government infrastructure investment and funding development in western China, Mongolia and along the Belt and Road place huge diverse demands on the financial system. The balancing act between monetary control via financial repression and facilitating these complex and interconnected demands is very challenging.

When the PBOC attempted to rein in credit growth from 2010, these growing and diverse needs saw the use of off-balance-sheet activity by banks accelerate sharply. These vehicles are not subject to interest rate controls, and they are less subject to financial repression. Reserve requirements on deposits are a tax on banks, while interest rate ceilings put a limit on banks' ability to attract deposits when inflation rises. Thus, when the PBOC raised reserve requirements twelve times in 2010–2011 (to 21.5%), banks, faced with strong demand, sought to avoid these restraints by using off-balance-sheet vehicles such as undiscounted bank acceptances, entrusted loans, trust company lending and wealth management products (WMPs).

Figure 9.9 compares the build-up of securitisation in the USA as a share of GDP, to shadow banking and WMPs in China.

Shadow bank lending rose rapidly from 2010. The authorities have always had an ambiguous attitude to the sector—wanting both to encourage it but also to contain it for financial stability reasons. The

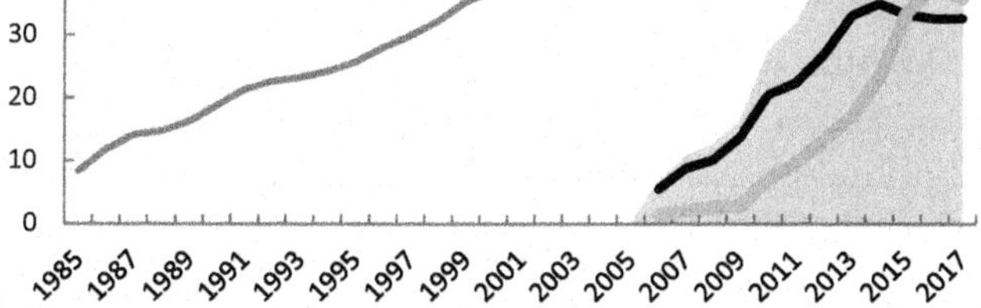

Fig. 9.9 US securitisation compared to China (*Source* SIFMA, Thomson Reuters, Bloomberg, author calculations. Shadow banking for China is the sum of undiscounted bank acceptances, Trust Company loans and entrusted loans. Wealth management products provided by banks are shown separately. The USA includes mortgage securities, CDOs, student loans, equipment, credit cards, automobile finance, including Fannie and Freddie. 'China total' is the sum of WMPs and Shadow Banking)

Macro-Prudential Assessment (MPA) framework seeks to look at '*social financing*' in a broader context and uses window guidance and quotas to try to contain it. With some success in containing shadow banking, banks were incentivised to accelerate disintermediation through WMPs. It is of some concern for the world economy that this activity has now moved to around 36% of Chinese GDP which, when combined with shadow banking, sums to around 68% of GDP. This is higher than the combined size of US bank securitisation and Fannie and Freddie securities in the USA on the eve of the global crisis. These concerns are compounded by a lack of transparency, since WMPs provide a useful way to shift doubtful loans out of reported bank non-performing loan numbers into asset management structures funded by formal or informal bank repo lending. There is little concern about transparency on loan quality because investors rely on an implicit guarantee that comes with management by state-owned banks—with all of the obvious moral hazards that have figured in past crises.

The above data do not include the *Dai Chi* repo market (a sort of '*held-on-behalf-of…*' market; see Kendall and Lees 2016), which is reputedly vast and is very difficult to control. Thus, if MPA policies seek to contain that which is measurable, this may simply push the market further into disintermediation through *Dai Chi*. In this market, like a repo, a bond can be sold for cash with an informal agreement to buy it back at a specific price and date later on. But unlike a normal repo this doesn't take place on the interbank market on an exchange. Instead, it is informal. The risk is that this market is not one consisting of legally enforceable contracts. Nevertheless, it has been estimated at CNY 12 trillion, twice the size of China's interbank market (Kendall and Lees 2017). The point about *Dai Chi* is that the sale of the bond can be used to take assets off a bank's balance sheet into 'thin air' as it was for the period of the loan—thereby completely circumventing regulations. The bond of course—being outside the interbank market—can be rehypothecated in a number of subsequent transactions. The development of this market is a perfect illustration of what happens when financial repression policy is combined with strong demand for credit.

These issues give rise to a China variant of counterparty risk and financial stability concerns (see the appendix). All of these markets (shadow banking, WMPs and *Dai Chi*) overflow into each other and involve banks, brokerages, asset managers and non-financial companies. Overlap via cross-ownership structures is high and growing larger. While *Dai Chi* contracts can't be legally enforced, walking away from an out-of-the-money trade in this informal market affects a firm's reputation and may create flow-on panics within wider markets with implications for lending and the economy. Much like US QSPEs during the crisis, which in theory were securities transferred to a third party, these were absorbed by the banks to maintain their reputations (and often under official pressure). Market participants assume there is an implicit guarantee for these contracts, as with Fannie's and Freddie's obligations in the USA, and this has proved correct to date. In China, the *Sealand Securities* bond default episode underlines the potential importance of these risks.[10]

Concluding Remarks

One measure of trade, investment and financial openness is the correlation between national saving and national investment.[11] The idea that the vast mineral deposits in the north of Western Australia should be funded by the saving of West Australian residents is a fairly silly proposition, and so it is for countries or groups of countries. Open economies should see a low or zero correlation between national saving and investment. Conversely, countries that are not open, or which are excessively selective in their openness, should see higher correlations. These

[10]Sealand is a brokerage with a local government ownership structure that became involved in the Dai Chi market. When bonds that it had to buy back were under water in December 2016, it stated that the trades had been forged by ex-employees. Signs of a panic in the market emerged. The CSRC stepped in and the losses were shared with various players using anonymous repo transactions.

[11]Feldstein and Horioka (1980) interpret the high correlation between national saving and investment in the 1970s and 1980s to imply that global savings are not sufficiently mobile to fund ex-ante demand for investment goods. The correlation itself is not due to econometric anomalies, such as the treatment of the endogeneity via instrumental variables. Obstfelt (1986), Summers and Carroll (1987), and Feldstein and Bacchetta (1991) respond to criticisms of an econometric nature, such as omitted variables, and dynamic effects.

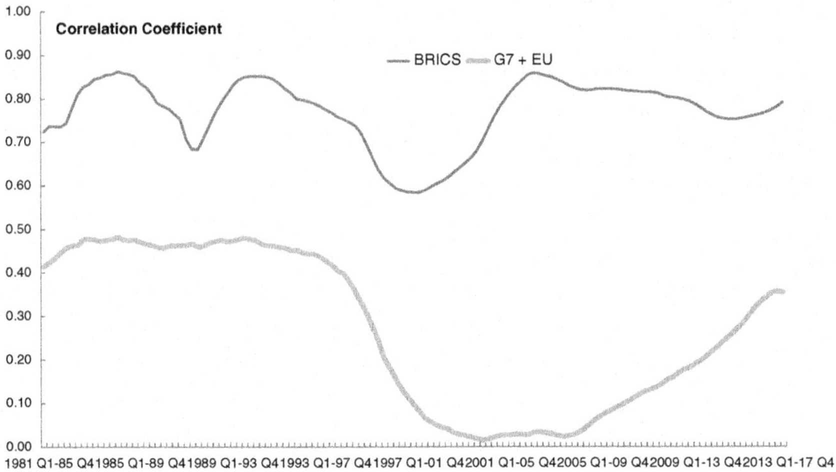

Fig. 9.10 Rolling 5-year saving–investment correlations, BRICS and G7/EU (lower correlations indicate greater openness) (*Source* OECD National Accounts, authors. A panel regression is run for each group with country's gross national capital formation (% GDP) as the dependent versus gross national saving (%GDP), using ordinary least squares. From 1981, the panel regressions are run in 5-year rolling sample period formats (adding and dropping observations for each new sample)

correlations are calculated for two subgroups of the global economy (the G7 plus the European Union, and the BRICS, i.e. Brazil, Russia, India, China and South Africa), shown in Fig. 9.10. Prior to the crisis, there is clear evidence of opening on the part of advanced countries, led by the G7 and the European Union. The most stable open period for this group is that which encompasses the samples after China was allowed to join the WTO (when US current accounts versus that country opened up) and up to 2008, when the crisis hit.

There is no empirical evidence to suggest that the BRICS have ever been seduced by a philosophy of market openness. The indicator is always in the high 0.60–0.84 range. Since around 2004, the very clear tendency is for effective openness to begin to decline in the G7 + EU group. This is likely due to a proliferation of bilateral treaties, anti-dumping duties on emerging economies (and especially with some justification versus China) and increasing resistance to Chinese FDI due to geopolitical concerns and economic issues such as the use of SOE bank finance. Policies to support financial repression through increased capital controls in emerging countries (China, Brazil, Indonesia, Taiwan, Thailand and Korea) are also important factors. Such policies dress up controls (motivated by cross-border flows and currency pressures related to financial repression) as 'macro-prudential tools' concerned with financial stability, e.g. due to currency and maturity mismatches in the foreign funding for domestic banks.[12] This is somewhat nonsensical, since currency mismatch can be controlled within existing internationally agreed policy instruments such as a variant of the Liquidity Coverage Ratio, which can be used to match currencies and maturities on both sides of bank balance sheet without restricting cross-border capital flows. Australia has huge foreign funding of its banks (more than many emerging countries), does not control capital flows, does not (even) ask for matching of currencies and maturities on both sides of the balance sheet and accepts the resulting volatility of its exchange rate.

Countries, acting in what they believe to be their national interest, negotiate bilateral trade deals and use financial repression instruments and subsidised funding to help gain market share or to buy strategic assets, without reciprocity, in the belief that the national interest trumps the collective interest. The evidence suggests that advanced countries appear to be responding to the success of China by moving towards more bilateral deals and raising restrictiveness as a response to dumping, import penetration and job losses. National security is also becoming an issue that leads to new restrictions. When this happens, the country affected complains and feels justified in its own forms of retaliation.

The US CFIUS reviews cover an extensive range of industries and play a role in blocking deals affecting companies of other countries when they own US subsidiaries. For example, the USA has blocked the Phillips

[12]It is unfortunate that IMF support for this can be found in many policy utterances, but sometimes via supposedly sound empirical research, such as in Ostry et al. (2010). This was reproduced and then criticised in Blundell-Wignall and Roulet (2013).

sale of its LED lighting division to a Chinese consortium. The proposed Foreign Investment Risk Review Modernisation Act (FIRRMA) looks to expand and strengthen the role of CFIUS where national security is concerned. The German Foreign Trade and Finance Ordinance law was amended in 2017: specifying critical industries (energy, information technology, water, finance, software, cloud computing, sophisticated parts of telecommunications, telematics as well as upgrading military sector coverage); introducing obligations to notify; and extending review periods. The deal to buy the German chipmaker Aixtron by Fujian Grand Chip Investment Fund had its approval by the German Government was withdrawn in 2017. In Australia, local government in the Northern Territory of Australia leased the port of Darwin to a Chinese company. Subsequently, geopolitical concerns have come to the fore since the port is used by US navy ships in proximity to the South China Sea, and US tracking stations are present in the Territory. This has led to stricter rules for foreign investment reviews and to a new Critical Infrastructure Centre set up in the Australia Attorney General's Department to assess all future deals. More recently, Australia is introducing new laws to match those in the USA, the UK and the EU on foreign political donations following the coming to light of Chinese political donations to key politicians.

Globalisation following the crisis appears to be in retreat. Whether China's BRI strategy will enable it to shrug off fears of a more restrictive international environment in the longer term remains an open question that will become clearer later in this century. Whether or not China has its own financial crisis stemming from its informal financial maze will be a part of the answer. Similarly, the failure to reform banking business models in Europe and the USA is a cause for concern—both in terms of the failure to build lower-cost funding for longer-term investment and the continuing presence of financial instability risks. Another major crisis would likely bring about major change in advanced economies affecting the role of the state and income distribution. What is at stake is enormous. Democratic Governments too often have a shorter focus and a lack of a coordinated vision compared, rightly or wrongly, to China's long-term (albeit risky) strategic view.

It is unlikely that large trade blocs and financial systems based on different and inconsistent principles can cohabitate very easily. In the long-term trade and investment, segmentation and possible financial crises will not be the way to a peaceful and prosperous future. A move to a more blended or mixed economic system would be likely if things do not go well in either of the two great parts of the world economy. Where the pressures for change will be greatest will be in the countries that do not prepare themselves well. Neither China nor large Western countries seem to have the right balance at this stage. Globalisation and finance really are at the crossroads.

Appendix to this Chapter: A Guide to the Chinese Financial System

The central bank in China, the Peoples Bank of China (PBOC), runs a monetary policy akin to that described by development economists like Ronald McKinnon (1973) as '*financial repression*'. The main instruments are reserve requirements, which must be met on average over an assessment period (but can be moderately lower than the minimum for that period on any day), central guidance on benchmark deposit and lending rates (often referred to as interest rate ceilings for banks), quantitative lending ceilings, a loan-to-deposits rule (75%) and 'window guidance' (a telephone call from the authorities). Foreign funding is contained by strict capital controls. More recently, the PBOC is experimenting with an 'interest rate corridor' approach, whereby its operations in the interbank market drive the repo rate which, in principle, has a transmission effect to the bond market.[13] The main borrowers and lenders in the interbank market consist of banks and, unlike in most advanced countries, asset managers and brokerage firms. China remains, however, very far from having a market-based interest rate transmission monetary policy system. As shadow banking and internet finance have taken off in China (partly as a consequence), the authorities have introduced a MPA framework to use all tools at their disposal to control this—window guidance being important in this context.

[13]See Ma et al. (2016).

Other than the PBOC, the banking system is made up of four main groups:

- *The four large state-owned commercial banks*: Industrial and Commercial Bank of China (ICBC); the Bank of China (BOC); the Agricultural Bank of China (ABOC); and the China Construction Bank (CCB). Backed by the full faith and credit of the state, these banks borrow cheaply in the interbank market (see below).
- *The Chinese Policy Banks*: also very large and focused on development lending (the China Development Bank, the Agricultural Development Bank of China, and the China Export–Import Bank). These banks are also heavily involved in financing the BRI. These state-controlled banks also borrow very cheaply in the interbank market. China Policy Banks fund themselves by issuing bonds and by the PBOC's *pledged supplementary lending facility*, in order to support lending related to development. This latter, in particular, is the source of the subsidy in the cost of capital for funding via Policy Banks.
- *'City' and 'rural' commercial banks*: smaller national state-owned banks in local areas. With lower creditworthiness, these borrow more expensively in the interbank market.
- *Joint stock banks*: these have a smaller presence, and funds in the interbank market are more expensive for them.

The asset managers consist of both stand-alone firms and financial vehicles that are owned by banks. The securities industry is overseen by the China Security Regulatory Commission (CSRC) while bank regulations are set by the Chinese Banking Regulatory Commission (CBRC)—which requires coordination with the PBOC, given the overlap between banking and asset management. The CBRC is to be merged with the China Insurance Regulatory Commission (CIRC) to improve coordination.

WMPs offered by banks are off-balance-sheet vehicles subject to lighter regulation (and in the past have been encouraged by the official sector to help deepen markets). This means they can offer better investment returns than controlled deposit and lending rates. Other off-balance-sheet activity of Chinese banks, often referred to as *shadow banking*, includes:

- *Undiscounted bank acceptances*: bills issued by companies that instruct the bank to pay a specified sum to a third party at a specified date. The bank acts as a guarantor, but unless the bill is discounted it doesn't appear on the bank balance sheet.
- *Entrusted loans*: Companies with idle funds provide finance to each other with a return above the deposit rate at a bank. The bank in principle is an intermediary only, and regulations in China require it not to offer guarantees.
- *Trust company loans*: Trust companies are financial entities owned by a bank, which administer funds (e.g. inheritances, endowments) on behalf of a third party. As such they are off-balance-sheet transactions for a bank.
- *The 'Dai Chi' market:* a large informal and not legally enforceable repo market.[14]

Smaller national and joint stock banks have more limited deposit bases than the large banks and issue negotiated certificates of deposit (NCD) as a means of additional wholesale funding. These instruments are traded in the interbank market. These companies borrow short-term and both lend and invest in WMPs, including those owned by larger banks.

Spreads in the interbank market depend on the quality of collateral issued and the creditworthiness of the borrower. The large state banks borrow more cheaply than the small banks. The biggest net lenders are the PBOC and the State Policy Banks, and the largest net borrowers are the smaller banks and the wealth management firms.

The repo market in China is different from the repo market in advanced countries (see Box 6.1), in that it is a 'pledged' market (as opposed to one involving outright transfers, conducted both on the interbank market and stock exchange). This means that the collateral is pledged by the borrower to the lender, but its economic ownership doesn't change hands—i.e. during the term of the contract, neither the lender nor the borrower can use the pledged securities. This precludes rehypothecation that is the hallmark of the Western system. This

[14]See Kendall and Lees (2017).

inability to reuse collateral means that much more of it is needed for the market to operate—there is no 'velocity' of collateral. Collateralised borrowing and lending are therefore more expensive, and hence, the term spread in the interbank market (say between overnight and 7 days) is much steeper. This is the basis of an interbank carry trade. The pledged repo also precludes shorting bonds through borrowing them and then selling them outright to exit repo positions (see Box 6.1). Thus, in order to have the necessary flexibility in trading, borrowers traditionally have used very short-term repos (including overnight).[15]

One consequence of this is that when the central bank operates in the overnight market, say to tighten policy, spread trading in the interbank market can result in carry losses for these segmented-in-quality participants. This creates financial stability risk through maturity mismatch in the bond carry trade, leverage risk (for levered carry trades) and the potential drying up of market liquidity as short rates rise. Smaller banks that use short-term funding to invest in WMPs could in the limit need to be bailed out in a squeeze. To help ameliorate this, the PBOC has introduced 14- and 28-day repos to help reduce volatility at the short end by facilitating longer carry contracts. However, the loss of control of leverage through bank off-balance-sheet vehicles has become a serious policy problem. China's MPA framework still very much relies on financial repression to achieve its stability goals. Thus, in January 2018, for example, China introduced window guidance to control the small-bank NCD issuance by quotas, to try to reduce the financial stability risks that are present there.

References

Blundell-Wignall, A., & Roulet, C. (2013). "Capital Controls on Inflows, the Global Financial Crisis and Economic Growth: Evidence for Emerging Economies". *OECD Journal, Financial Market Trends*, (2), 1–14.

Buffet, W. (2001). Warren Buffet on the Stock Market (with Carol Loomis). *Fortune Magazine.* Available at: http://archive.fortune.com/magazines/fortune/fortune_archive/2001/12/10/314691/index.htm.

[15]See Kendall and Lees (2017) and the references therein for an excellent discussion of the Chinese repo market.

Campbell, J. Y., Lo, A. W., & MacKinlay, A. C. (1997). *The Econometrics of Financial Markets.* Princeton: Princeton University Press.

Feldstein, M., & Bacchetta, P. (1991). National Saving and International Investment. In B. D. Bernheim & J. B. Shoven (Eds.), *National Saving and Economic Performance,* Chicago: University of Chicago Press, 201–226.

Feldstein, M., & Horioka, C. (1980, June). Domestic Savings and International Capital Flows. *The Economic Journal, 90,* 314–329.

Fukuyama, F. (1989). The End of History. *National Interest,* Summer.

Kendall, R., & Lees, J. (2017, June). The Chinese Interbank Repo Market. *Reserve Bank of Australia Bulletin,* 75–86.

Ma, J., Hong, H., Jia, Y., Zhang, S., Yin, L. H., & An, G. (2016). *The Role of Yield Curves in Monetary Policy Transmission* (PBOC Working Paper No. 2016/1). People's Bank of China.

McKinnon, R. I. (1973). *Money and Capital in Economic Development.* Washington, DC: Brookings Institution.

Obstfelt, M. (1986, January). Capital Mobility in the World Economy: Theory and Measurement. *Carnegie-Rochester Conference Series on Public Policy, 24*(1), 55–103.

OECD & EUIPO. (2016). *Trade in Counterfeit and Pirated Goods: Mapping the Economic Impact.* Paris: OECD.

Ostry, J. D., Ghosh, A. R., Habermeier, K., Chamon, M., Qureshi, M. S., & Reinhardt, D. B. S. (2010). *Capital Inflows: The Role of Controls.* IMF Staff Position Note 10/04, 19 February. Washington: International Monetary Fund. Available at: www.imf.org/external/pubs/ft/spn/2010/spn1004.pdf.

Patil, S. (2015, May), "OBOR and India's Security Concerns". *Gateway House.* Available at: http://www.gatewayhouse.in/security-implications-of-chinas-transnational-corridors/.

Summers, L., & Carroll, C. (1987). Why Is U.S. National Saving So Low? *Brookings Papers on Economic Activity, 18*(2), 607–642 (Economic Studies Program, The Brookings Institution).

UK Parliament. (2009, March). Memorandum from Deutsche Bank. Available at: https://publications.parliament.uk/pa/cm200809/cmselect/cmtreasy/144/144iii25.htm.

Williamson, J. (2004, 24–25 September). *A Short History of the Washington Consensus.* Paper Commissioned by Fundación CIDOB for a Conference "From the Washington Consensus Towards a New Global Governance," Barcelona.

Erratum to: Globalisation Sets the Background to the Crisis

Erratum to:
Chapter 1 in: A. Blundell-Wignall et al.,
***Globalisation and Finance at the Crossroads*,**
https://doi.org/10.1007/978-3-319-72676-2_1

The original version of the book was inadvertently published with misspelt author name "Blundell-Wignal et al." in the opening page footnote of Chapter 1, which has to be now corrected to read as "Blundell-Wignall et al.". The erratum chapter and the book have been updated with the change.

The updated online version of this chapter can be found at
https://doi.org/10.1007/978-3-319-72676-2_1

A. Blundell-Wignall et al., *Globalisation and Finance at the Crossroads*,
https://doi.org/10.1007/978-3-319-72676-2_10

Bibliography

Abraham, S. (2017). *The History of Options Contracts*. https://www.investopedia.com/articles/optioninvestor/10/history-options-futures.asp.

Allison, G. (2015, September). The Thucidides Trap. *The Atlantic*.

Autor, D. H., Dorn, D., & Henderson, G. H. (2016). *The China Shock: Learning from Labour Market Adjustment to Large Changes in Trade* (NBER Working Paper No. 21906). National Bureau of Economic Research.

Ayadi, R., De Groen, W. P., Sassi, I., Mathlouthi, W., Rey, H., & Aubry, O. (2015). *Banking Business Models Monitor 2015, Europe*. Montreal: HEC Montreal.

Bagehot, W. (1873). *Lombard Street: A Description of the Money Market*. New York: Scribner and Sons.

Bakker, A. F. P. (1996). *The Liberalization of Capital Movements in Europe*. Dordrecht and Boston: Kluwer Academic.

Bank for International Settlements. (2007). *Annual Report*. Basel.

Bank for International Settlements. (2009). *Comments Received on the Consultative Documents 'Strengthening the Resilience of the Banking Sector' and 'International Framework for Liquidity Risk Measurement, Standards and Monitoring'*. http://www.bis.org/publ/bcbs165/cacomments.htm.

Basel Committee on Banking Supervision. (1988, July). *International Convergence of Capital Measurement and Capital Standards*.

A. Blundell-Wignall et al., *Globalisation and Finance at the Crossroads*,
https://doi.org/10.1007/978-3-319-72676-2

Basel Committee on Banking Supervision. (2004, June). *International Convergence of Capital Measurement and Capital Standards: A Revised Framework*.

Basel Committee on Banking Supervision. (2006, June). *International Convergence of Capital Measurement and Capital Standards: A Revised Framework*—Comprehensive Version.

Basel Committee on Banking Supervision. (2013a, January). Regulatory Consistency Assessment Program (RCAP). *Analysis of Risk Weighted Assets for Market Risk*.

Basel Committee on Banking Supervision. (2013b, January). *Basel III: The Liquidity Coverage Ratio and Liquidity Risk Monitoring Tools*.

Basel Committee on Banking Supervision. (2014, January). *The Standardised Approach for Measuring Counterparty Credit Risk Exposures*. Available at: https://www.bis.org/publ/bcbs279.pdf.

Basel Committee on Banking Supervision. (2016a, January). *Minimum Capital Requirements for Market Risk*. Available at: https://www.bis.org/bcbs/publ/d352.pdf.

Basel Committee on Banking Supervision. (2016b, July). *Revisions to the Securitisation Framework*. Available at: https://www.bis.org/bcbs/publ/d374.pdf.

Basel Committee on Banking Supervision. (2017a, December). *High-Level Summary of Basel III Reforms*. Basel. Available at: https://www.bis.org/bcbs/publ/d424_hlsummary.pdf.

Basel Committee on Banking Supervision. (2017b, December). *Finalising Basel III Reforms*. Basel. Available at: https://www.bis.org/bcbs/publ/d424.pdf.

Berka, M., Devereux, M. B., & Engel, C. (2014, September). *Real Exchange Rates and Sectoral Productivity in the Eurozone* (NBER Working Paper No. 20510). National Bureau of Economic Research.

Bernanke, B. (2005). The Global Saving Glut and the U.S. Current Account Deficit. Federal Reserve Board. *Homer Jones Lecture*.

Bernanke, B. S. (2007, May). The Subprime Mortgage Market. At the *Federal Reserve Bank of Chicago's 43rd Annual Conference on Bank Structure and Competition*, Chicago, IL. https://www.federalreserve.gov/newsevents/speech/bernanke20070517a.htm.

Black, F., & Scholes, M. (1973). The Pricing of Options and Corporate Liabilities. *Journal of Political Economy*, *81*(3), 637.

Blundell-Wignall, A. (2007, June). An Overview of Hedge Funds and Structured Products. *OECD Journal Financial Trends, 2007*(1), 37–57.

Blundell-Wignall, A. (2007, November). Structured Products: Implications for Financial Markets. *OECD Journal, Financial Trends* (2). http://www.oecd.org/daf/fin/financial-markets/39654605.pdf.

Blundell-Wignall, A. (2008). The Subprime Crisis: Size, Deleveraging and Some Policy Options. *OECD Journal Financial Market Trends, 2008*(1), 1–25.

Blundell-Wignall, A. (2012). Ratings Agencies Issues, Presentation to the French Senate. http://www.oecd.org/daf/fin/financial-markets/50018884.pdf.

Blundell-Wignall, A. (2012). Solving the Financial and Sovereign Debt Crisis in Europe. *OECD Journal, Financial Trends, 2011*(2), 1–23.

Blundell-Wignall, A. (2013, March 21). Cyprus: Further Compressing the Coiled Spring. *OECD Insights.* Available at: http://oecdinsights.org/2013/03/21/cyprus-further-compressing-the-coiled-spring/.

Blundell-Wignall, A., & Atkinson, P. E. (2008). The Subprime Crisis: Causal Distortions and Regulatory Reform. In Kent & Bloxham (Eds.), *Lessons from the Financial Turmoil of 2007 and 2008*. Reserve Bank of Australia. http://www.rba.gov.au/PublicationsAndResearch/Conferences/2008/Blundell-Wignall_Atkinson.pdf.

Blundell-Wignall, A., & Atkinson, P. E. (2009). Origins of the Financial Crisis and Requirements for Reform. *Journal of Asian Economics*. https://doi.org/10.1016/j.asieco.07.009.

Blundell-Wignall, A., & Atkinson, P. E. (2010). Thinking Beyond Basel III: Necessary Solutions for Capital and Liquidity. *OECD Journal, Financial Market Trends,2010*(1), 9–33.

Blundell-Wignall, A., & Atkinson, P. E. (in collaboration with Samuel Eddins) (2011). Global SIFIs, Derivatives and Financial Stability. *OECD Journal, Financial Market Trends, 2011*(1), 1–34.

Blundell-Wignall, A., & Atkinson, P. E. (2012). Deleveraging, Traditional Versus Capital Markets Banking and the Urgent Need to Separate GSIFI Banks. *OECD Journal, Financial Market Trends, 2012*(1), 1–42.

Blundell-Wignall, A., & Atkinson, P. E. (2015). Basel Regulation Needs to Be Rethought in an Age of Derivatives. In J. Danielsson (Ed.), *Post-crisis Banking Regulation: Evolution of Economic Thinking as It Happened on Vox*. London: CEPR Press.

Blundell-Wignall, A., Atkinson, P. E., & Roulet, C. (2012). The Business Models of Large Interconnected Banks and the Lessons of the Financial Crisis. *National Institute Economic Review, 221*, 31–44.

Blundell-Wignall, A., Atkinson, P. E., & Roulet, C. (2013a). Bank Business Models and the Separation Issue. *OECD Journal, Financial Market Trends, 2012*(2), 1–23.

Blundell-Wignall, A., Atkinson, P. E., & Roulet, C. (2013b). Integration Versus Interdependence and Complexity in Global Trade and Finance in the Post-war Period. In Morten & Gnan (Eds.), *50 Years of Money and Finance: Lessons and Challenges*. SUERF 50th Anniversary Volume. Larcier.

Blundell-Wignall, A., Atkinson, P. E., & Roulet, C. (2013c). Bank Business Models and the Basel System: Complexity and Interconnectedness. *OECD Journal, Financial Market Trends,* (2), 1–26.

Blundell-Wignall, A., Atkinson, P. E., & Se Hoon, L. (2009a). The Current Financial Crisis: Causes and Policy Issues. *OECD Journal, Financial Trends,* (1), 1–21.

Blundell-Wignall, A., Atkinson, P. E., & Se Hoon, L. (2009b). Dealing with the Crisis and Thinking About the Exit Strategy. *OECD Journal Financial Market Trends, 2009*(1), 1–18.

Blundell-Wignall, A., & Roulet, C. (2012). Bank Business Models and the Distance to Default. *OECD Journal, Financial Trends, 2012*(2), 7–34.

Blundell-Wignall, A., & Roulet, C. (2013a). Bank Business Models, Capital Rules and Structural Separation Policies: An Evidence-Based Critique of Current Policy Trends. *Journal of Financial Economic Policy, 5*(4), 339–360.

Blundell-Wignall, A., & Roulet, C. (2013b). Capital Controls on Inflows, the Global Financial Crisis and Economic Growth: Evidence for Emerging Economies. *OECD Journal, Financial Trends* (2), 1–14.

Blundell-Wignall, A., & Roulet, C. (2014). Problems in the International Financial System. *OECD Journal, Financial Trends, 2014*(1), 1–23.

Blundell-Wignall, A., & Roulet, C. (2016). Evaluating Capital Flow Management Measures Used as Macro-prudential Tools. *OECD Journal, Financial Market Trends, 2016*(1), 1–36.

Blundell-Wignall, A., Wehinger, G., & Slovik, P. (2009). The Elephant in the Room: The Need to Focus on What Banks Do. *OECD Journal, Financial Market Trends, 2009*(2), 1–27.

Brown, K., & Enrich, D. (2008, November 29). Rubin Under Fire Defends His Role at Citi. *Wall Street Journal*.

Brunsden, J. (2017, October 24). European Commission Withdraws Bank Separation Proposal. *Financial Times*. Available at: https://www.ft.com/content/ddbedcd9-2dea-3b68-b8e2-2e1bc1eda13f.

Buffet, W. (2001). Warren Buffet on the Stock Market (with Carol Loomis). *Fortune Magazine*. Available at: http://archive.fortune.com/magazines/fortune/fortune_archive/2001/12/10/314691/index.htm.

Cai, F., Park, A., & Yao, Z. (2008). The Chinese Labour Market in the Reform Era. In L. Brandt & T. Rawski (Eds.), *China's Great Economic Transformation*. Cambridge: Cambridge University Press.

Campbell, J. Y., Lo, A. W., & MacKinlay, A. C. (1997). *The Econometrics of Financial Markets*. Princeton: Princeton University Press.

Corsetti, G. P., Pesenti, P., & Roubini, N. (1998). *What Caused the Asia Currency and Financial Crisis: The Policy Debate* (NBER Working Paper No. w6834). National Bureau of Economic Research.

Dodd-Frank. (2010). Wall Street Reform and Consumer Protection Act (See US Congress).

Dombrovskis, V. P. (2016, September 29). Embracing Disruption. *Speech to the European Banking Federation*.

Dooley, M., & Isard, P. (1980, April). Capital Controls, Political Risk, and Deviations from Interest-Rate Parity. *Journal of Political Economy, 88*(2), 370–384. University of Chicago Press.

Duffie, D. (2012). *Market Making Under the Proposed Volcker Rule* (Working Paper). Stanford University Graduate School of Business. Available at: www.darrellduffie.com/uploads/policy/DuffieVolckerRule.pdf.

EBA. (2016). *Recommendation on Harmonisation of Covered Bond Frameworks in the EU*. Brussels.

Eichengreen, B. (1999). *Towards a New International Financial Architecture: A Practical Post-Asia Agenda*. Washington: Institute for International Economics.

Ericsson, N. R., & Mackinnon, J. G. (2002). Distributions of Error Correction Tests for Cointegration. *Econometrics Journal, 5*, 285–318.

FDIC. (2005). Capital and Accounting News: Basel II and the Potential Effects on Insured Institutions in the United States: Results of the Fourth Quantitative Impact Study (QIS4). *Supervisory Insights* (Winter), vol. 2, Issue 2, 27–32.

Federal Reserve. (2012, December 14). Proposed Rules to Strengthen the Oversight of US Operations of Foreign Banks.

Federal Reserve. (2013, March 14). Comprehensive Capital Analysis and Review 2013: Assessmant Framework and Results.

Feldstein, M., & Bacchetta, P. (1991). National Saving and International Investment. In B. D. Bernheim & J. B. Shoven (Eds.), *National Saving and Economic Performance* (pp. 201–226). Chicago: University of Chicago Press.

Feldstein, M., & Horioka, C. (1980, June). Domestic Savings and International Capital Flows. *The Economic Journal, 90*, 314–329.

FHFA. (2017, August 7). *Dodd-Frank Act: Stress Test Results: Severely Adverse Scenario.*

Financial Stability Forum. (2007, May). *Update of the FSF Report on Highly Leveraged Institutions.* Basel. http://www.fsb.org/wp-content/uploads/r_0705.pdf.

FINMA. (2013, July). *FINMA Position Paper on the Resolution of Systemically Important Banks, Swiss Financial Market Supervisory Authority* (FINMA). Switzerland. Available at: www.finma.ch/e/aktuell/Pages/mm-pos-sanierung-abwicklung-20130807.aspx.

FOMC. (2007). Meeting of the Federal Open Market Committee on August 7.

French Ministry for the Economy, Industry and Employment. (2009, February). The Credit Default Swap (CDS) Market. Trésor-Economics, No. 52. Available at: https://www.tresor.economie.gouv.fr/Ressources/file/327008.

FSB. (2015). *Principles on Loss-Absorbing and Recapitalisation Capacity of G-SIBs in Resolution.* Basel. Available at: http://www.fsb.org/2015/11/total-loss-absorbing-capacity-tlac-principles-and-term-sheet/.

Fukao, M. (1990, September). The Liberalization of Japanese Exchange Controls and Structural Changes in the Balance of Payments. *The Bank of Japan Monetary and Economic Studies, 8*(2), 101–165. Tokyo.

Fukuyama, F. (1989). The End of History. *National Interest*, Summer.

General Accounting Office. (2007). *Agencies Engaged in Consolidated Supervision Can Strengthen Performance Measurement and Consolidation*, GA-07-154. Washington, DC, March, p. i.

Goodhart, C. A. E. (2013). The Optimal Financial Structure, LSE Financial Markets Group Paper Series, Special Paper 220.

Goos, M., Manning, A., & Soloman, A. (2014). Explaining Job Polarisation: Routine Biased Technological Change and Offshoring. *American Economic Review, 104*(8), 2509–2526.

Gordy, M. D. (2003). A Risk-Factor Model Foundation for Ratings-Based Bank Capital Rules. *Journal of Financial Intermediation, 12*, 199–232.

Gurría, A. (2008, October 11). *Statement by the Secretary-General of the OECD*, before the International Monetary and Financial Committee, Washington, DC.

Haldane, A. (2012). The Dog and the Frisbee, Speech Given at the Federal Reserve Bank of Kansas City's 36th Economic Policy Symposium, The Changing Policy Landscape, Jackson Hole, WY.

Helpman, E., Melitz, M. J., & Yeaple, S. R. (2004). Export Versus FDI with Heterogeneous Firms. *American Economic Review, 94*(1), 300–316.

Hoenig, T. (2013, April). *Basel III Capital: A Well-Intended Illusion, Speech Delivered to the International Association of Deposit Insurers*, Basel.

Hoenig, T. (2016, November 9). *Strengthening Global Capital: An Opportunity Not to Be Lost*—Remarks by FDIC Vice Chairman Thomas M. Hoenig to the 22nd Annual Risk US Conference, New York.

IMF. (2007a, April). *Global Financial Stability Report*. Washington, DC.

IMF. (2007b). *Staff Report on the United States*. Washington, DC.

Isaksson, M., & Celik, S. (2013). *Who Cares? Corporate Governance in Today's Equity Markets* (OECD Corporate Governance Working Paper No. 8).

Johnson, C. (1982). *MITI and the Japanese Miracle: The Growth of Industrial Policy, 1925–1975*. Stanford, CA: Stanford University Press.

Kendall, R., & Lees, J. (2017, June). The Chinese Interbank Repo Market. *Reserve Bank of Australia Bulletin*.

Kiernan, K. (2015, May 20). *From Ancient Greece to Wall Street: A Brief History of the Options Market*. FINRA (https://www.FINRA.org).

King, M. (2012, May 2). *The 2012 BBC Today Programme Lecture*. London. Available at: https://www.bankofengland.co.uk/-/media/boe/files/speech/2012/bbc-today-programme-lecture.

Lewis, M. (1989). *Liar's Poker*. New York: W. W. Norton.

Liikanen, E. (2012, October). *High-Level Expert Group on Reforming the Structure of the EU Banking Sector: Final Report*. Brussels. Available at: http://ec.europa.eu/internal_market/bank/docs/high-level_expert_group/report_en.pdf.

Lipsey, R. G., & Lancaster, K. (1956). The General Theory of the Second Best. *The Review of Economic Studies, 24*(1), 11–32.

Liu, L. (2005, March). Bidding Farewell to This Year's Laid off Workers. *China News Weekly*, Vol. 220.

Lumpkin, S. (2008). Resolutions of Weak Institutions: Lessons Learned from Previous Crises. *OECD Journal Financial Market Trends, 2008*(1), 1–42.

Ma, G., Roberts, I., & Kelly, G. (2016). A Rebalancing Chinese Economy: Challenges and International Implications. In *Structural Change in China: Implications for Australia and the World*. Reserve Bank of Australia.

Ma, G., & Wang, Y. (2010, June). *China's High Saving Rate: Myth and Reality* (BIS Working Paper No. 312). Bank for International Settlements.

Ma, J., Hong, H., Jia, Y., Zhang, S., Yin, L. H., & An, G. (2016). *The Role of Yield Curves in Monetary Policy Transmission* (PBOC Working Paper No. 2016/1). People's Bank of China.

Mathis, W. S. (2017). *A Brief History of Derivatives*. http://www.realmarkits.com/derivatives/3.0history.php.

McLean, B., & Nocera, J. (2011). *All the Devils Are Here*. New York: Penguin.

McKinnon, R. I. (1973). *Money and Capital in Economic Development*. Washington, DC: Brookings Institution.

Melitz, M. J., & Redding, S. J. (2012). *Heterogeneous Firms and Trade* (NBER Working Paper No. 18652). National Bureau of Economic Research.

Mnuchin, S. T., & Phillips, C. S. (2017). *A Financial System That Creates Economic Opportunities: Banks and Credit Unions*. US Department of the Treasury.

Moss, D., & Kintgen, E. (2010, November 10). *The Dojima Rice Market and the Origins of Futures Trading*. Harvard Business School, revised.

Obstfelt, M. (1986, January). Capital Mobility in the World Economy: Theory and Measurement. *Carnegie-Rochester Conference Series on Public Policy, 24*(1), 55–103.

OECD. (2002). *Forty Years' Experience with the OECD Codes of Liberalisation of Capital Movements*. Paris: OECD.

OECD. (2007, June). *Economic Outlook, 2007/1 No. 81, June,* OECD Publishing, Paris.

OECD. (2009a). *The Financial Crisis: Reform and Exit Strategies*. Paris: OECD. Available at: www.oecd.org/dataoecd/55/47/43091457.pdf.

OECD. (2009b, June). *Corporate Governance and the Financial Crisis: Key Findings and Main Messages*. Paris: OECD.

OECD. (2015a). *Business and Finance Outlook*. Paris: OECD.

OECD. (2015b). *Economic Survey of Japan*. Paris: OECD.

OECD. (2017). *Business and Finance Outlook*. Paris: OECD.

OECD & EUIPO. (2016). *Trade in Counterfeit and Pirated Goods: Mapping the Economic Impact*. Paris: OECD.

Ostry, J. D., Ghosh, A. R., Habermeier, K., Chamon, M., Qureshi, M. S., & Reinhardt, D. B. S. (2010). *Capital Inflows: The Role of Controls*. IMF Staff

Position Note 10/04, 19 February. Washington: International Monetary Fund. Available at: www.imf.org/external/pubs/ft/spn/2010/spn1004.pdf.

Radelet, S., & Sachs, J. (1998). The East Asian Financial Crisis: Diagnosis, Remedies, Prospects. *Brookings Papers on Economic Activity, 1*, 1–90.

Resti, A. (2017, March). Fines for Misconduct in the Banking Sector: What Is the Situation in Europe. *In Depth Analysis*. European Parliament.

Ritholtz, B. (with Aaron Task). (2009). *Bailout Nation.* Hoboken, NJ: Wiley.

Rodrik, D. (2008). The Real Exchange Rate and Economic Growth. *Brookings Papers on Economic Activity, 39*(2) (Fall), 365–439.

Sarin, N., & Summers. (2016, September). *Have Big Banks Gotten Safer.* Brookings Papers on Economic Activity, Conference Draft.

SEC. (2008, September 25). *SEC's Oversight of Bear Stearns and Related Entities: The CSE Program* (Report No. 446-A), pp. viii–ix.

Shigehara, K., & Atkinson, P. (2011). *Surveillance by International Institutions: Lessons from the Global Financial and Economic Crisis* (Economics Department Working Paper No. 860). Paris: OECD.

Sirri, E. (2008, May 7). Testimony Concerning the Turmoil in Credit Markets: Examining the Regulation of Investment Banks by the Securities and Exchange Commission, Before the Subcommittee on Securities, Insurance and Investment. United States Senate.

Sorkin, A. R. (2010, March 15). At Lehman, Watchdogs Saw It All. *New York Times*. Available at: http://www.nytimes.com/2010/03/16/business/16sorkin.html.

Stiglitz, J., & Yusuf, S. (2001). *Rethinking the East Asian Miracle.* New York: Oxford University Press.

Summers, L. (2007, March 25). As America Falters, Policy Makers Must Look Ahead. *The Financial Times.*

Summers, L., & Carroll, C. (1987). Why Is U.S. National Saving so Low? *Brookings Papers on Economic Activity, 18*(2), 607–642 (Economic Studies Program, The Brookings Institution).

Tarullo, D. K. (2008). *Banking on Basel: The Future on International Bank Regulation*. Washington: Peterson Institute for International Economics.

The White House. (2004, September 2). President George W. Bush, "Increasing Affordable Housing and Expanding Home Ownership", Press Release.

Tica, J., & Druzic, I. (2006). *The Harrod-Balassa-Samuelson Effect: A Survey of Empirical Evidence* (Working Paper Series No. 06–07). University of Zagreb.

Treasury Committee. (2007). *The Run on The Rock: Fifth Report, Session 2007–08*, Vol. 2: Oral, EV. 47.

Turner, A. (2009, March). *The Turner Review: A Regulatory Response to the Global Banking Crisis* (Vol. 7). London: Financial Services Authority.

UBS. (2008, April). *Shareholder Report on UBS Write-Downs*. UBS AG.

UK Government. (2011a, April). *Interim Report: Consultation on Reform Options*. Independent Commission on Banking. London. Available at: https://s3-eu-west-1.amazonaws.com/htcdn/Interim-Report-110411.pdf.

UK Government. (2011b, September). *Independent Commission on Banking: Final Report Recommendations* (Vickers Report). London. Available at: http://webarchive.nationalarchives.gov.uk/20131003105424/https:/hmt-sanctions.s3.amazonaws.com/icb%20final%20report/icb%2520final%2520report%5B1%5D.pdf.

UK Parliament. (2009, March). Memorandum from Deutsche Bank. Available at: https://publications.parliament.uk/pa/cm200809/cmselect/cmtreasy/144/144iii25.htm.

United States Department of the Treasury. (2016, October). *Foreign Exchange Rate Policies of Major Trading Partners of the United States. Semi-Annual Report to Congress*.

US Congress. (2010). Dodd-Frank Wall Street Reform and Consumer Protection Act (2009). H.R. 4173—111th Congress. Available at: www.govtrack.us/congress/bill.xpd?bill=h111-4173.

Wallis, S. (1997). *Financial System Inquiry Final Report*. Treasury, Canberra. Available at: http://fsi.treasury.gov.au/content/FinalReport.asp.

Warren, D. R. (2015). *Developments in Banking Law*. Review of Banking and Financial Law, Vol. 34 (pp. 439–450, Section V, on 'Congress's Rollback of the Dodd-Frank Swaps Push-Out Rule').

White, W. R. (2006, June). *Opening Address, Financial Globalisation*. 5th Annual BIS Research Conference. Brunnen. Available at: http://www.bis.org/speeches/sp060619.htm.

Williamson, J. (2004, September 24–25). *A Short History of the Washington Consensus*. Paper Commissioned by Fundación CIDOB for a Conference "From the Washington Consensus Towards a New Global Governance." Barcelona.

Wyplosz, C. (2001). *Exchange Rate Regimes: Some Lessons from Postwar Europe* (CEPR Discussion Paper No. 2723). Centre for Economic Policy Research.

Index

A. Blundell-Wignall et al., *Globalisation and Finance at the Crossroads*,
https://doi.org/10.1007/978-3-319-72676-2

Printed by Printforce, United Kingdom